Butcher Block Projects

Butcher Block Projects

Kenn Oberrecht

CREATIVE HOMEOWNER PRESS®

Manufactured in United States of America

Current printing (last digit)
10 9 8 7 6 5 4 3 2 1

Produced by Roundtable Press, Inc.

Project editor: Donald Nelson
Managing editor: Marguerite Ross
Illustrations: Norman Nuding
Design: Jeffrey Fitschen
Jacket design: Jerry Demoney
Jacket photo: David Arky
Art production: Nadina Simon
Illustrated techniques and project photos: Kenn Oberrecht

LC: 87-5408
ISBN: 0-932944-83-3 (paper)
        0-932944-84-1 (hardcover)

CREATIVE HOMEOWNER PRESS®
BOOK SERIES

A DIVISION OF FEDERAL
MARKETING CORPORATION
24 PARK WAY,
UPPER SADDLE RIVER, NJ 07458

KEY TO SYMBOLS

The projects in this book are rated by the length of time you can expect them to take and by the relative level of difficulty involved. These ratings are indicated by symbols at the beginning of each project. In addition, when it is required that you protect your eyes, you'll find a small pair of safety goggles as a reminder.

Afternoon

Overnight

More than one day

Easy

Moderate

Difficult

Safety goggles

Introduction

Not long ago, the only butcher-block item most of us ever saw was the butcher's meat-cutting block at the corner grocery store. As supermarkets and mini-markets forced the little grocer out of business, butcher blocks ended up on auction blocks, where they commanded premium prices from homeowners, apartment dwellers, and decorators who recognized the utilitarian and aesthetic value of their sturdy hardwood construction, simple lines, and adaptability to various decors.

When demand exceeded supply, furniture makers began producing new butcher blocks, and soon, all manner of furnishings in the butcher-block motif started appearing in furniture stores everywhere. Now they are widely available and are among the most popular of furnishings. They are extremely rugged and handsome, and they accommodate a variety of decorating needs.

Commercially manufactured butcher-block furniture is expensive, mainly because the building techniques don't readily lend themselves to inexpensive mass production. Furthermore, buyers expect butcher-block products to be hefty, all-wood furnishings, so substituting cheap materials is out of the question.

The same cost disadvantages that put high price tags on butcher-block furnishings and fixtures make them ideal for do-it-yourselfers. Building materials the manufacturers use are readily available to the home craftsman, but more important, high labor costs are eliminated by the person who fashions his own butcher-block projects.

Armed with the right tools and the proper skills, you can turn out butcher-block projects that rival anything in the stores, but at a fraction of the cost. Moreover, you can use these same skills to custom-build furnishings that aren't available anywhere else for any price.

The butcher-block top is made of strips of maple, laminated end-grain-up with waterproof plastic-resin glue.

In the pages that follow, you will be introduced to the tools and techniques of butcher-block building. You will learn about the various materials and finishing processes. And you will find more than two dozen projects described in a text that's easy to follow, accompanied by clear, step-by-step illustrations.

A complete list of required tools and a bill of materials are included with every project. The more ambitious projects also include cutting schedules, diagrams, and parts lists to aid you in the construction process.

You will find simple, easy projects that are fun to build and make excellent gifts. There are projects for the kitchen, dining room, living room, family room, den, and home office—everything from a simple serving tray, candle holders, and coaster set to a table lamp, accent tables, a computer desk, an executive-size oak pedestal desk, and much more. And, of course, there are

plans for building a traditional butcher's block, but one slightly modified for the modern kitchen. Like its predecessors, this one is made of solid maple, but its lines are leaner, it rides on casters for mobility, and it doubles as a sturdy microwave cart.

The first part of the book is a brief guide to the tools, materials, and techniques of butcher-block building. Then each project shows you how to use these tools, materials, and techniques for specific tasks.

Much of what you learn in one project, in fact, can be applied to other projects—even to plans not found here. You can use the skills you will learn in this book to adapt many project plans for custom-building butcher-block furnishings of all sorts.

In short, you will not only learn how to build specific projects, but you will also learn how to manufacture your own laminated wood products that you can substitute wherever you desire.

By using the techniques and materials covered here, you can laminate table tops, desk tops, benches, doors, drawer faces, shelving, cabinet panels, and more—all butcher-block style. What's more, your creations will be beautiful, naturally finished products that are sturdier, stabler, and more durable than anything built with conventional materials and processes.

So this book goes well beyond what's contained between its covers. The tools you acquire for building the various projects described here will, of course, serve you on many more jobs for years to come. More important, though, the skills you master while working on the following projects can be applied to other woodworking projects you read about elsewhere or design yourself.

You will gain experience as solid and durable as the butcher-block furnishings themselves. They will last you a lifetime.

Contents

Work Surfaces and Supports

Just as houses never seem to have enough closet space and offices never have enough desktop space, workshops of all sizes often lack sufficient bench space. Even those craftsmen fortunate enough to own large shops often need extra work surfaces for layout, cutting, and assembly.

A pair of sturdy sawhorses will provide extra surface and adequate support for many projects. You'll find sawhorse brackets or folding metal legs available at home-improvement centers. With these, you can make your own sawhorses with 2 × 4s or other two-by stock.

You can make your sawhorses much more useful by ripping two scraps of ¾-inch plywood to five-inch widths, then cutting them to match the length of the horizontal 2 × 4 on each horse. Counterbore and drill the plywood, and attach it to the top of the 2 × 4 with three or more ¼ × 2½ lag bolts and flat washers. This makes each sawhorse a mini-bench that you can clamp material to for drilling, cutting, and other operations. Lay a slab of ¾-inch plywood atop the sawhorses, and you have a temporary workbench.

One of the handiest and most versatile accessories for any workshop, no matter its size, is the Black & Decker Workmate®. Its two-piece surface provides additional work space, but also functions as a large vise.

Trim a sheet of ¾-inch plywood to 30 by 60 inches, attach a 60-inch 2 × 4 to the center of the underside with screws, and you have a spacious benchtop that conveniently clamps into the jaws of the Workmate® or stands against a wall when you don't need it.

Similarly, you can make plywood bases for your miter box and various benchtop power tools, store them out of the way, and when you need one, simply secure it in the Workmate®'s jaws for a portable but stable foundation.

Swivel grips, hold-down clamps, and other accessories make the Workmate® even more versatile, and the unit collapses for easy storage.

A pair of sawhorses provides support for work pieces of all sizes. Those shown have five-inch-wide plywood tops attached with lag bolts.

The Workmate® is not only a handy work surface and super vise, but it also serves as a foundation for bench tools.

Workmate® swivel grips allow the clamping of thin stock and even odd-shaped items for sanding, drilling, and other operations.

Drills and Drilling

The first power tool that most do-it-yourselfers own is an electric drill, since it's one of the most useful tools and best bargains available.

If you're buying your first drill or have decided it's time to replace an old ¼-inch, fixed-speed model, look for a top-quality, ⅜-inch, variable-speed, reversing drill. Of course, the bigger drills with ½-inch chucks will accept larger bits, but there's seldom a need for them. Such drills are usually heavier and bulkier, which makes them awkward and tiring to handle.

A 13-piece set of twist-drill bits, ranging in size from ¹⁄₁₆ to ¼ of an inch in diameter, will see to most of your needs. Buy the larger sizes as specific projects require.

Brad-point bits are excellent for fine woodworking, since they don't tend to walk off the mark as twist-drill bits will, and they make perfectly clean entry holes. You can buy them in sets or individually. You will probably find ⅜-inch and ½-inch the most useful; these are the only sizes required for projects in this book.

There are numerous accessories and specialty bits available for electric drills. By and large, you can buy them as needs dictate. Some projects in this book call for drill stops and a dowel jig.

There are adjustable drill stops that fit several sizes of bits, and there are metal collars, made to fit specific bit diameters, that attach with set screws. Each type is designed to allow you to drill to a set depth.

There are a number of relatively inexpensive dowel jigs on the market. The best for projects in this book is one that is self-centering.

There are some drilling jobs that simply can't be done with a hand-held drill or are better accomplished with a drill press. But you needn't take out a second mortgage to make a down payment on a drill press. If your shop budget is tight, consider buying a drill-press stand that fits your electric drill. It will bolt securely to a bench or base, will adequately perform all necessary

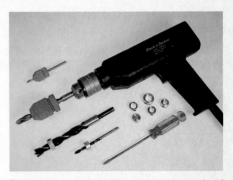

Twist-drill bits (in chuck and next below) are all-purpose bits. Brad-point bits (center) won't walk, and make clean entry holes. Forstner bits (bottom) are the finest wood bits available.

Drill stops permit drilling to predetermined depths. Adjustable stops (red plastic) come in two sizes and fit most standard bits. Metal collars are made to fit bits of specific sizes.

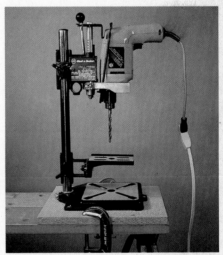

A self-centering dowel jig assures perfectly centered holes in stock of almost any thickness.

A drill-press stand, clamped to a solid work surface, turns an electric drill into a drill press.

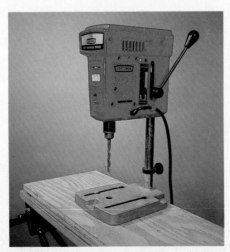

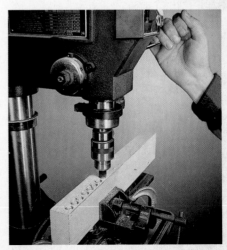

An inexpensive benchtop drill press—this one attached to a plywood base and clamped in a Workmate®—will see to most drilling jobs.

With a drill press and plug cutter, you can turn scraps into useful wood plugs. Here, scrap is held secure in a drill-press vise.

functions, and will probably cost less than $50. Its chief drawback is that connecting and disconnecting the drill each time you use it takes some time. If that's a nuisance you can live with, this might be your best buy and is definitely a good way to begin learning about drill-press operation.

Popular bench-type drill presses range in price from under $100 to more than $200, depending on size, capacity, speeds, and a few other options. You can bolt the tool to a bench or Workmate® base, and it might prove to be all the drill press you will ever need.

Forstner bits are finely made, precision boring instruments that should be used with a drill press. They're expensive—from about $8 (⅝-inch) to $25 (two-inch)—so you will probably want to buy them one at a time, as required. But they're about the best wood bits made and with proper care should last a lifetime.

Plug cutters also must be used with a drill press or drill-press stand. They come in several sizes, with ⅜-inch and ½-inch probably the most useful. With a plug cutter you can turn scraps of wood into plugs for screw holes.

A drill-press vise is a handy item for securing work pieces and for setting up the drill press for repetitive drilling. In the absence of a vise, you can use C-clamps or spring clamps for securing work when necessary; for repetitive operations, use a scrap of wood as a fence attached to the drill-press base with C-clamps.

Whether you're using a hand-held drill or drill press, the most important part of any drilling operation is the preliminary work. With an electric drill, that means carefully measuring, marking, and then center-punching a starter hole. With a drill press, skip the center-punching, but take time to set up the machine for perfectly placed holes.

A steel tape rule and combination square are the most useful tools for measuring and marking, especially for repetitive drilling. When setting up a series of holes in a matched set of 1 × 2s, for example, you can use the rule to mark one strip, then scribe lines across several strips at a time with the combination square. Then set the square for ¾ of an inch and mark the

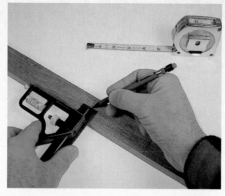

Careful measuring and marking beforehand assure accurate placement of holes in all drilling operations. The most important tools for this are a steel tape rule and combination square.

You can use wood plugs that you make yourself with a plug cutter to plug screw holes in furniture and other projects.

center of each line for holes centered on the broad side, or ⅜ of an inch for holes centered on the narrow edge.

To make perfectly placed holes, use a center punch to keep the bit from walking off its mark. It takes little extra time, and the results will show in the finished product.

With a drill press, you needn't worry about the bit moving off its mark, but you must make sure it hits the mark. To ensure this, take the time to accurately measure and mark guide lines on your work pieces; then adjust the drill-press vise or set a fence on the base so the bit hits the guide line exactly where it should.

Several projects in this book call for counterboring and drilling through as a means of sinking screw heads. The

A 1 × 2 ripped in half shows the advantages of counterboring (with a 3/8-inch brad-point bit) and then drilling through (with an 11/64-inch twist-drill bit): the 1¼ × 8 screws get a better bite.

Whenever you use a hand-held drill, keep the bit from walking off the mark by center-punching a starter hole first.

technique offers several advantages over simple countersinking, in which the screw head is left flush with the wood surface.

To counterbore, drill a hole of sufficient diameter to accommodate the screw head. For most projects, a ⅜-inch brad-point bit is best. Then drill through the center of the first hole with a twist-drill bit that's slightly larger in diameter than the screw shank.

Counterboring sets screws deeper than countersinking does and thereby provides a better bite and tighter joint, while reducing the chances of stripping the screw hole. When the technique is used to attach trim and other exterior pieces, the holes are plugged with flathead or button plugs for a professional-looking finishing touch.

Saws and Sawing

Even in small, moderately equipped workshops, most handsaws have been replaced by power saws. So the beginning do-it-yourselfer would do well to follow the example set by veterans. With few exceptions, power saws are not only much faster than handsaws, but also do a better job.

One tool combination—the miter box and backsaw—is a notable exception and is indispensable in the woodworker's shop. With it, you can precisely crosscut molding, framing strips, cleats, dowel rods, and other strips of wood, either squarely or at various angles.

The simplest miter boxes are no more than three-sided wood boxes with saw slits that enable you to cut at 45- and 90-degree angles. Next best are the metal or wood-and-metal models that allow for cutting at other angles as well. The best are adjustable for fine tuning, lock firmly at any angle between 0 and 45 degrees, have positive stops at 0, 15, 30, and 45 degrees, and, with a 26-inch backsaw, will handle wood up to eight or nine inches wide.

There are many jobs this combination will do that no portable power saw can accomplish. Of course, stationary and bench-type power saws—table, power-miter, radial-arm, and bandsaws—will crosscut and cut miters, but each is limited in some way and none is more accurate than a good miter box and backsaw.

Price is not always an indication of quality. You should be able to find an adequate combination for under $50 and the best setup for under $100. Some selling for $150 or more sport needless frills. Be wary of those designed for cutting compound miters, as they might not do a good job on the simpler, more frequent cuts.

Another handsaw required for some of the projects in this book is a dovetail saw, used here primarily for cutting the heads off wooden plugs. The best for such purposes is an offset dovetail saw that can be used in either the left or right hand and will make flush cuts on

any surface, regardless of size.

The most versatile portable power saw is a 7¼-inch circular saw. It will see to most cutting jobs and is a good saw to start with. In fact, even though table and radial-arm saws are easier and faster to set up for many cutting chores, there are some jobs a circular saw simply does better. So it's not only a good saw to start with, but one to stay with.

An essential accessory for the circular saw is a saw guide. Of course, you can fashion your own guides from straight strips of wood, or you can use yardsticks or straightedges on some jobs, but you would do well to invest in one of the commercially made guides—such as the Strate-Cut—which is a two-piece aluminum guide that can be used with stock up to eight

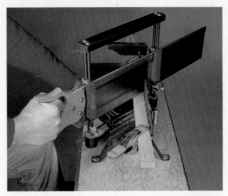
A miter box and backsaw are indispensable in any woodworking shop. This one is attached to a plywood base that's clamped in a Workmate®

An offset dovetail saw is handy for cutting the heads off wood plugs.

A table saw is ideal for ripping wide stock into narrow stock. Keep blade guard in place and use push blocks.

A table saw is also a good tool for crosscutting small pieces and cutting grooves, dadoes, and rabbets.

A saw guide is essential for making accurate cuts with a circular saw. Such guides are attached with C-clamps and keep the saw running true.

feet. This and similar guides clamp in place with C-clamps and ensure that your saw (or router) travels in a straight line. Cutting a straight line without such an aid is as difficult as drawing a straight line without a ruler.

There's a standing controversy over which stationary saw is best—the table saw or the radial-arm saw. Most serious woodworkers eventually conclude they need both. So the question amounts to which to buy first. For the projects in this book, many of which require ripping wide stock into narrow strips, the table saw is the best choice.

A bandsaw, though slower than a table saw, will also do an adequate job of ripping for most projects. And this tool is superior for crosscutting thick stock and ripping narrow strips from thin stock.

Of course, if you already own a power-miter or radial-arm saw, you know its capabilities and limitations and when to substitute it for the recommended tools. If you own no stationary power saws and are working on a limited budget, don't overlook the bench-type tools, as they will see to every project in this book.

Regardless of what kind of saw you are using, as with drilling, the most important part of any cut is preparation. Measure carefully, and measure again. The old rule is: "Measure twice and cut once."

No matter how skilled and experienced you are now or eventually become, measurements have a way of going awry. You'll avoid wasting wood by exercising as much care in setting up a cut as you do in making the cut.

When ripping wood on a table saw, don't trust the saw's rip scale. Always measure from the fence to the blade with a steel tape rule or yardstick for accuracy; then check the setup by running a piece of scrap wood through the saw and readjusting as necessary.

Saw blades make the cleanest cuts on the entry surface of the wood and tend to splinter along the kerf on the exit side, particularly when crosscutting hardwood plywood and other laminates. So when using a circular, radial-arm, or power-miter saw, make sure the best surface of the work piece is face down. With a table saw, the good

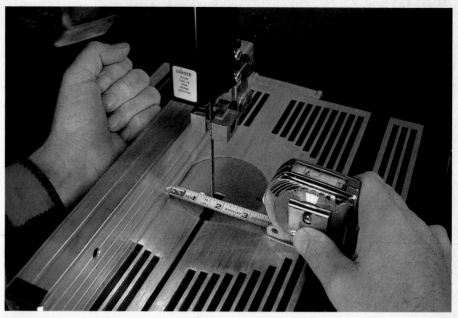

Always measure and double check the distance between the blade and fence, even if your saw is equipped with a rip scale.

Left and right pieces of oak plywood show entry and exit surfaces cut with a 80-tooth, carbide-tipped blade designed for smooth cuts. Splintered center piece was cut with a similarly priced 40-tooth, carbide-tipped blade.

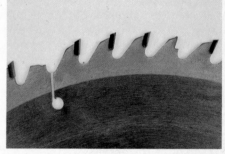

The result of moving material too fast through a saw is shown here. This expensive blade was severely damaged when it hit hard burl wood, breaking one tooth off and knocking off several carbide tips.

surface should be up.

Splintering is much less a problem with certain blades, such as fine-tooth plywood, hollow-ground planer, and 60-tooth and 80-tooth carbide-tipped blades. These are slower than other blades with fewer teeth, but they make much cleaner crosscuts.

Keep blades sharp for optimum performance. Ask your local lumber or hardware supplier to recommend a professional sharpener.

Often a blade that seems dull merely needs cleaning. Resins and pitch from most woods and adhesives used in plywood and other manufactured wood products collect on blades and resist most cleaning methods. An easy way to dissolve them is to spray blades with Easy-Off oven cleaner, let stand for 20

minutes, and hose the residues away.

When power sawing, it's important to proceed at the right speed. If you saw too slowly, the blade will overheat from excessive friction and burn the wood. If you force the tool or material, the saw motor will lug or even stall. Move the saw or material quickly and smoothly without straining the motor.

Wood densities vary from species to species and even in the same piece of wood. Generally, you can cut softwoods faster than hardwoods, and you can usually rip faster than crosscut. But always slow down as you approach knots and burl wood, as the grain is much denser and the wood harder there. Trying to zip through such areas can cause kickback or even break teeth off the blade.

Clamps and Clamping

Among the most important tools in any woodworker's shop are clamps, in their various forms and sizes. They're used for securing work pieces to solid foundations, setting up sawing and drilling operations, laminating wood, attaching molding, and gluing all wood joints.

C-clamps are the most common and are put to many uses in the shop. You should own at least one pair, and three-inch clamps are a good size to start.

Spring clamps are meant for light-duty work and are excellent for some tool setups and for gluing small pieces. They're faster than C-clamps, especially if you pick a pair with cushioned jaws.

Though more expensive than C-clamps, bar clamps are often the better choice, particularly for clamping large pieces. They are commonly available in sizes from six to 36 inches, or even larger on special order.

Heavy-duty bar clamps larger than 24 inches are relatively expensive. An inexpensive alternative is a set of pipe-clamp fixtures, with which you can make clamps of any size with iron pipe.

One of the best clamps for woodworking is the sliding bar clamp, which has a metal bar with hardwood—usually hornbeam—jaws. These are the fastest-acting clamps available, and their cork-faced jaws eliminate the need for clamp cushions.

Corner clamps are handy for miter and butt joints. A set of four will serve well on most projects.

For attaching edge trim or molding, edge clamps are ideal. Start with a pair, and buy others as you need them.

The cheapest and most useful clamps for butcher-block projects are threaded-rod clamps you can make for about a dollar apiece. For each you'll need a $5/16$-by-36-inch threaded rod, two $1/4$-inch flat washers, two $5/16$-inch hex nuts, and two three-inch pieces of parting bead with $3/8$-inch-diameter center holes.

With these clamps, you can laminate wood slabs of any thickness and length and widths up to 30 inches.

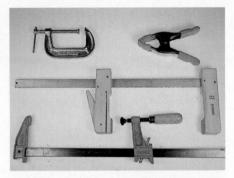

Here are the most useful clamps. Top are the popular C-clamp and faster-acting but lighter-duty spring clamp. Center is a sliding bar clamp with cushioned jaws. Bottom is a bar clamp.

Corner clamps are ideal for clamping stock for gluing and fastening. The clamps can be used for miter joints or butt joints.

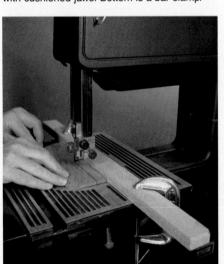

C-clamps are used for all sorts of tool setups. Here a scrap of wood is C-clamped to a saw table to function as a fence.

Spring clamps are ideal for quick tool setups. Here, stock is clamped to a Workmate® to allow a two-handed grip on the drill.

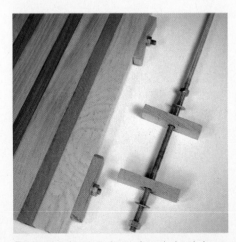

For butcher block projects, threaded-rod clamps are the most useful of all. Each clamp consists of a threaded rod, two flat washers, two hex nuts, and two cushions.

Threaded-rod clamps are tightened with two wrenches: an adjustable wrench (left) held steady, and a socket wrench (right) turned clockwise.

Sanding and Finishing

Although sanders are useful in some forming and shaping operations, sanding must be considered part of the finishing process, because the better job you do with abrasives, the better the final finish will be.

The two types of sanders essential for projects in this book are the portable belt sander and pad sander.

Certainly, if you own a stationary belt sander, by all means, use it whenever possible. A good substitute, though, is a portable belt sander clamped upside down in the jaws of a Workmate®. For finish-sanding small pieces, clamp a pad sander the same way.

The belt sander is what you will use for rough-sanding laminated stock, so you will need a heavy-duty model that uses 3-by-21-inch or larger belts. For most jobs, you will need only medium (80-grit) and fine (120-grit) belts.

Start with the medium belt and sand the surface to a smooth, even finish, always with the sander running with the grain. You can then sand the same surface with the fine belt, or begin finish-sanding with a pad sander.

Your best choice for finish-sanding is a half-sheet pad sander. Start with 120-grit sandpaper and sand the surface until all scratches left by the belt sander are removed. For most projects, another sanding with 220-grit paper is essential. For an even finer finish, follow that with 320-grit paper.

Finishing options and combinations are many. There are dozens of stains, sealers, oils, varnishes, and lacquers available, and all have different effects on the various species of softwoods and hardwoods.

The best advice is to spend some time at a local home-improvement center examining the options and reading product labels and literature. Decide what effect you want to achieve, and test the product on scraps of wood before using it on any project.

You can also follow the recommendations in this book and use the finishing materials that have already been tested for you.

A belt sander is an essential tool for rough-sanding stock of all sorts, including the laminated panels for butcher block projects.

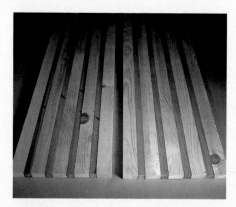

Laminated panel on left has not been sanded and shows blade marks and flaws. Panel on right has been rough-sanded to a smooth, even finish with a belt sander.

A half-sheet pad sander is the ideal tool for finish-sanding. The sander is shown here rounding over a sharp edge.

For finish-sanding small pieces, clamp a pad sander upside down in a Workmate® and press the piece against the sander by hand.

Laminated spice container on right has not been sanded. Container on left has been rough-sanded with a stationary belt sander.

Twenty-four Tips on Shop Safety

If you're a beginning do-it-yourselfer, there are some potential workshop hazards you should know about. Even if you're a veteran craftsman, you would do well to review the following tips, as old-timers sometimes tend to take safety measures for granted.

By exercising some common sense and keeping safety in mind during every phase of every workshop task, you'll be able to enjoy shop projects while avoiding injury.

1. Store your tools safely out of the reach of children, and keep children out of the workshop unless you're teaching them. The first lesson for any youngster should be one on shop safety.

2. When you have finished with tools, hardware, extension cords, and the like, put them away. Keep your work area free of clutter.

3. When sawing, drilling, routing, and performing other chores, secure work pieces to a solid surface with clamps or a vise. Not only will this allow you to use your tools safely, but will also reduce the chances of errors while increasing accuracy.

4. Keep saws, knives, bits, and chisels sharp. Dull cutting tools are dangerous. Moreover, dull bits and blades will put unnecessary strain on tool motors.

5. When ripping narrow stock with a table saw or bandsaw, use push blocks to keep your fingers away from the blade.

6. Remove the table-saw blade guard *only* to make cuts that do not fully penetrate the wood, as in cutting rabbets and dadoes. Replace the guard immediately after such cuts, and leave it in place for all other work.

7. When crosscutting or miter-cutting with a table saw or bandsaw and miter gauge, remove the fence from the saw. Never use both the miter gauge and the fence together; it can lead to saw damage and serious injury.

8. When sawing large boards or panel stock with a circular saw, the cut halves will collapse toward the blade if not properly supported, causing

When cutting panel stock and wide boards with a circular saw, always support the kerf with Kerf-Keeper clamps.

In the absence of Kerf-Keepers, use a bar clamp and wood scraps to support the kerf when cutting with a circular saw.

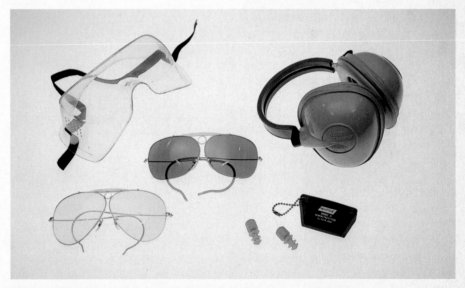

When working with power tools and striking tools (hammers and punches), wear eye protection: goggles, safety glasses, or shooting glasses. Guard your hearing with approved protectors.

kickback. Prevent injury and damage to stock by supporting the work piece near both sides of the kerf and using Kerf-Keeper clamps. In the absence of Kerf-Keepers, support the kerf with deep-throated C-clamps or bar clamps and scraps of one-by stock.

9. Read instruction manuals that come with new power tools before operating the tools, and review the manuals periodically to make sure you haven't developed any bad habits. Before setting to work with any new tool, practice with it on scrap material.

10. Wear some sort of goggles or safety glasses when working with power tools and hammers. If you're working outdoors on a sunny day, wear sunglasses with impact-resistant lenses.

11. Protect your hearing when using noisy power tools. Any tool that causes your ears to ring for 10 minutes or more is probably causing permanent ear damage. Don't just stuff your ears with cotton; use approved ear protectors, such as those designed for target shooting.

12. Maintain your tools for long life—yours and the tools'. Keep them clean, free of corrosion, and well lubricated. Replace worn or damaged electric cords promptly.

13. Make sure power tools are switched off before plugging them in. Always disconnect power-tool plugs before changing bits or blades or making necessary adjustments. Unplug all tools at the end of the work session.

14. Power tools must be properly grounded. If the tool is equipped with a three-conductor cord and three-prong plug, make sure the outlet is a proper, grounding-type receptacle. Extension cords should also be grounded, and any used outdoors should be designed for outdoor use and so labeled.

15. Before operating any power tool, make sure power cords and extension cords are out of the way and will not interfere with tool operation.

16. Don't wear jewelry or loose-fitting clothing when operating any tools or machinery that might entangle it and cause personal injury. Remove watches, rings, and other metal when operating any portable power tool that isn't double insulated.

17. When working with sanders, grinders, and other tools that create dust, wear a dust mask. If you suffer from any sort of respiratory ailment, consult a physician about the type of mask you should wear for maximum protection.

18. If a power tool stalls during operation, release the trigger or switch the machine off immediately. Then unplug the tool and work it loose in safety. Before resuming operation, correct the cause of the stall.

19. Always grip a portable power tool

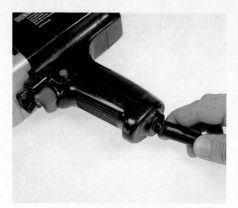

Check power-tool electrical cords for damage. This one should be replaced before the tool is used again.

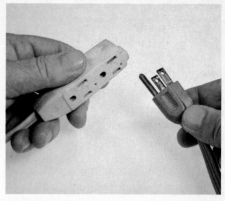

Make sure power tools are properly grounded. Use those with three-prong plugs only with three-prong extension cords and outlets.

When using sanders and other tools that create dust, wear a face mask or a respirator recommended by your physician.

Read the labels on all products used in the shop, and pay special attention to CAUTION, WARNING, and DANGER notices.

firmly before switching it on, as the torque of the motor could cause you to lose your grip. Whenever possible, grip the tool with both hands.

20. When working with acids, solvents, chemicals, and adhesives that can cause skin damage, always wear rubber or chemical-proof plastic gloves.

21. Lacquers, thinners, cleaners, solvents, and adhesives that produce toxic, flammable, or explosive fumes should only be used in a well-ventilated area, away from sources of heat or open flame. Do not use power tools around any flammable substances, as fumes might be ignited by electrical arc when the tool is switched on.

22. Read the labels on all materials used in the shop. Pay special attention to bold CAUTION and WARNING notices. When in doubt about the safe handling of any material, phone or write the manufacturer.

23. When working with a heavy piece of lumber or plywood, don't misjudge its weight. Test it by moving it slightly. Be aware of possible injury before you attempt to lift it. Get help if you need it. Keep your back straight while lifting, bend your legs instead of stooping over the object, and let your legs do all the work.

24. Most important, use common sense on every workshop project, and concentrate on the task at hand.

Serving Tray

A good way to become familiar with butcher-block building techniques is to make this simple but functional and attractive serving tray.

Made of oak 1 × 2 stock and employing oak cabinet-door pulls as handles, this tray has many uses in the home. It also makes a fine gift or craft-show item.

This project introduces you to a lamination process that uses threaded-rod clamps. Not only are these among the handiest tools for butcher-block construction, they are also the least expensive. Moreover, you can make them yourself from materials readily available everywhere.

The basic techniques you will learn building this tray will serve you well on many other projects, too.

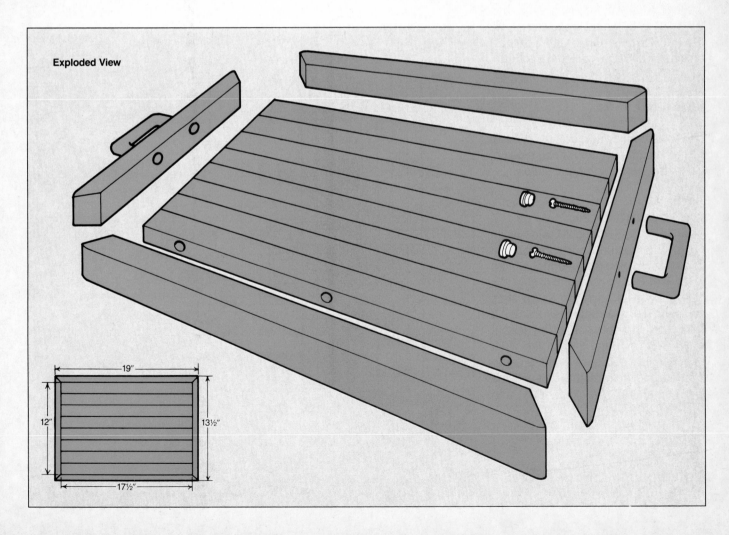

Exploded View

19"

12"   13½"

17½"

BILL OF MATERIALS

Qty	Size	Material	Qty	Size	Material	Qty	Size	Material
18'	1 × 2	Oak	2	#P674	Belwith drawer pulls			Deft Clear Wood Finish
4	3/8"	Oak button plugs		120-grit	Sandpaper			Watco Medium Walnut
		Carpenter's or white glue		220-grit	Sandpaper			Danish Oil Finish
		Five-minute epoxy cement		320-grit	Sandpaper			Tack cloth

TOOLS

Steel tape rule	Miter box and backsaw	3/8" brad-point bit
Combination square	24" bar clamps (3)	3/16" twist-drill bit
Pencil	5/16" threaded-rod clamps (3)	Table saw or circular saw and guide
Claw hammer	1/2" or adjustable wrenches (2)	Belt sander
Center punch	Drill press or drill-press stand	Pad sander
Screwdriver	Electric drill	Paintbrush

STEP 1
CUTTING AND MARKING 1 × 2s

Cut eight strips of 1 × 2 to 18 inches, lay them broad side up, and sort them in a contrasting grain pattern. Then turn them on narrow edges, with broad sides together, and number ends from 1 to 8. Clamp them with a pair of bar clamps, and scribe lines across them at the center and one inch from each end.

STEP 2
DRILLING 1 × 2s

With a drill press or electric drill and drill-press stand, use a 3/8-inch bit to drill holes through the narrow sides of each strip, centered on the lines.

STEP 3
LAMINATING 1 × 2s

Arrange strips numerically, wide faces up, on a protected work surface. Run threaded-rod clamps through the three holes in strip 1. Apply a coat of glue to a narrow edge of each remaining strip, and slide the strips onto the rods. Put a clamp cushion, flat washer, and hex nut on each clamp, and tighten the nuts. Wipe excess glue away with a damp sponge, and let the slab stand until the glue sets. Remove the rods and cushions.

STEP 4
SANDING THE SLAB

Sand the slab top and bottom with a belt sander and medium belt. Then use a pad sander and 120-grit paper. Fin-

MARKING 1 × 2s

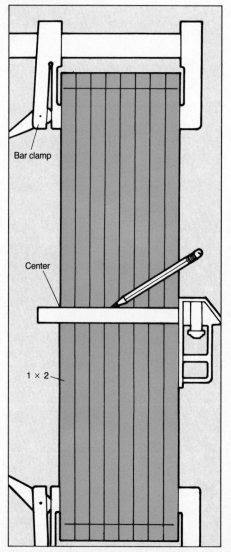

Bar clamp

Center

1 × 2

Align and clamp the 1 × 2s together with two bar clamps. Then scribe lines across the narrow edges at the center and one inch from each end.

DRILLING 1 × 2s

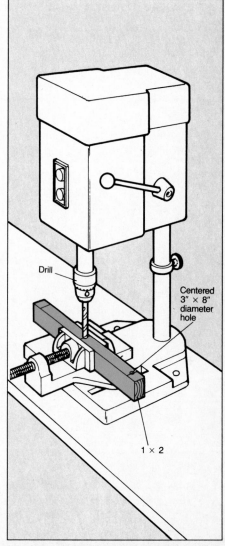

Drill

Centered 3" × 8" diameter hole

1 × 2

Drill a 3/8-inch-diameter hole through the center of each 1 × 2 at each of the three scribed lines.

ish-sand the top with 220-grit and 320-grit paper.

STEP 5
CUTTING 1 × 2 TRIM

With a miter box and backsaw, cut four pieces of 1 × 2 to fit the edges of the slab with 45-degree miters at each end.

STEP 6
ATTACHING SIDE TRIM

Mix a small amount of epoxy cement, and apply a thin coat to each long edge of the slab. Then clamp the long miter-cut trim pieces to the slab with three bar or cam clamps. Let the trim stand for five minutes.

STEP 7
DRILLING HANDLE HOLES IN END TRIM

Lay the small miter-cut trim pieces on a bench, inside broad surfaces up. Scribe a center line across each. Measure 1¾ inches left and right of the center line, and scribe two more lines; then mark these lines for drill-starter holes ⅜ of an inch from the top.

Center-punch starter holes; counterbore ⅜-inch-diameter, ¼-inch-deep holes; and drill with a ³⁄₁₆-inch bit.

STEP 8
ATTACHING END TRIM

Attach end pieces with epoxy cement and bar clamps, as in Step 6, and let stand for five minutes. Then sand trim pieces with a pad sander and 120-, 220-, and 320-grit paper.

STEP 9
ATTACHING HANDLES AND PLUGGING HOLES

Attach the handles with screws. Then press a button plug into each screw hole, or use a hammer and block of wood to tap the plugs in.

STEP 10
FINISHING THE TRAY

Vacuum all sanding dust from the tray; then clean all surfaces with a tack cloth.

To duplicate the finish shown, apply a coat of Watco Medium Walnut Danish Oil; follow manufacturer's directions. Let stand for 72 hours. Then apply three coats of Deft Semi-Gloss Clear Wood Finish.

LAMINATING 1 × 2s

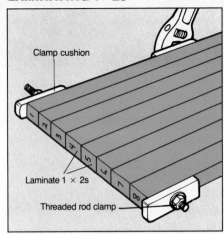

Laminate the 1 × 2s, using wood glue and three threaded-rod clamps, installed with clamp cushions. When the glue dries, sand the slab to an extra-fine finish.

ATTACHING SIDE TRIM

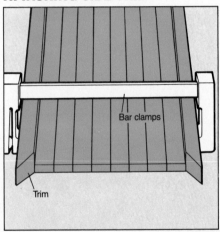

Attach the two longest pieces of trim to the sides of the slab, using epoxy cement and securing the assembly with three bar clamps.

ENDS AND HANDLES

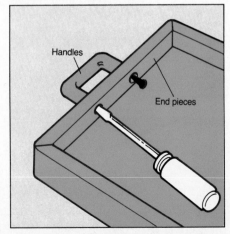

After attaching end pieces with epoxy cement and bar clamps, install handles with screws.

CUTTING 1 × 2 TRIM

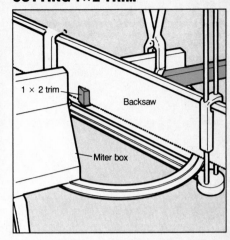

Use a miter box and backsaw to cut four pieces of 1 × 2, with 45-degree mitered ends, to fit the slab sides.

DRILLING HANDLE HOLES

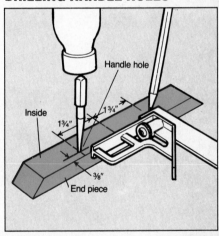

Mark inside end pieces for centered handles, ⅜ inch from the top.

PLUGGING HOLES

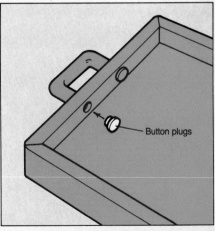

Plug the handle screw holes with button plugs, and apply desired finish.

Carving Board

A good carving board is essential in any kitchen. With this efficiently designed board, you will find it a pleasure to slice and carve fowl, roasts, and hot or cold meats of all sorts.

Designed specifically for meat cutting and carving, the grooved top helps hold the meat in place while allowing juices to drain from the cutting surface to the spacious gutters.

Because of its strength, durability, and grain structure, maple has long been the favored wood for cutting boards. Consequently, this one is made entirely of maple 1 × 2s.

If you have any trouble locating 1 × 2 stock, use any width available, and rip it into 1 × 2s with a table saw.

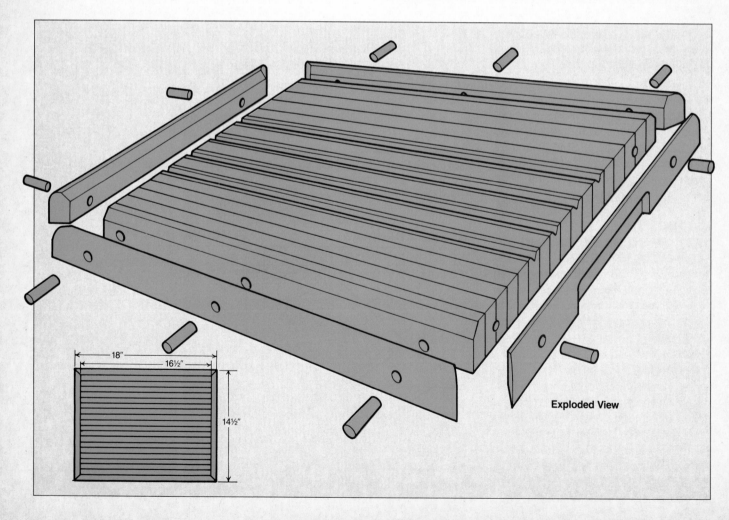

Exploded View

18″
16½″
14½″

BILL OF MATERIALS

Qty	Size	Material	Qty	Size	Material	Qty	Size	Material
40'	1 × 2	Maple	4	1¼ × 8	Flathead wood screws		Medium/	Abrasive sponge
10	⅜"	Flathead tapered wood plugs		120-grit	Sandpaper		Fine	
		Plastic resin glue		220-grit	Sandpaper			Tack cloth
		Urethane Bond		Medium	Sanding drum			Olive oil
				Fine	Sanding drum			

TOOLS

Steel tape rule
Combination square
Pencil
Claw hammer
Center punch
Screwdriver
Miter box and backsaw
Dovetail saw
C-clamps (2)

⁵⁄₁₆" threaded-rod clamps (3)
Edge clamps (2)
½" or adjustable wrenches (2)
Drill press or drill-press stand
Electric drill
⅜" brad-point bit
³⁄₃₂" and ¹¹⁄₆₄" twist-drill bits
¾" drum-sanding attachment
Table saw

Belt sander
Pad sander
Router
½" straight router bit
⅜" V-groove router bit
Workmate® (optional)
Paintbrush

STEP 1
CUTTING AND DRILLING 1 × 2s

Cut 17 pieces of 1 × 2 to 17 inches. Sort them in a contrasting grain pattern, number the ends, and lay them broad side up.

Mark each for centered holes in the middle and one inch from each end. Then drill a ⅜-inch-diameter hole at each spot marked.

STEP 2
LAMINATING 1 × 2s

Mix about a half-cup of plastic resin glue according to the manufacturer's directions.

Insert the three rod clamps with cushions into the holes in strip 1. Apply a coat of glue to a broad side of strip 2, and slide it onto the rods, down to strip 1. Continue assembling this way until all strips are on the rods.

Put cushions, flat washers, and nuts on the rods, and tighten the nuts. Install a bar clamp with cushions. Let the slab stand overnight. Remove the rods and clamp. Then sand the top and bottom with a belt sander and medium belt.

STEP 3
TRIMMING AND BEVELING THE SLAB

Set the table-saw fence 16¾ inches from the far teeth of the blade, and trim one end of the slab. Reset the fence at 16½ inches, and trim the opposite end.

Set the blade at 45 degrees, and,

MARKING 1 × 2s

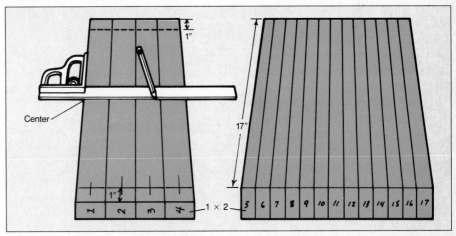

Scribe lines across the broad sides of all the 17-inch 1 × 2s at the center and one inch from each end.

DRILLING 1 × 2s

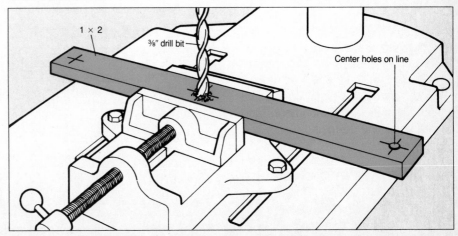

Use a ⅜-inch bit to drill three holes through each 1 × 2, centered on the scribed lines.

with the slab top on the saw table, cut a ⅜-inch bevel along each edge.

Similarly, cut a bevel along one edge of the remaining 1 × 2 stock.

STEP 4
SANDING THE SLAB

Sand all surfaces with a pad sander and 120-grit paper. Then sand the top and beveled edges with 220-grit paper.

STEP 5
ROUTING V-GROOVES

With a router guide (or straightedge), router, and ⅜-inch V-groove bit set for a ¼-inch depth, rout a groove the length of the sixth and eighth strip from each side, marking four grooves in all.

STEP 6
MITER-CUTTING AND MARKING BEVELED 1 × 2s

With a miter box and backsaw, cut four pieces of beveled 1 × 2, with 45-degree angles at the ends, to fit the edges of the slab. Then sand the beveled edges of the 1 × 2 with 120-grit and 220-grit sandpaper.

Lay the pieces inside surface down, and scribe lines across the long pieces in the middle and 1½ inches from each end. Scribe lines across the short pieces 1½ inches from each end. Mark the center of each line for a screw hole.

STEP 7
ROUTING HAND HOLDS

Clamp a small, straight scrap of wood to each end of each short piece, aligned with the lines, and simultaneously clamp the piece to the edge of a benchtop or Workmate®.

Set the router's edge guide ¾ of an inch from the base-plate center line and the straight bit for a ⅜-inch depth. Then run the router inside the wood-scrap guides to rout out a hand hold in each piece, about 1 × 6 × ⅜ inches.

Sand hand holds with an electric drill, drum-sanding attachment, and medium and fine drums.

STEP 8
DRILLING AND ATTACHING EDGE PIECES

Drill a ⅜-inch-diameter hole at each spot marked on the long miter-cut edge pieces. Counterbore a ⅜-inch-diame-

GLUING 1 × 2s

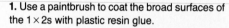

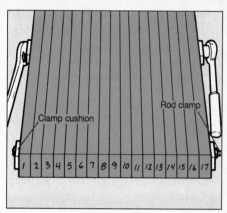

1. Use a paintbrush to coat the broad surfaces of the 1 × 2s with plastic resin glue.

2. Run three rod clamps through the holes in the 1 × 2s, and tighten clamp nuts.

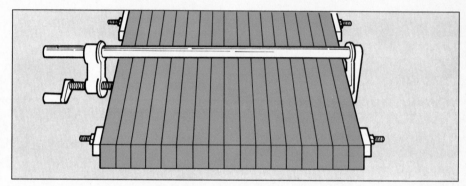

3. Clamp 1 × 2s with two bar clamps between the rod clamps, and let stand overnight.

TRIMMING THE SLAB

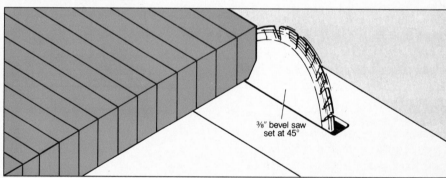

Use a table saw to trim a half-inch from each end of the rough-sanded slab; then set the blade at 45 degrees and cut a ⅜-inch bevel along all top edges.

ROUTING V-GROOVES

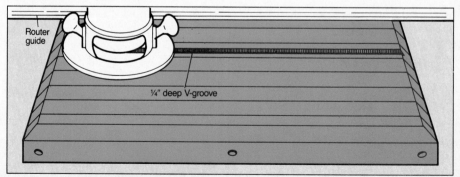

After the slab has been finish-sanded, rout ¼-inch-deep V-grooves in the centers of the sixth and eighth strips, counting in from each side.

ter, ⅜-inch-deep hole at each spot marked on the short pieces; then drill through with an ¹¹⁄₆₄-inch bit.

Mix a small amount of glue according to the manufacturer's directions. Then apply a coat to the inside surfaces of the long, miter-cut 1 × 2s, and attach them to the slab with rod clamps, with beveled edges up.

Lightly clamp the short pieces to the ends of the slab with a bar clamp, and drill pilot holes into the slab with a ⅛-inch bit. Be sure the hand holds open down.

Remove the clamps, and attach each end piece with glue and two 1¼ × 8 screws. Let the board stand overnight.

STEP 9
PLUGGING HOLES AND SANDING

Squeeze a small amount of Urethane Bond into each hole in the edge trim, and plug each hole with a ⅜-inch tapered hardwood plug. Let the board stand for an hour; then cut off plug heads with a dovetail saw.

Sand the edges and plug heads smooth with a belt sander and medium belt. Then sand the edge trim with a pad sander and 120- and 220-grit sandpaper. Then sand hand holds, beveled edges, and V-grooves with medium and fine abrasive sponges.

STEP 10
OILING THE CARVING BOARD

Remove the top from a bottle of olive oil, and set the bottle in a pan of warm water on a stove and slowly heat the water on a low burner setting. When the oil is warm to the touch, hand-rub a liberal amount into all surfaces of the cutting board, and let the board stand overnight.

Repeat this process until the board will accept no more oil. After final oiling, wipe the board dry with paper towels.

To keep the board in good shape, wipe it clean with a damp cloth or wash it quickly with soapy water, but never let it soak. Rinse it, wipe it dry, and let it air dry overnight.

Periodically sand out knife marks with 220-grit sandpaper. Apply more oil every few months, or as often as required.

MITER-CUTTING 1 × 2s

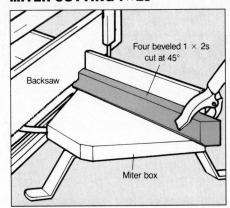

Use a miter box and backsaw to cut four pieces of beveled 1 × 2 with 45-degree angles at each end to fit slab sides.

ROUTING HAND HOLDS

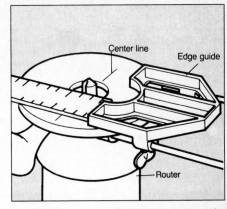

1. Set the router's edge guide at ¾ inch from the base-plate center line.

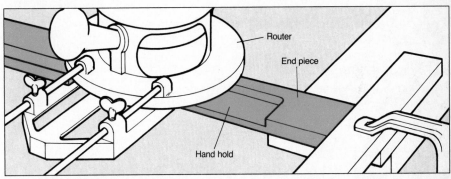

2. Then rout hand holds in end pieces according to the directions given in the text.

ATTACHING SIDES AND ENDS

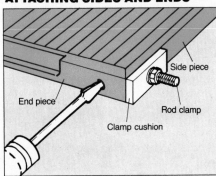

1. Attach side pieces with glue and rod clamps, and end pieces with glue and screws.

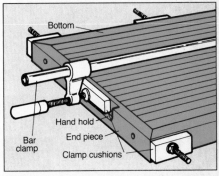

2. Then clamp the end pieces to the slab with one bar clamp attached at hand holds.

PLUGGING HOLES

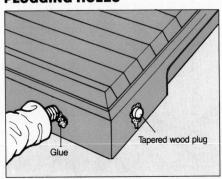

Squeeze a small amount of Urethane Bond into each screw hole, and then plug it with a tapered wood plug.

FINAL SANDING

After finish-sanding trim, use an abrasive sponge to sand V-grooves and gutters.

Salt, Pepper & Picks

In this simple project, you'll laminate contrasting hardwoods to make a set of pieces that will grace any dining table. Extra sets are great for all gift-giving occasions.

Plans call for oak 1 × 3 and walnut micro wood, because they are such compatible woods and contrast nicely. You could also combine other common hardwoods, such as cherry and maple, mahogany and birch, or even more exotic woods, such as rosewood, myrtle, cocobolo, and tulipwood.

If you wish, you can use more than two kinds of wood—in fact, up to eight different species.

You need only browse through the hardwood display at a home-improvement center to recognize the possibilities.

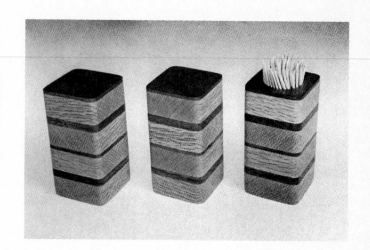

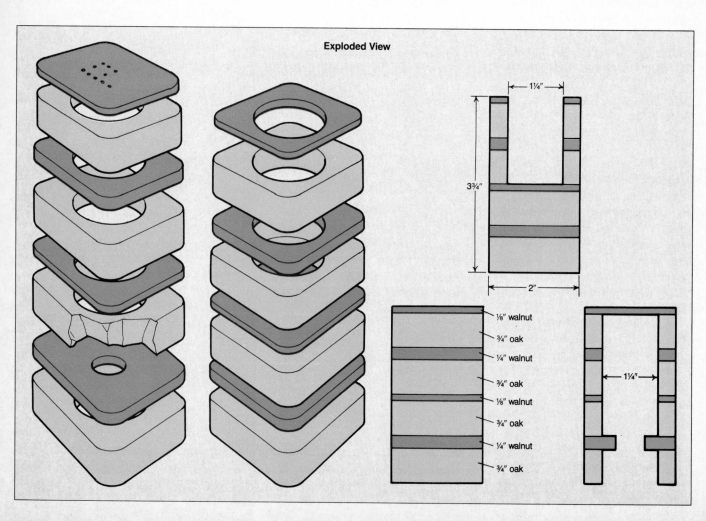

Exploded View

1¼″

3¾″

2″

⅛″ walnut
¾″ oak
¼″ walnut
¾″ oak
⅛″ walnut
¾″ oak
¼″ walnut
¾″ oak

1¼″

BILL OF MATERIALS

Qty	Size	Material	Qty	Size	Material	Qty	Size	Material
26"	1 × 3	Oak		120-grit	Sandpaper	2	¾" × 1"	Tapered cork stoppers
13"	⅛"	Walnut micro wood		220-grit	Sandpaper	18	⅛" × 3½"	Rubber bands
13"	¼"	Walnut micro wood		320-grit	Sandpaper			Tack cloth
		Carpenter's or white glue			Deft Clear Wood Finish			

TOOLS

Steel tape rule
Combination square
Pencil
Claw hammer
Center punch
C-clamps (2)

Drill press or drill-press stand
Drill-press vise
Electric drill
³⁄₃₂" and ⁷⁄₆₄" twist-drill bits
⅝" and 1¼" Forstner bits
Bandsaw

Belt sander
Pad sander
Workmate®
Paintbrush

STEP 1
CUTTING WALNUT AND OAK

Set the fence on the bandsaw or clamp a straight strip of wood two inches from the blade, and rip the ⅛-inch and ¼-inch walnut micro wood and oak 1 × 3 to two inches. Then turn each strip perpendicular to the fence, and crosscut six squares of ⅛-inch walnut, six squares of ¼-inch walnut, and 12 squares of ¾-inch oak.

STEP 2
MARKING AND DRILLING SQUARES

Set a combination square for one inch, and mark the centers of three ⅛-inch walnut squares, five ¼-inch walnut squares, and ten ¾-inch oak squares for holes.

With a drill press and 1¼-inch Forstner bit, drill a hole through the center of three ⅛-inch walnut squares, three ¼-inch walnut squares, and ten ¾-inch oak squares. Switch to a ⅝-inch Forstner bit, and drill through the centers of two ¼-inch walnut squares. Be sure to put a scrap of wood beneath each square when drilling, and clamp the work securely in a drill-press vise.

STEP 3
MARKING AND DRILLING S AND P HOLES

On two of the remaining ⅛-inch walnut squares, scribe perpendicular center lines. Then on each, scribe two horizontal lines ⅜ of an inch above and below the horizontal center line, and

CUTTING WALNUT AND OAK

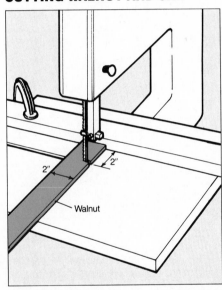

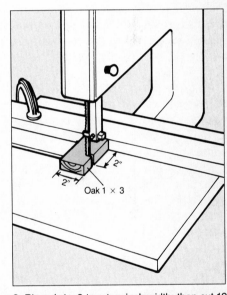

1. Rip ⅛-inch and ¼-inch walnut micro wood into two-inch-wide strips; then cut six two-inch squares from each.

2. Rip oak 1 × 3 to a two-inch width; then cut 12 two-inch squares.

MARKING SQUARES

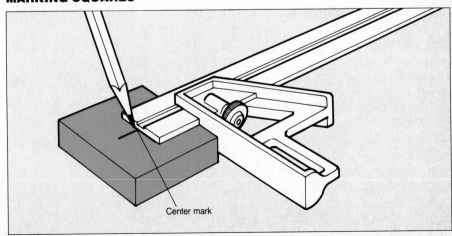

Mark the centers of three ⅛-inch walnut squares, five ¼-inch walnut squares, and 10 oak squares for drilling holes.

vertical lines ¼ of an inch left and right of the vertical center line.

Mark for drill-starter holes and center-punch starter holes. Then drill salt holes with a ³⁄₃₂-inch bit and pepper holes with a ⁷⁄₆₄-inch bit.

STEP 4
LAMINATING SHAKERS AND PICK HOLDER

Arrange the shaker squares according to the exploded diagram, and apply a coat of glue to the top of the bottom drilled oak square. Lay the walnut square with the ⁵⁄₈-inch hole atop that, apply glue to the top and bottom of another oak square, and lay that on top. Then apply glue to the top of a ⅛-inch walnut square, another oak square, and a ¼-inch walnut square, and stack them in that order.

Cap the assembly with a ⅛-inch walnut shaker top, and secure with six doubled rubber bands. Assemble the other shaker the same way.

Use the same pattern for the pick holder, starting with a solid oak square on the bottom, followed by a solid ¼-inch walnut square, solid oak square, and solid ⅛-inch walnut square.

Next, glue a drilled oak square, ¼-inch walnut square, and ⅛-inch walnut square, in that order. Secure with rubber bands as before, and let all three stand overnight.

STEP 5
SANDING SHAKERS AND PICK HOLDER

Rough-sand shaker and holder sides with a belt sander and medium belt. Then clamp a pad sander upside down in a Workmate®, and sand all surfaces with 120-, 220-, and 320-grit sandpaper.

STEP 6
FINISHING SHAKERS AND HOLDER

Thoroughly vacuum shakers and holder, and wipe them down with a tack cloth. Then apply three coats of Deft Clear Wood Finish.

When lacquer dries, fill holder with tooth picks, and shakers with salt and pepper; then put cork stoppers in bottoms of shakers.

DRILLING SQUARES

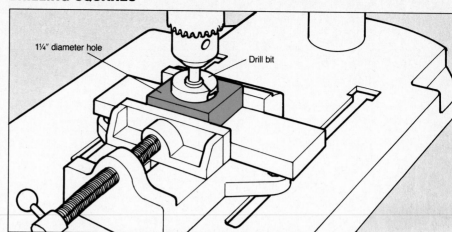

Drill 1¼-inch-diameter holes through the centers of three ⅛-inch walnut squares, three ¼-inch walnut squares, and 10 oak squares. Drill ⅝-inch-diameter holes through two ¼-inch walnut squares.

MARKING S AND P HOLES

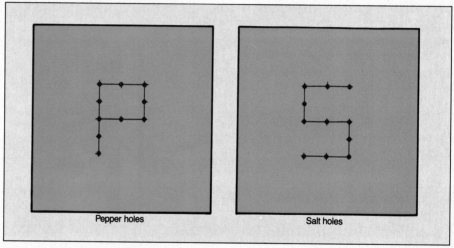

Pepper holes   Salt holes

Mark two ⅛-inch walnut squares for drill-starter holes according to these diagrams. Center-punch holes and then drill as explained in the text.

LAMINATING THE SET

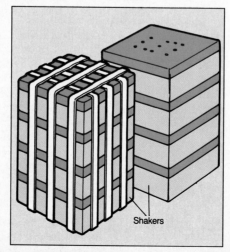

Shakers

Arrange squares according to diagrams, glue shakers and pick holder, and secure each assembly with rubber bands.

FINISHING THE SET

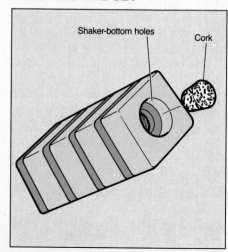

Shaker-bottom holes   Cork

After sanding the three pieces, apply three coats of lacquer. Plug the bottom holes in shakers with cork stoppers.

Candle Holders

Here's a project you can make from scraps or from wood you buy specifically for it. If the latter is the case, there's a bonus: another simple project you can make from the leftovers.

The materials list calls for 10-inch scraps of all required wood, because that's all you need to make the three candle holders.

Micro wood comes in 24-inch lengths. So if you choose to buy it for this project, either trim it to 10-inch lengths, or make a longer laminated block so that you have enough material for an extra gift set or napkin rings to match. From a 20-inch block, for example, you can cut a set of candle holders and eight matching napkin rings, or two complete sets of candle holders.

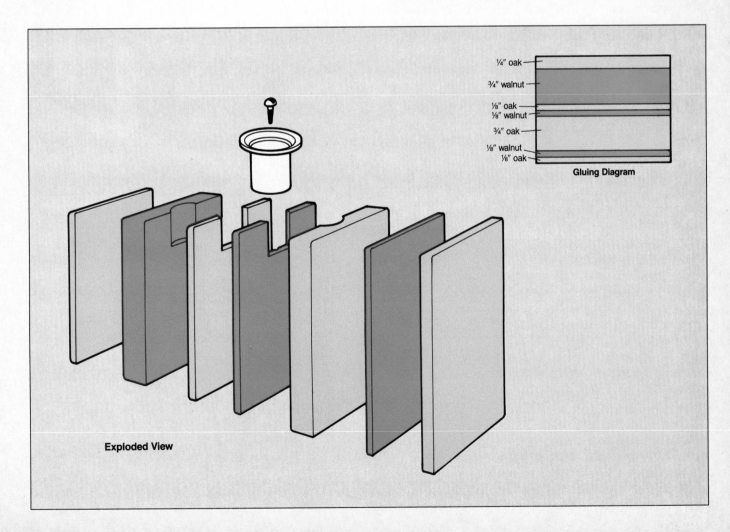

¼" oak
¾" walnut
⅛" oak
⅛" walnut
¾" oak
⅛" walnut
⅛" oak

Gluing Diagram

Exploded View

BILL OF MATERIALS

Qty	Size	Material	Qty	Size	Material	Qty	Size	Material
10″	1×3	Oak			Carpenter's or white glue		320-grit	Sandpaper
10″	1×3	Walnut	3		Brass candle cups		Medium	Sanding drum
10″	⅛″	Oak micro wood	3	½×6	Brass roundhead screws			Deft Clear Wood Finish
10″	¼″	Oak micro wood		120-grit	Sandpaper			Tack cloth
10″	⅛″	Walnut micro wood		220-grit	Sandpaper	12	⅛″×3½″	Rubber bands

TOOLS

Steel tape rule	3″ or larger C-clamps or bar clamps (6)	Bandsaw
Ruler or carpenter's square	Drill press or drill-press stand	Bench or belt sander
Pencil	Electric drill	Pad sander
Screwdriver	³⁄₃₂″ twist-drill bit	Workmate®
Miter box and backsaw	⅞″ and 1½″ Forstner bits	Paintbrush

STEP 1
RIPPING OAK AND WALNUT

Set the bandsaw fence or clamp a straight strip of wood to the bandsaw table 2¼ inches from the blade. Then rip all oak and walnut to a 2¼-inch width.

STEP 2
LAMINATING WOOD STRIPS

Lay strips out in this order: ¼-inch oak, ¾-inch walnut, ⅛-inch oak, ⅛-inch walnut, ¾-inch oak, ⅛-inch walnut, and ⅛-inch oak.

Brush an even coat of glue onto all but the last strip. Stack the strips in order, put clamp cushions against the outside strips, and secure with 12 evenly spaced rubber bands.

Clamp the block with six bar clamps or C-clamps, and let stand overnight.

STEP 3
CUTTING CANDLE HOLDERS AND NAPKIN RINGS

With a miter box and backsaw, slice about a quarter-inch off one end of the block. For each candle-holder set, use the miter box and backsaw, a bandsaw, or any stationary power saw to cut a two-inch, three-inch, and four-inch block. For each napkin ring, cut off a one-inch slice.

STEP 4
ROUGH-SANDING CANDLE HOLDERS AND NAPKIN RINGS

With a stationary or bench-model belt sander or a portable belt sander mounted upside down in a Workmate®,

RIPPING OAK AND WALNUT

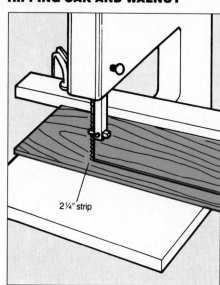

2¼″ strip

Rip two strips of ⅛-inch oak, two of ⅛-inch walnut, one of ¼-inch oak, oak 1 × 3, and walnut 1 × 3 to a 2¼-inch width.

LAMINATING STRIPS

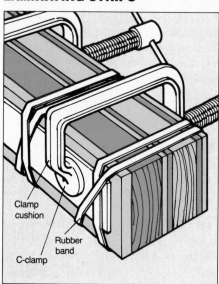

Clamp cushion

Rubber band

C-clamp

Glue strips together according to the diagram and secure the assembly with rubber bands and clamps.

CUTTING LAMINATED BLOCK

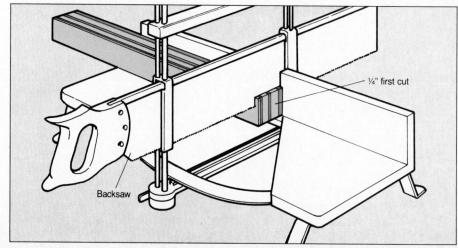

¼″ first cut

Backsaw

Trim a quarter-inch from one end of the block; then cut a two-inch, three-inch, and four-inch block for each holder set, and a one-inch slice for each napkin ring.

sand the laminated edges flat on each candle holder and napkin ring.

STEP 5
DRILLING HOLDERS AND RINGS

Scribe intersecting lines from corner to corner on one end of each candle holder and napkin ring.

Where lines intersect on candle holders, use a drill press and 7/8-inch Forstner bit to drill 3/4-inch-deep holes. Then drill a 3/32-inch pilot hole about 1/2-inch deep in the center of each existing hole.

Check candle cups for fit in the candle holders. Sand holes, as required, with an electric drill, drum-sanding attachment, and medium drum.

On napkin rings, drill through the centers with a 1½-inch Forstner bit. Be sure to put a scrap of wood under the napkin rings when drilling.

STEP 6
FINISH-SANDING HOLDERS AND RINGS

Clamp a pad sander upside down in a Workmate®. Sand all surfaces of the candle holders and napkin rings with 120-grit sandpaper. Then sand all surfaces but the holder bottoms with 220- and 320-grit paper.

STEP 7
FINISHING HOLDERS AND RINGS

Vacuum the candle holders and napkin rings, and wipe them down with a tack cloth to remove all dust. Then apply the finish of your choice.

To duplicate the finish of the objects pictured here, apply three coats of Deft Semi-Gloss Clear Wood Finish.

STEP 8
INSTALLING CANDLE CUPS

Press a brass candle cup into the hole in each candle holder. Then secure each candle cup with a ½ × 6 brass roundhead screw.

DRILLING HOLDERS AND RINGS

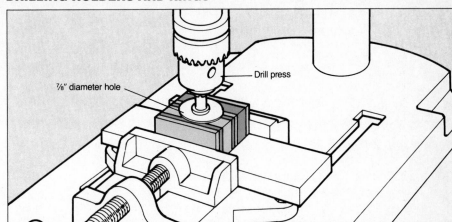

Drill a ⅞-inch-diameter, ¾-inch-deep hole in the top of each candle holder, and a 1½-inch-diameter hole through each napkin ring.

SANDING HOLDERS AND RINGS

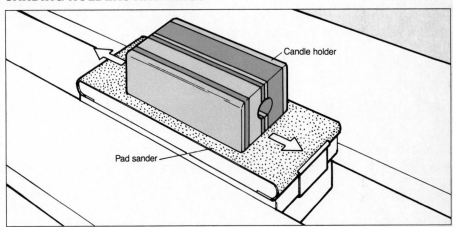

With a pad sander mounted in a Workmate®, finish-sand all the holders and rings with 120-grit sandpaper; then sand all surfaces but the holder bottoms with 220- and 320-grit paper.

INSTALLING CANDLE CUPS

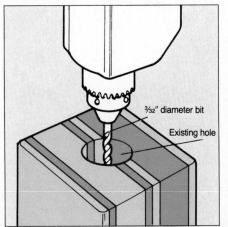 

1. Drill a ³⁄₃₂-inch-diameter, ½-inch-deep hole in the bottom center of each existing hole in the candle holders.

2. Install a brass candle cup in each holder with a brass screw.

Coaster Set

These coasters are an attractive means for protecting your finely finished furniture from unsightly glass rings. The three-coat lacquer finish is resistant to both water and alcohol, and the felt cushions attached to the bottoms prevent scratches.

You can make the coaster set from any available scraps that are six inches in length or longer. If you want to make extra sets for gifts or to sell at craft shows, you will need four inches of laminated stock for each set of eight.

The set shown is made of oak and walnut, because these woods are very compatible and contrast well. Many other hardwood combinations are appropriate, but use a dark wood with a light wood for the best effect.

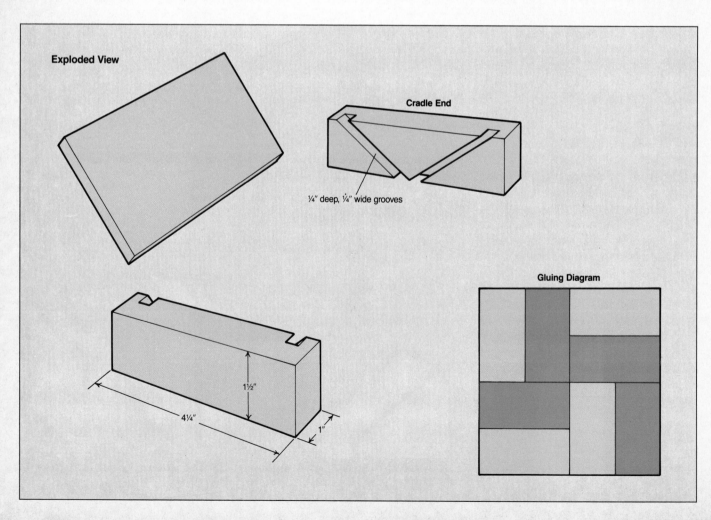

Exploded View

Cradle End

¼" deep, ¼" wide grooves

1½"

4¼"

1"

Gluing Diagram

BILL OF MATERIALS

Qty	Size	Material	Qty	Size	Material	Qty	Size	Material
7"	¼"	Oak micro wood			Five-minute epoxy cement			Tack cloth
36"	1×2	Oak		120-grit	Sandpaper			Deft Clear Wood Finish
24"	1×2	Black walnut		220-grit	Sandpaper			
		Carpenter's or white glue		320-grit	Sandpaper	1	6"×18"	Self-adhesive felt pad

TOOLS

Steel tape rule	4" C-clamps or bar clamps (6)	Belt sander
Straightedge	X-Acto knife	Pad sander
Pencil	Table saw	Workmate®
Miter box and backsaw	Bandsaw (optional)	Paintbrush

STEP 1
GLUING AND CLAMPING 1×2s
Apply an even coating of glue to a broad side of a 24-inch piece of oak 1×2. Then clamp a 24-inch piece of walnut 1×2 to it with at least four bar clamps or C-clamps to form a 2×2; let it stand until the glue sets.

STEP 2
CUTTING AND GLUING 2×2s
Sand any uneven spots along the seams of the 2×2s with a belt sander and medium belt.

With a miter box and backsaw, cut the laminated 2×2 in half. Then glue and clamp the two pieces together, according to the diagram, to form a 2×4.

STEP 3
CUTTING AND GLUING 2×4s
When glue has set, sand the seams of the 2×4 with a belt sander, as required.

Use a miter box and backsaw to cut the 2×4 in half. Then glue and clamp the two halves together, according to the diagram, to form a 4×4 (actual dimensions: three by three inches).

STEP 4
SANDING 4×4 BLOCK
Sand all surfaces except the ends of the laminated block with a belt sander and medium belt. Then sand with a pad sander and 120- and 220-grit sandpaper.

STEP 5
CUTTING COASTERS
With a miter box and backsaw, trim about a quarter-inch from one end of

GLUING 1×2s

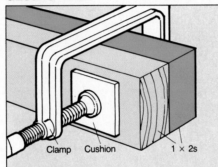

Apply a coat of glue to broad side of oak 1×2, and clamp it to a piece of walnut 1×2.

GLUING 2×4s

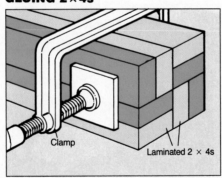

Glue two laminated 2×4 halves and clamp them together to form one 4×4.

ATTACHING FELT

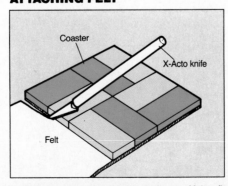

1. Using coasters as guides, cut pieces of felt to fit with an X-Acto knife and attach them to the coaster bottoms.

GLUING 2×2s

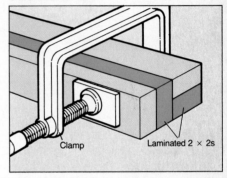

Glue two laminated 2×2 halves and clamp them together to form one 2×4.

CUTTING COASTERS

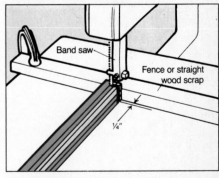

Use a bandsaw or a miter box with a backsaw to cut eight ⅜-inch coaster slices from the laminated 4×4 block.

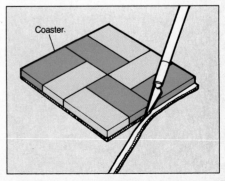

2. Carefully trim off excess felt around the coaster edges with an X-Acto knife.

the 4×4 block. Then, with either a miter box or a bandsaw with fence set ³⁄₈ of an inch from the blade, cut eight ³⁄₈-inch-thick slices from the block.

STEP 6
SANDING AND FINISHING COASTERS

Sand the end grain on both sides of each coaster with a belt sander and medium belt. Then secure a pad sander upside down in the jaws of a Workmate®, and sand all but the bottom surfaces of the coasters with 120- or 220-, and 320-grit paper.

Vacuum all dust from the coasters, and wipe them clean with a tack cloth. Then apply three coats of Deft Clear Wood Finish to all surfaces.

STEP 7
ATTACHING FELT TO COASTER BOTTOMS

Lay self-adhesive felt pad, cloth surface down, and use a straightedge and X-Acto knife to cut it in half lengthwise.

Using the coasters as guides, carefully cut pieces of felt to fit each. Peel off release paper, and affix felt to coaster bottoms.

Lay coasters felt side down on work surface, and carefully trim away excess felt with the point of the X-Acto knife.

STEP 8
GROOVING CRADLE ENDS

Set the table saw blade for a ¼-inch depth and miter gauge at 45 degrees.

Scribe a guide line on a narrow edge

GROOVING CRADLE ENDS

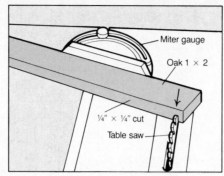

1. Cut a ¼-inch-deep, ¼-inch-wide groove in broad side of oak 1 × 2, using a table saw with the miter gauge set at 45 degrees.

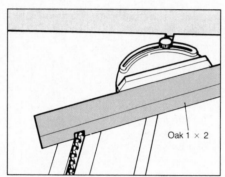

2. With the miter gauge on the opposite side of the blade, cut a second groove in the oak 1 × 2 to form a V to match the diagram on page 30.

CUTTING CRADLE PIECES

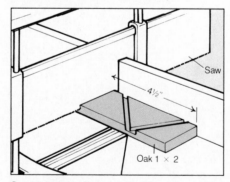

Cut 4¼ inches off each end of the grooved 1 × 2 to form cradle ends.

ASSEMBLING CRADLE

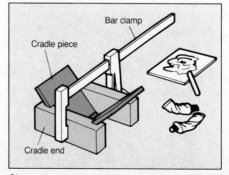

Glue oak micro wood into cradle-end grooves with epoxy cement; install a bar clamp.

of a 12-inch piece of oak 1 × 2, ¼ of an inch from the end. Then cut a diagonal ¼-inch-deep groove into a broad surface of the 1 × 2, just inside the guide line. Make another pass over the blade to widen the groove to ¼ of an inch.

Set the miter gauge on the opposite side of the blade, and do the same to form V-shaped grooves.

Make the same cuts at the opposite end of the 1 × 2 to make another V-shaped pair of grooves.

STEP 9
CUTTING AND SANDING CRADLE PIECES

Measure 4¼ inches from each end of the 1 × 2, mark, and cut off ends square with a miter box and backsaw.

Then stack coasters between the cradle ends, measure from the groove in one cradle end to the groove in the other, and cut two pieces of ¼-by-3-inch micro wood to that width (about 3⅞ inches).

Sand cradle pieces with 120- and 220-grit sandpaper.

STEP 10
ASSEMBLING AND FINISHING CRADLE

Mix a small amount of epoxy cement, and glue the cradle ends to the micro pieces. Secure with a bar clamp or C-clamp, and let stand five minutes.

Apply three coats of Deft Clear Wood Finish to the cradle. When the lacquer dries, fill the cradle with the coasters.

Planter Box

Ornamental planter boxes, built according to the instructions given for this project, hold house plants in pots up to eight inches in diameter. They can sit on tables, countertops, shelves, or on the floor with equal facility.

These boxes are meant for indoor use only. For outdoor use, construct them with pressure-treated lumber, cedar, or redwood, all of which resist the ravages of insects and the effects of weather.

If you use this design to build outdoor planters, you should also substitute a waterproof adhesive, such as plastic resin glue, and finish the planters with a more durable, weather-resistant finish, such as marine spar varnish or exterior polyurethane.

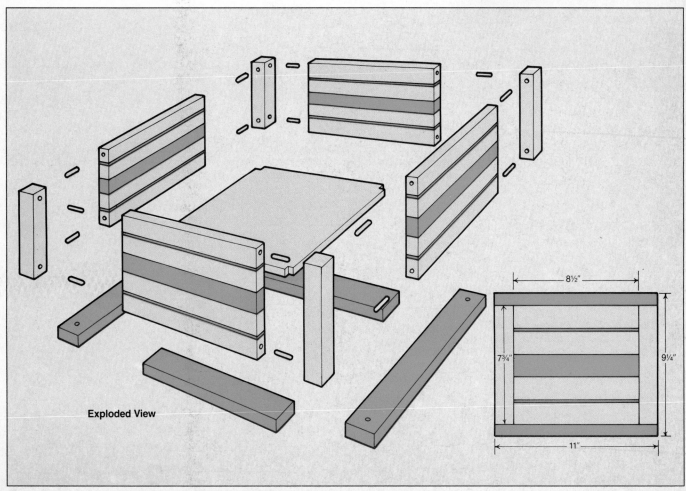

Exploded View

8½"

7¾"

9¼"

11"

BILL OF MATERIALS

Qty	Size	Material	Qty	Size	Material	Qty	Size	Material
1	9″ × 9″	¼″ or ½″ oak plywood scrap	16	5⁄16″	Fluted dowel pins			Deft Clear Wood Finish
12′	1 × 2	Oak			Carpenter's or white glue			Watco Natural Danish Oil Finish
12′	1 × 2	Walnut			Five-minute epoxy cement			
24″	⅛″	Walnut micro wood	4	⅞″	Leveling furniture glides			Watco Medium Walnut Danish Oil Finish
3′	2 × 2	Oak		120-grit	Sandpaper			Tack cloth
				220-grit·	Sandpaper			

TOOLS

Steel tape rule
Combination square
Pencil
Claw hammer
Soft-faced mallet
Center punch
Miter box and backsaw

Bar clamps (4–8)
Dowel jig
Electric drill
5⁄16″ twist-drill bit
⅜″ brad-point bit
5⁄16″ drill stop or collar
Portable jig saw

Table saw
Bandsaw
Belt sander
Pad sander
Workmate® or woodworker's vise
Paintbrush

STEP 1
CUTTING AND RIPPING WOOD STRIPS

With a miter box and backsaw, cut four pieces of oak 2 × 2 to 7¾ inches, eight pieces of oak 1 × 2 and two pieces of walnut 1 × 2 to 18 inches, and two pieces of walnut 1 × 2 to 40 inches.

Set the bandsaw fence or clamp a straight piece of wood 1¼ inches from the blade, and rip the 40-inch pieces of walnut to that width.

Reset the fence for a ¾-inch rip, and rip the ⅛-inch walnut micro wood into four strips. Then trim those to 18 inches.

STEP 2
LAMINATING THE WOOD STRIPS

Laminate the 18-inch strips into two 7¾-by-18-inch slabs by gluing in this order: oak 1 × 2, ⅛-inch micro wood, oak 1 × 2, walnut 1 × 2, oak 1 × 2, ⅛-inch micro wood, and oak 1 × 2. Clamp each set with four bar clamps, and let it stand for about an hour.

STEP 3
ROUGH-SANDING SLABS

Secure laminated slabs on the Workmate® top with swivel grips, and rough-sand both sides with a belt sander and medium belt. Then sand with a pad sander and 120-grit sandpaper.

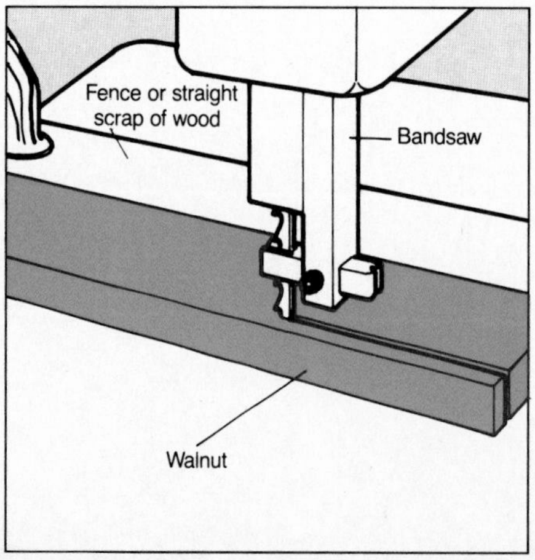

CUTTING WOOD STRIPS

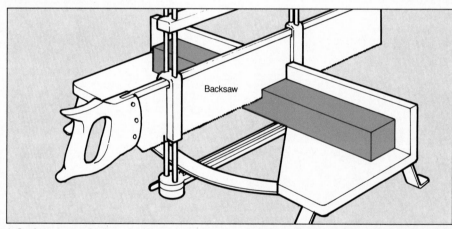

1. Cut four pieces of oak 2 × 2 to 7¾ inches, eight pieces of oak 1 × 2 and two 1 × 2 walnuts to 18 inches, and two 1 × 2 walnuts to 40 inches.

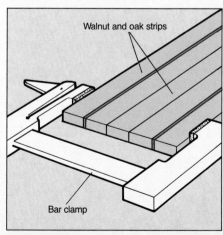

2. Rip the 40-inch walnut 1 × 2s to a 1¼-inch width and the walnut micro wood into four ¾-inch strips.

LAMINATING STRIPS

Apply glue to two sets of 18-inch oak and walnut strips, clamp each set with four bar clamps, and let the assembly stand an hour.

STEP 4
CUTTING PLANTER SIDES

Set the table-saw fence 17¾ inches from the near teeth of the blade, and trim one end of each slab. Reset the fence for 8½ inches, and, with the trimmed end of the slab against the fence, cut two planter sides.

STEP 5
MARKING AND DRILLING FOR DOWEL PINS

Mark each end of each planter side ¾ of an inch from the top and bottom; then use a dowel jig aligned with the marks and a 5⁄16-inch bit to drill a hole about an inch deep at each spot.

Mark two adjacent sides of each 2×2 corner piece for matching holes, and with a drill stop or collar on the bit set for a ½-inch depth, drill four holes in each corner piece.

Then finish-sand outer surfaces of planter sides with a pad sander and 220-grit sandpaper.

STEP 6
ASSEMBLING PLANTER SIDES

Pour a small amount of glue into a jar lid, dip four dowel pins in glue, insert them in the side holes of two corner pieces, and tap them with a soft-faced mallet to seat them.

Dip the pin ends of one corner piece in glue, and insert them in one end of a planter side; then tap home with a block of wood and soft-faced mallet.

Attach a corner piece to the opposite end the same way, and attach two more corner pieces to another side, with open holes in each facing the same direction. Glue and tap pins into open holes. Then dip pins of one side assembly in glue, and lay assembly on bench, pins up.

Tap the other side pieces onto the side assembly, as before, and let the unit stand for 30 minutes.

STEP 7
CUTTING AND ATTACHING BOTTOM TRIM

Turn the planter box upside down, measure from one outside corner to another, and cut a piece of ripped walnut 1×2 to fit. Cut another to fit the opposite side.

DRILLING FOR DOWEL PINS

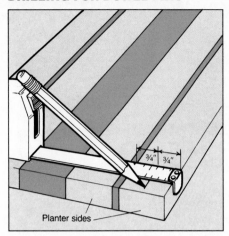

1. Mark each end of the planter sides ¾ of an inch from top and bottom; also mark the 2×2 corner pieces in the same way.

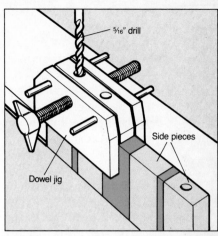

2. Use a dowel jig and a 5⁄16-inch bit to drill dowel holes in the corner pieces and the planter sides.

ASSEMBLING PLANTER SIDES

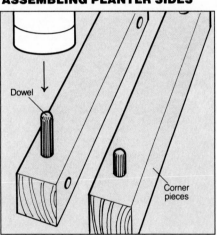

1. Apply glue to the ends of the dowel pins, and tap them firmly into the corner 2×2s with a soft-faced mallet.

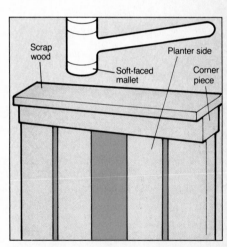

2. Glue dowel ends, and tap corner pieces into planter side with mallet and wood scrap.

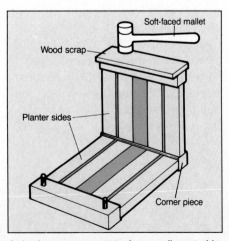

3. In the same way, attach two adjacent sides using glue and dowel pins.

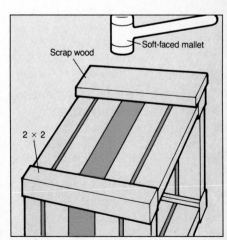

4. Attach the third and fourth sides with glue and dowel pins in the same way.

Mix a small amount of epoxy cement; apply a thin bead to the bottom edges of two opposing sides, and a small amount to the bottom of the corner 2×2s. Then clamp each piece of trim in place with two bar or cam clamps, and let stand for five minutes.

Cut two more pieces of walnut to fit between those installed, and attach them with epoxy and clamps.

STEP 8
CUTTING AND INSTALLING THE BOTTOM

Trim a scrap of ¼-inch or ½-inch plywood to nine by nine inches. With a portable jig saw or a backsaw, cut a ¼-inch square notch in each corner.

With the planter upright, run a bead of glue along the top edges of the bottom trim, lay the bottom panel in place, put a heavy object on it, and let stand for 30 minutes.

STEP 9
ATTACHING TOP TRIM AND FINISH-SANDING

Cut four pieces of ripped walnut 1×2 as you did for the bottom trim, and attach them to the planter top the same way.

Then sand the trim with a pad sander and 120- and 220-grit paper, rounding over corners and sharp edges.

STEP 10
MARKING AND DRILLING FOR FURNITURE GLIDES

Turn the planter upside down. Set a combination square for ⅝ of an inch, measure in that far from each bottom corner, and mark for a centered hole.

Center-punch a drill-starter hole, and drill a ⅜-inch-diameter hole one inch deep at each spot.

STEP 11
FINISHING THE PLANTER BOX AND INSTALLING GLIDES

Vacuum the planter box, and wipe it down with a tack cloth. Then apply the finish of your choice.

ATTACHING BOTTOM TRIM

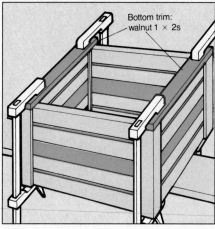

Bottom trim: walnut 1 × 2s

Attach ripped walnut 1×2 to bottom of planter with epoxy cement and bar clamps.

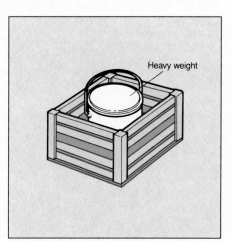

Heavy weight

2. Glue bottom in place, set a heavy object on it, and let it stand for 30 minutes.

Let stand 72 hours; then apply three coats of Deft Clear Wood Finish.

When lacquer dries, turn planter box upside down, and tap a glide barrel into each hole. Then screw a glide into each.

To duplicate the finish shown, mix equal parts of Watco Natural and Medium Walnut Danish Oil Finish, and follow manufacturer's directions.

INSTALLING PLANTER BOTTOM

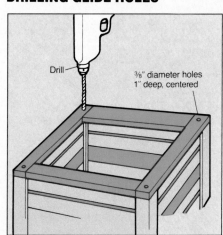

¼" × ¼" notch in each corner

9" × 9" plywood scrap

1. Cut a piece of plywood scrap to nine-by-nine-inch size. Then cut a ¼-inch square notch into each corner of the piece.

DRILLING GLIDE HOLES

Drill

⅜" diameter holes 1" deep, centered

Drill a centered ⅜-inch-diameter hole an inch deep in each corner of the bottom.

INSTALLING GLIDES

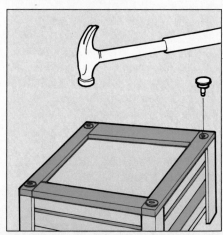

Tap a glide barrel into holes in bottom trim. Screw a glide into each barrel.

Adjustable Bookrack

Most households have a collection of books of one kind or another. So whether you are a homeowner with a large library and shelf units spanning entire walls, or an apartment dweller with only a few volumes in need of organized storage, this useful rack will keep your favorite books in order, close at hand.

This adjustable bookrack fits as well atop a desk in the home office, study, or den as it does in a child's room or on the kitchen countertop where it will conveniently organize cookbooks.

Inasmuch as the bookrack makes an excellent gift, you might want to make several for your home and others for friends. If you like the idea of turning a profit on your hobby, the rack is a dandy craft-show product.

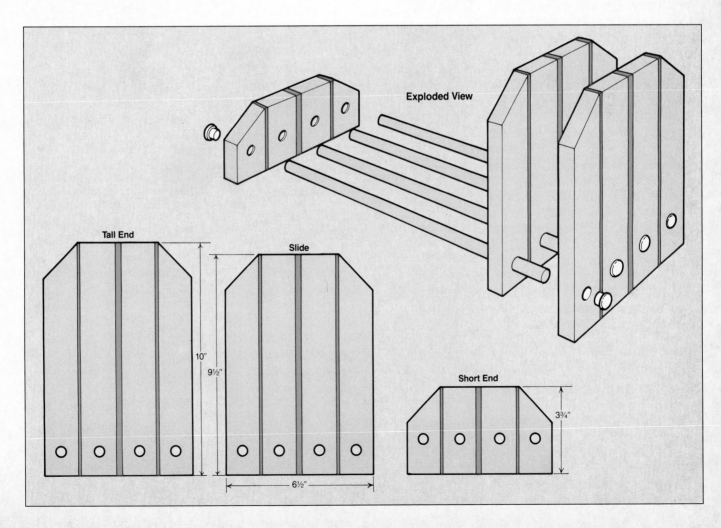

Exploded View

Tall End

Slide

10"

9½"

6½"

Short End

3¾"

BILL OF MATERIALS

Qty	Size	Material	Qty	Size	Material	Qty	Size	Material
8'	1 × 2	Oak			Carpenter's or white glue			Oil Finish
24"	⅛"	Walnut micro wood	120-grit		Sandpaper			Watco Medium Walnut
24"	¼"	Walnut micro wood	220-grit		Sandpaper			Danish Oil Finish
8	½"	Oak button plugs			Deft Clear Wood Finish			Tack cloth
2	½" × 36"	Oak dowel rods			Watco Natural Danish			

TOOLS

Steel tape rule
Combination square
Pencil
Claw hammer
Soft-faced mallet
Center punch
Miter box and backsaw

Spring clamps or C-clamps (2)
Bar clamps (4)
Drill press or drill-press stand
½" brad-point bit
⅜" cylindrical grinding point
1" conical grinding point
Bandsaw

Belt sander
Pad sander
Bench disc sander (optional)
Workmate®
Paintbrush

STEP 1
CUTTING OAK AND WALNUT

Cut an eight-foot oak 1 × 2 or trim four scraps to 24 inches. Set the bandsaw fence ¾ of an inch from the blade, and rip two 24-inch strips of ⅛-inch and one strip of ¼-inch walnut micro wood to ¾-inch widths.

STEP 2
GLUING STRIPS

Sort oak in a contrasting grain pattern and number the ends from 1 to 4. Stand oak strips on narrow edges, and apply an even coat of glue to the top edges of strips 1, 2, and 3. Apply glue to a broad edge of each strip of walnut.

Lay the oak strips on their broad sides, and sandwich a ⅛-inch walnut strip between strips 1 and 2, another between 3 and 4, and the ¼-inch strip between 2 and 3. Clamp the strips together with four bar clamps, and let the assembly stand for 30 minutes.

STEP 3
SANDING AND CUTTING THE SLAB

Sand both broad surfaces of the slab with a belt sander and medium belt. Then sand with a pad sander and 120- and 220-grit paper.

With a miter box and backsaw, cut ¼ of an inch off one end of the slab. Then

RIPPING WALNUT STRIPS

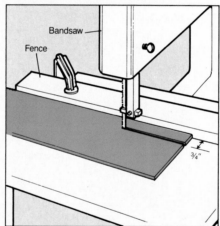

Set the bandsaw fence ¾ of an inch from the blade. Then rip two strips of ⅛-inch and one strip of ¼-inch walnut micro wood.

MARKING DOWEL HOLES

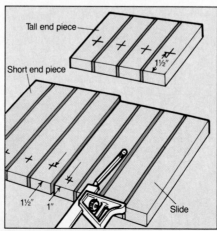

Mark the center of each oak 1 × 2 strip 1½ inches from the bottom on both rack ends and one inch from the bottom on the smaller slide.

GLUING OAK AND WALNUT

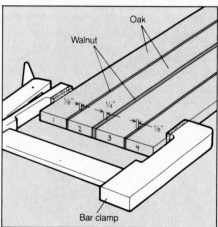

Glue ⅛-inch walnut strips between oak strips 1 and 2, and between 3 and 4; glue a ¼-inch strip between oak strips 2 and 3; then clamp.

BEVELING DOWEL HOLES

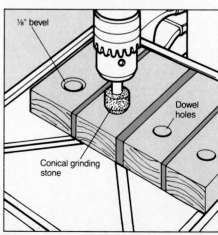

Put a ⅛-inch bevel in each dowel hole, using a conical grinding point.

cut a 10-inch end piece, 3¾-inch end piece, and 9½-inch slide.

STEP 4
MARKING AND DRILLING COMPONENTS

Mark the center of each oak 1 × 2 strip 1½ inches from the bottom on each end piece and one inch from the bottom on the slide.

Center-punch a drill-starter hole and drill a ½-inch-diameter hole at each spot.

STEP 5
CUTTING AND SANDING DOWEL RODS

Cut each dowel rod exactly in half. Hand-sand each rod with 120- and 220-grit sandpaper. Then, either by hand or with a stationary disk sander, bevel each end of each rod about ⅛ of an inch.

STEP 6
GRINDING AND BEVELING DOWEL HOLES

With a drill press or drill-press stand and electric drill and ⅜-inch cylindrical grinding point, polish the holes in the end pieces so dowel-rod ends fit snugly. Enlarge and polish holes in the slide until rods slide freely in them.

Use a conical grinding point to put a ⅛-inch bevel on the inside of each hole in the end pieces and both sides of each hole in the slide.

STEP 7
CUTTING CORNERS AND FINISH-SANDING COMPONENTS

With a miter box and backsaw set at 45 degrees, cut the top corners off each component to the ⅛-inch walnut strips.

Clamp a pad sander upside down in a Workmate®, and sand the narrow edges of the components with 120-grit paper. Then sand all but the bottom edges with 220-grit paper, slightly rounding over corners and sharp edges as you proceed.

TRIMMING TOP CORNERS

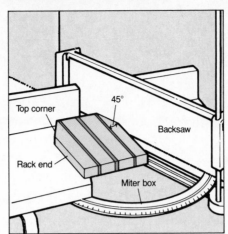

Cut off the top corners of both rack ends and the slide at a 45-degree angle, using a miter box with a backsaw.

SLIDE AND SHORT END

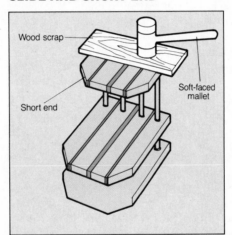

Put the slide onto the rods; then put the short end on the rods, and tap in place with a soft-faced mallet and a scrap of wood.

STEP 8
ASSEMBLING THE BOOKRACK

Lay the tall end piece on a workbench, with inside surface facing up, twist a dowel rod into each hole, and tap each lightly with a soft-faced mallet until firmly seated. Put the slide onto the rods, and press the short end piece onto the rods. With a block of wood and hammer or soft-faced mallet, tap the short end piece to seat the rods.

At the outside of each end-piece hole, squeeze in a small amount of glue, insert a button plug, and tap lightly with a soft-faced mallet to seat. Let stand for two hours or overnight.

INSTALLING DOWEL RODS

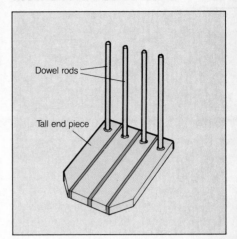

Twist a dowel rod into each hole in the tall end piece.

PLUGGING HOLES

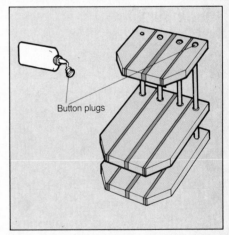

Put a small amount of glue in each dowel hole at each end, and plug the holes with button plugs, tapping them gently into place.

STEP 9
FINISHING THE BOOKRACK

Check the slide for proper functioning. If it doesn't slide freely along the entire length of the rods, hand-sand the rods with 220-grit sandpaper, as required.

Vacuum the bookrack to remove dust, and wipe the unit with a tack cloth. It's now ready for the finish of your choice.

To duplicate the finish of the rack shown, mix equal parts of Watco Natural and Medium Walnut Danish Oil Finish, apply according to the manufacturer's directions, and let stand for 72 hours. Then apply three coats of Deft Clear Wood Finish.

Shelf Unit

Whether you need a compact unit with adjustable shelves to house a few books, stereo components, and other items, or several walls of floor-to-ceiling shelves to hold a large library, here's a project that will serve you well. What's more, the unit shown can be easily expanded to fit your needs. It can be finished in any way you wish, or left unfinished to serve as utility shelving.

The laminated shelves are considerably stronger than dimensional lumber cut to the same length and are much less susceptible to cupping and checking.

The unit's uprights are braced between floor and ceiling by means of tension devices at the top. To add on to the unit, simply make another upright and seven more shelves for every 30 inches of wall space to be covered.

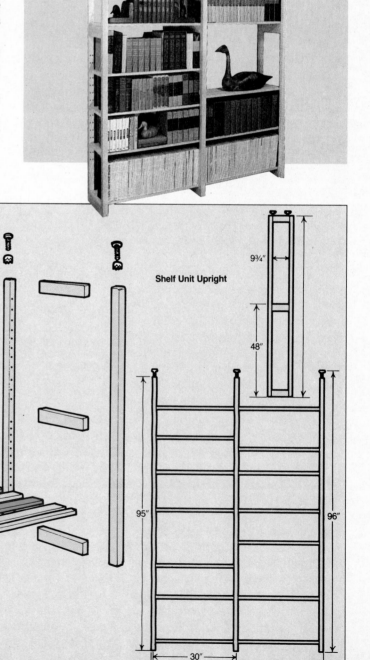

Exploded View

Shelf Unit Upright

9¾″

48″

95″

96″

30″

61½″

PARTS LIST

Part Name	Qty	Description	Part Name	Qty	Description
Upright vertical	6	1½" × 1½" × 95" fir or pine	Shelf strip	84	¾" × 1½" × 31" fir or pine
Upright horizontal	9	1½" × 3" × 9¾" fir or pine	Shelf-face trim	14	½" × ¾" × 30" parting bead

BILL OF MATERIALS

Qty	Size	Material	Qty	Size	Material	Qty	Size	Material
9	1" × 6" × 8'	K.D. pine or fir			Wood filler	220-grit		Sandpaper
1	1" × 6" × 4'	K.D. pine or fir			Carpenter's or white glue			Watco Natural Danish
6	2" × 2" × 8'	Clear fir or pine		1"	Brads			Oil Finish
1	2" × 4" × 8'	Clear fir or pine	36	8d	Finishing nails			Deft Clear Wood
4	½" × ¾" × 8'	Parting bead	56		Shelf-bracket pins			Finish
1	½" × ¾" × 6'	Parting bead	6		Tension devices			Tack cloth
				120-grit	Sandpaper			

TOOLS

Steel tape rule	Miter box and backsaw	⁷⁄₆₄", ⁵⁄₁₆", and ¼" twist-drill bits
Carpenter's square	Large spring clamps (2)	⅜" brad-point bit
Combination square	Threaded-rod clamps (4 or more)	Circular saw and guide
Pencil	Corner clamps (4)	Table saw or bandsaw
Felt-tipped pen	½" or adjustable wrenches (2)	Belt and pad sanders
Claw hammer	Putty knife	Two sawhorses or Workmate®
Nail set	Drill press or drill-press stand	Paintbrush
Center punch	Electric drill	

STEP 1
CUTTING AND RIPPING WOOD

Use a miter box and backsaw to trim six 2 × 2s to one inch less than ceiling height (95 inches for a standard eight-foot ceiling).

Cut an eight-foot 2 × 4 into nine 9¾-inch pieces. Then set a table saw or bandsaw fence a quarter-inch from the *near* teeth of the blade, and run each piece through the saw to square one edge. Reset the blade at three inches, and run each piece through again with the squared edge against the fence.

From each eight-foot 1 × 6, cut three 31-inch pieces; then cut another from the four-foot 1 × 6. With a table saw or bandsaw, rip a quarter-inch from one edge of each piece. Then set the fence 1½ inches from the *near* teeth of the blade, and rip 84 strips.

Cut the four eight-foot parting beads into 12 30-inch strips. From the six-footer, cut two more 30-inch strips.

STEP 2
DRILLING VERTICALS

Sort the six 2 × 2s into three sets of two, and mark the top of each front and rear

RIPPING UPRIGHTS

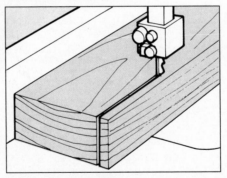

Use a bandsaw or table saw to rip each 9¾-inch 2 × 4 to a three-inch width.

MARKING VERTICALS

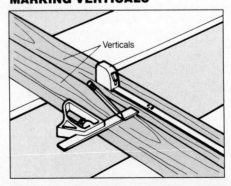

1. Scribe lines across the inside surfaces of verticals, two at a time, 48 inches from the bottom. Clamp pairs together at top and bottom.

CUTTING 1 × 6s

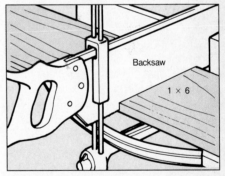

Use a miter box and backsaw to cut 28 pieces of 1 × 6 to 31 inches each.

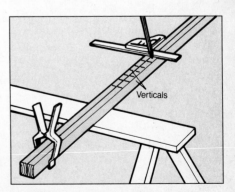

2. Scribe lines across the inside surfaces at two-inch intervals, 12 to 40 inches from the bottom and 8 to 36 inches from the top.

piece: 1F and 1R, 2F and 2R, and 3F and 3R.

Lay each pair side by side, inside surfaces up. Measure 48 inches from the bottom, and scribe a line across each pair with a combination square. Then, using that as a guide line, scribe lines across the adjacent sides of each piece.

Carefully align one pair of 2 × 2s, and clamp them top and bottom with two spring clamps or C-clamps.

Extend a steel tape rule from the bottom, and make marks at two-inch intervals from 12 to 40 inches from the bottom. Then extend the steel tape rule from the top and do the same, from 8 to 36 inches.

Use a combination square to scribe a line across the inside surfaces of both 2 × 2s in each set at each spot marked. Then set the square for 3/8 of an inch, and mark each line (except those at 48 inches) at 3/8 of an inch from the left and right edges.

Center-punch a drill-starter hole and drill a 1/4-inch-diameter, 1/2-inch-deep hole at each spot.

Rotate the 2 × 2s so outside surfaces are up, and scribe lines across each at one and two inches from the top and bottom and 46 and 47 inches from the bottom.

Set the combination square for 3/4 of an inch, and mark the center of each line. Then center-punch a drill-starter hole and drill a 7/64-inch-diameter pilot hole at each spot.

STEP 3
ASSEMBLING UPRIGHTS

Sand the inside surface of each 2 × 2 vertical with a pad sander and 120- and 220-grit sandpaper, but avoid the guide lines scribed earlier.

Butt a 9¾-inch horizontal to the top inside of a front vertical, dry-clamp it with a corner clamp, and adjust for fit. Remove the horizontal, apply glue to one end, and let stand for several minutes. Apply more glue, as required, clamp the horizontal to the vertical, and secure it with two 8d finishing nails, driven through the pilot holes. Countersink the nails.

Attach another horizontal to the bottom inside of the vertical the same way. Then attach a third vertical with its top

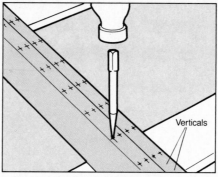

3. Mark each line 3/8 of an inch from each side, and center-punch a drill-starter hole at each spot.

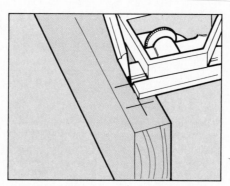

5. Mark for centered holes on the outside surfaces of the verticals at one and two inches from the top and bottom and 46 and 47 inches from the bottom.

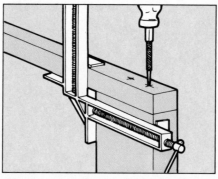

2. Attach the other vertical to the assembly the same way, with glue, corner clamps, and nails; then countersink the nails.

2. Drill 3/8-inch-diameter holes through the strips, centered on the lines.

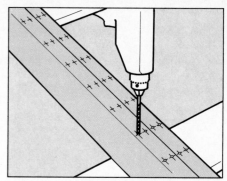

4. Drill a 1/4-inch-diameter, 1/2-inch-deep hole at each spot, two per line.

ASSEMBLING UPRIGHTS

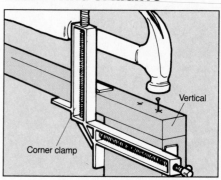

1. Glue and clamp a 3-by-9¾-inch horizontal to the top inside of a vertical, secure with two 8d finishing nails, and countersink the nails.

DRILLING SHELF STRIPS

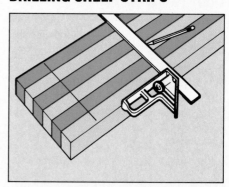

1. Scribe lines across the narrow edges of the shelf strips at 1½ and 11 inches from each end.

LAMINATING SHELVES

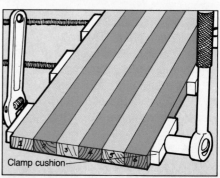

Laminate each set of six strips with glue and four rod clamps.

edge aligned with the guide lines 48 inches from the bottom.

Turn the assembly over, and apply glue to the upright ends of the horizontals. Then attach the rear vertical with 8d nails, and countersink the nails. With a corner clamp at the bottom front corner and another at the top rear corner, let the assembly stand for at least an hour.

Assemble two more uprights the same way.

STEP 4
SORTING, MARKING, AND DRILLING SHELF STRIPS

Sort the 31-inch shelf strips into 14 sets of six, and sequentially number one end of each set.

Rotate the strips in each set so they're standing on narrow edges, align them, and scribe lines across each set at 1½ and 11 inches from each end.

With a drill press or drill-press stand and electric drill, drill ⅜-inch-diameter holes through each strip, centered on the lines.

STEP 5
LAMINATING THE SHELVES

Insert a rod clamp into each hole in the first strip of one set. Brush an even coat of glue onto a narrow edge of the second strip, and slide it onto the rod clamps, down to the first strip. Continue applying glue to the remaining strips and sliding them onto the clamps.

Attach a cushion, flat washer, and hex nut to the end of each clamp, and tighten clamp nuts with a pair of ½-inch or adjustable wrenches. Wipe excess glue from the shelf with a damp sponge, and let stand two hours or overnight.

Assemble 13 more shelves in the same manner.

STEP 6
CUTTING AND TRIMMING THE SHELVES

Use a circular saw to cut a half-inch off each end of each shelf, for a finished length of 30 inches. Then, with a miter box and backsaw, cut 14 pieces of parting bead to 30 inches.

Prenail each piece of parting bead with five one-inch brads. Stand each

ATTACHING PARTING BEAD

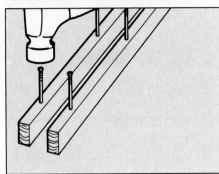

1. Prenail each 30-inch parting-bead strip with five one-inch brads.

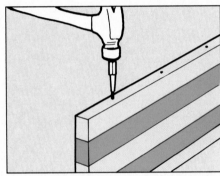

2. Attach parting bead to the front edge of each shelf with glue and brads, and countersink the brads.

INSTALLING TENSION DEVICES

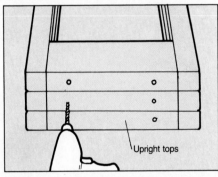

1. Drill ⁵⁄₁₆-inch-diameter, one-inch-deep holes in the tops of the uprights, centered three inches from the front and rear.

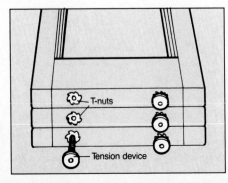

2. Tap a T-nut into each hole in the tops of the uprights. Screw a tension device into each T-nut.

shelf on its rear edge, and run a thin bead of glue along its front edge. Lay a parting-bead strip on the shelf's front edge, and countersink the brads.

STEP 7
FILLING AND SANDING

Fill brad and nail holes in the shelf and upright fronts with wood filler, and let stand until the filler hardens.

Sand top and bottom surfaces of the shelves to a smooth, even finish with a belt sander and medium belt. Then sand tops and fronts with a pad sander and 120- and 220-grit sandpaper, slightly rounding over front edges as you proceed.

Sand the uprights with a pad sander and 120- and 220-grit sandpaper, slightly rounding over corners and edges as you sand.

STEP 8
INSTALLING TENSION DEVICES

Lay the uprights on one side atop a Workmate® or pair of sawhorses. Measure in three inches from the front and rear edges and scribe lines across each top horizontal. Then mark the center of each line for a drill-starter hole.

Center-punch a drill-starter hole, and drill a ⁵⁄₁₆-inch-diameter hole about an inch or so deep at each spot. Tap a T-nut into each hole, and screw a tension device into each T-nut.

STEP 9
FINISHING THE SHELF UNIT

The shelf unit is now ready for the finish of your choice. You can either stain the uprights and shelves or finish them naturally. Then apply the oil, varnish, or lacquer that best suits your needs.

You also have the option of leaving the unit unfinished, which you may prefer if you plan to use it for utility shelving in a basement, garage, or workshop.

The unfinished shelving also works well in any room where walls are covered with rustic paneling or unfinished tongue-and-groove planks. The unfinished shelves and uprights will darken naturally with age and can always be stained and varnished or lacquered later.

Cutlery Block

If there's a kitchen without cutlery, it's probably also a kitchen without a cook. In fact, in most households, kitchen knives are the most important tools the home chef owns. Yet, in far too many instances, quality cutlery is thrown carelessly into a drawer, along with other utensils, where it can be dangerous to hands, and where it is inevitably dulled and nicked.

One of the best places to store an assortment of knives is in a hardwood block made for the purpose. For this project, you will learn how to make a block designed to hold a butcher's steel and up to 12 knives ranging in size from small parers and peelers to large carvers and chef's knives.

Made of oak and finished to show off the wood's beauty, this cutlery block should fit the decor of any kitchen.

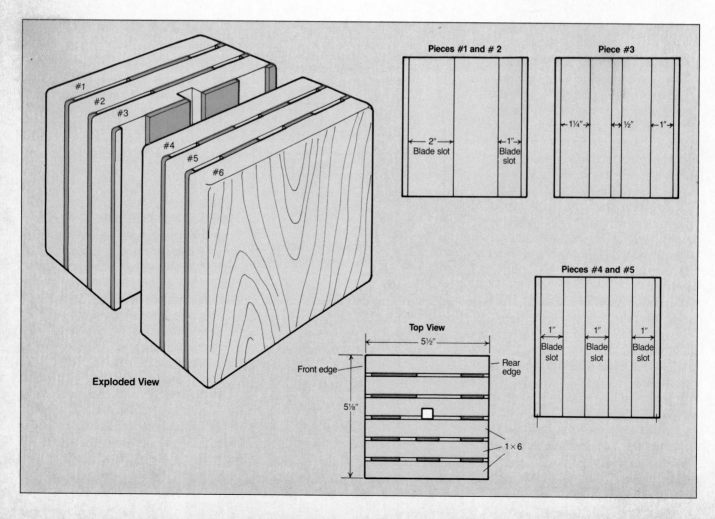

Exploded View

#1 #2 #3 #4 #5 #6

Pieces #1 and #2

2" Blade slot   1" Blade slot

Piece #3

1¼"   ½"   1"

Pieces #4 and #5

1" Blade slot   1" Blade slot   1" Blade slot

Top View

Front edge   Rear edge

5½"

5⅛"

1 × 6

BILL OF MATERIALS

Qty	Size	Material	Qty	Size	Material	Qty	Size	Material
1	1″×6″ ×6′	Oak		220-grit	Sandpaper			Danish Oil Finish
			1		Emery board			Deft Clear Wood Finish
3	⅛″×3″* ×24″	Oak micro wood	4	½″	Rubber protector pads			Tack cloth
		Carpenter's or white glue			Watco Medium Walnut			
	120-grit	Sandpaper						

TOOLS

Steel tape rule	Spring clamps (4)	Belt sander
Combination square	12″ bar clamps (4)	Pad sander
Pencil	Table saw	Workmate® (optional)
Miter box and backsaw	Bandsaw	Paintbrush

STEP 1
CUTTING AND RIPPING WOOD

With a miter box and backsaw, cut six pieces of oak 1×6 to 10¼ inches. Then, from three ⅛-inch oak micro wood strips, cut six pieces to 10¼ inches.

Set the bandsaw fence or clamp a strip of wood ¼ of an inch from the blade, and rip five ¼-inch strips from two 10¼-inch pieces of micro wood. Reset the fence at one inch, and rip another strip. Reset the fence, and rip a 1¼-inch strip.

Set the fence ⅞ of an inch from the blade, and rip a strip from each of the remaining 3-by-10¼ inch pieces of micro wood. Reset the fence two inches from the blade, and rip two more strips.

STEP 2
MARKING OAK 1×6

Find the two 1×6 pieces with the best grain, and use them as the exterior pieces. Then number each piece from 1 to 6.

Set a combination square for 2¼ inches, and make several pencil marks parallel to the front edges on pieces 1 and 2.

Set the square for 1½ inches, and make several marks parallel to the front edges of pieces 4 and 5. Reset the square for 1¼ inches, and make several marks parallel to the rear edges on the same pieces.

CUTTING AND RIPPING WOOD

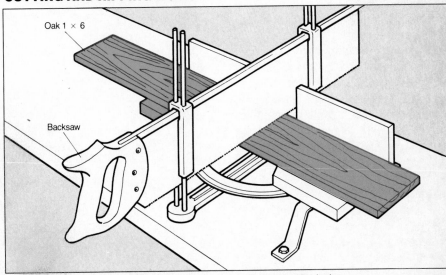

Oak 1 × 6

Backsaw

1. Use a miter box and backsaw to cut six pieces of oak 1 × 6 to 10¼ inches.

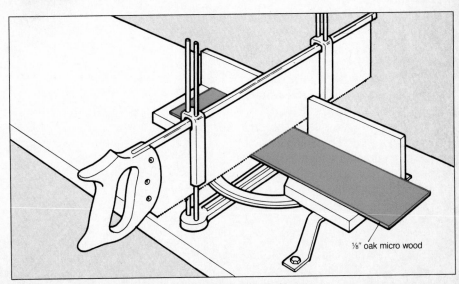

⅛″ oak micro wood

2. Then cut six pieces of ⅛-inch oak micro wood to 10¼ inches.

STEP 3
GROOVING 1 × 6 PIECE NO. 3

Set the table-saw blade for a ³⁄₈-inch depth and the fence 2½ inches from the *near* teeth. Then, with the front edge of 1 × 6 piece No. 3 against the fence, run it over the blade to cut a ³⁄₈-inch-deep groove the length of the piece.

Reset the fence three inches from the *far* teeth of the blade, and cut another groove. Then reset the fence and make two more passes to remove all material between the first two cuts, creating a ³⁄₈-inch-deep, ½-inch-wide groove the length of the piece.

STEP 4
GLUING MICRO STRIPS AND 1 × 6 PIECES

Brush a thin coat of glue onto one side of two ¼-inch-wide micro strips, and press them in place flush with the front and rear edges of 1 × 6 piece No. 1. Apply a thin coat of glue to a two-inch-wide strip, and press it in place, aligned with the marks scribed in Step 2. Brush a coat of glue onto the tops of the strips, lay 1 × 6 piece No. 2 on top, and clamp the pieces with four spring clamps or bar clamps. Let stand for 30 minutes.

While the glue sets, attach two more ¼-inch strips flush with the front and rear edges of 1 × 6 piece No. 4. Brush a thin coat of glue onto two ⁷⁄₈-inch-wide micro strips, and align these inside the guide lines scribed in Step 2. Brush glue onto the tops of the strips, clamp 1 × 6 piece No. 5 on top, and let stand for 30 minutes.

When the glue has set, attach micro strips to 1 × 6 piece No. 2 the same as to No. 1, and clamp piece No. 3 to the assembly. Attach micro strips to 1 × 6 piece No. 5 the same as to No. 4, and clamp piece No. 6 to it. Let both assemblies stand for 30 minutes.

When glue has set, brush a thin coat of glue onto the two remaining ¼-inch-wide strips, and attach them flush with the front and rear edges of 1 × 6 piece No. 3. Apply glue to the inch-wide strip, and press it in place along the front edge of the center groove. Glue the 1¼-inch-wide strip along the rear edge of the groove. Then apply glue to the tops of the strips, clamp the two block halves together with four bar clamps,

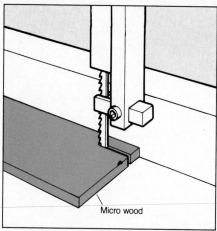

3. Use a bandsaw to rip micro wood into 10¼-inch, four ⁷⁄₈-inch, one one-inch, one 1¼-inch, and two two-inch strips.

MARKING OAK 1 × 6

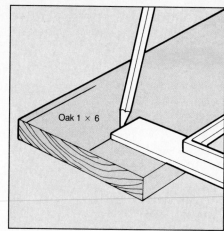

Oak 1 × 6

Use a combination square to make guide marks on 1 × 6 pieces for aligning micro wood strips.

GROOVING 1 × 6 NO. 3

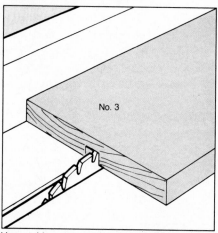

No. 3

Use a table saw to cut a ³⁄₈-by-½-inch groove into 1 × 6 piece No. 3.

MICRO STRIPS AND 1 × 6s

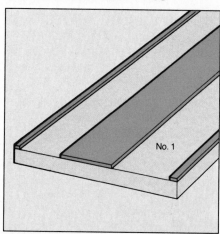

No. 1

1. Glue a ¼-inch micro wood strip along each edge of 1 × 6 piece No. 1 and a two-inch strip along the guide lines.

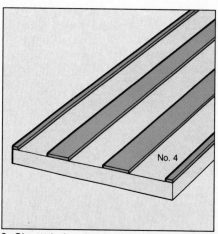

No. 4

2. Glue ¼-inch strips flush with front and rear edges of 1 × 6 piece No. 4. Then attach two ⁷⁄₈-inch strips inside the guide lines.

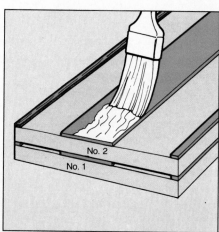

No. 2
No. 1

3. Attach strips to 1 × 6 piece No. 2 the same as to piece No. 1. Then brush a coat of glue onto the top of the strips.

and let stand two hours or overnight.

STEP 5
SANDING THE BLOCK

Sand all surfaces smooth with a belt sander and medium belt. Then sand with a pad sander and 120- and 220-grit sandpaper, carefully rounding over the top edges and corners and vertical corners as you proceed. Only slightly round over the bottom edges—just enough to prevent splintering.

Use the fine side of an emery board to sand the edges of the knife slits to remove splinters and small fibers.

STEP 6
FINISHING THE BLOCK

Vacuum the block to remove dust, and wipe it down with a tack cloth. Then apply the finish of your choice.

To duplicate the finish of the block shown, apply Watco Medium Walnut Danish Oil Finish according to the manufacturer's directions. During application, keep the top end grain well saturated with oil. Before the second application, invert the block, and keep the bottom end grain saturated.

When the block has been wiped dry with paper towels, stand it on a double layer of paper towels, and let it stand for 72 hours. During the first 24 hours, invert the block about every eight hours, and replace the paper towels it stands on to allow excess oil to drain from the slots and seep from the end grain.

When the Danish Oil Finish has completely cured, apply three coats of Deft Clear Wood Finish to all surfaces of the block.

Finally, turn the block upside down. Then attach a ½-inch, self-adhesive, rubber protector pad just inside each bottom corner of the block.

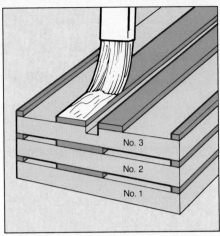

4. Glue strips to 1 × 6 piece No. 5 the same as to piece No. 4. Then brush a coat of glue onto the strips and clamp 1 × 6 No. 6 to it.

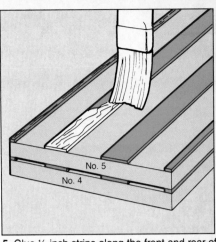

5. Glue ¼-inch strips along the front and rear of 1 × 6 piece No. 3, glue a one-inch strip along the front edge of the groove, glue a 1¼-inch strip along the rear edge of the groove, and apply glue to the tops of the strips.

SANDING EDGES

1. Sand block and round over edges and corners with a pad sander and 120- and 220-grit sandpaper.

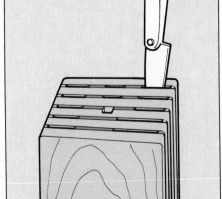

6. Clamp block halves together with four bar clamps, and let stand overnight.

2. Sand inside edges of the slots with the fine side of an emery board.

ATTACHING RUBBER FEET

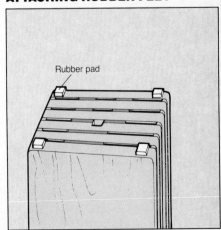

Rubber pad

Attach a ½-inch, self-adhesive rubber protector pad inside each bottom corner of the block.

Wine Rack

The popularity of wine in America has grown tremendously in recent years. As a result, gift shops, wine shops, and department stores, nationwide, now stock wine racks of all sorts.

The most attractive racks are constructed of finely finished hardwoods and serve as handsome furniture as well as functional storage units. And their prices are usually just the other side of outrageous.

With a few dollars' worth of oak and walnut and several pleasant hours in the workshop, you can build a wine rack you will be proud to show off. The rack is designed to hold a case of wine and will stand on the floor, in a shelf unit, or just about anywhere else you want to put it.

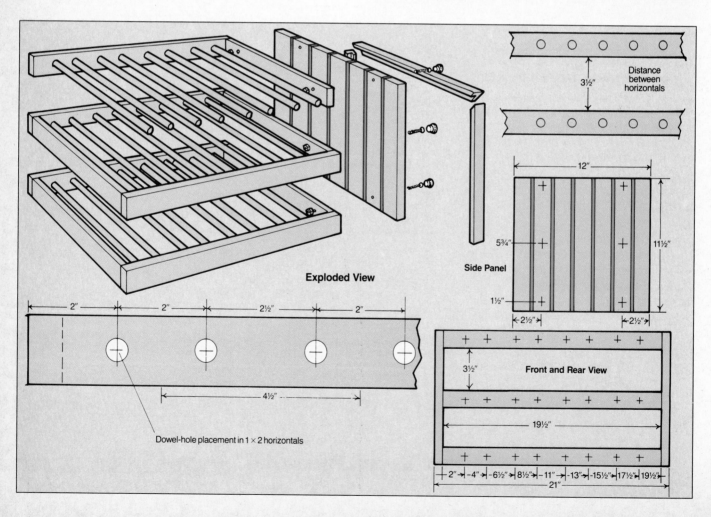

Exploded View

Distance between horizontals

3½"

12"

5¾"

11½"

Side Panel

1½"

2½"   2½"

2"   2"   2½"   2"

4½"

Dowel-hole placement in 1 × 2 horizontals

3½"

Front and Rear View

19½"

2" 4" 6½" 8½" 11" 13" 15½" 17½" 19½"

21"

BILL OF MATERIALS

Qty	Size	Material	Qty	Size	Material	Qty	Size	Material
4	1″ × 2″ × 8′	Oak	12	10–24 × 1½	Stainless-steel machine screws		120-grit	Sandpaper
8′	½″ × 1⅛″	Walnut box frame molding					220-grit	Sandpaper
3	¼″ × 3″ × 24″	Walnut micro wood	12	10–24	Stainless-steel hex nuts			Deft Clear Wood Finish
12	½″	Oak button plugs						Watco Natural Danish Oil Finish
8	⅝″ × 36″	Oak dowel rods	12	#10	Stainless-steel flat washers			Watco Medium Walnut Danish Oil Finish
		Carpenter's or white glue						Tack cloth
		Five-minute epoxy cement						

TOOLS

Steel tape rule
Combination square
Pencil
Claw hammer
Soft-faced mallet
Center punch
Screwdriver
Miter box and backsaw

C-clamps or spring clamps (4)
18″ bar clamps (5)
24″ bar clamps (2)
Adjustable wrench
Drill press or drill-press stand
Electric drill
⅜″ brad-point bit
⅝″ Forstner bit

¹³⁄₆₄″ twist-drill bit
Bandsaw
Belt sander
Pad sander
Paintbrush
Workmate®

STEP 1
CUTTING OAK 1 × 2 AND DOWEL RODS

With a miter box and backsaw, cut seven pieces of oak 1 × 2 to 24 inches, six pieces to 19½ inches, and six to 9½ inches. Then cut 24 pieces of ⅝-inch dowel rod to 10⅛ inches. Note: Save time by cutting two or more pieces of dowel rod at a time with the miter box and backsaw.

STEP 2
RIPPING WALNUT STRIPS

Set the fence on the bandsaw or clamp a straight piece of wood ¾ of an inch from the blade. Then rip two ¾-inch-wide strips from each of three 24-inch pieces of ¼-inch walnut micro wood.

STEP 3
LAMINATING OAK AND WALNUT STRIPS

For best results, laminate 24-inch oak and walnut strips in three phases.

First, arrange four oak 1 × 2s with a strip of walnut between each. Apply glue to a narrow edge of each but the last 1 × 2 and a broad surface of each walnut strip. Sandwich strips together, and clamp with five bar clamps. Let stand for 30 minutes.

Similarly, arrange the remaining strips and apply glue. Clamp them and let stand for 30 minutes.

LAMINATING OAK AND WALNUT STRIPS

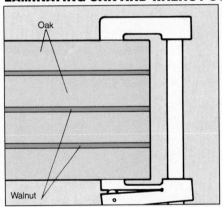

1. Glue four oak strips with a strip of walnut between each, and three oak strips with two walnut strips between, to make two slabs.

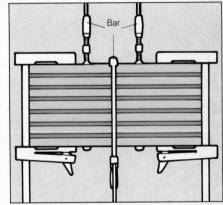

2. Glue the two slabs together and secure the assembly with five bar clamps.

MARKING DOWEL HOLES

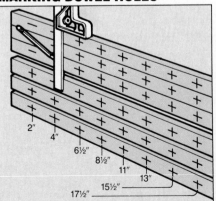

Mark the center of each 1 × 2 oak horizontal at 2, 4, 6½, 8½, 11, 13, 15½, and 17½ inches from one end.

DRILLING DOWEL HOLES

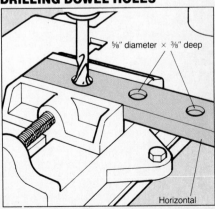

Drill a ⅝-inch-diameter, ⅜-inch-deep hole at each spot marked on horizontals.

Then apply glue to the narrow edge of the outside oak 1 × 2 in the first slab, clamp the two slabs together with five clamps, and let the assembly stand for an hour.

When glue has dried, rough-sand both broad surfaces with a belt sander and medium belt.

STEP 4
MARKING HORIZONTALS FOR DOWEL HOLES

Align 19½-inch 1 × 2s in two sets of three, and mark one strip in each set at 2, 4, 6½, 8½, 11, 13, 15½, and 17½ inches from one end. Use a combination square to scribe a pencil mark across each strip in each set at those marks. Then set the square for ¾ of an inch, and mark the center of each line for a centered hole.

STEP 5
PUNCHING AND DRILLING DOWEL HOLES

Center-punch a drill-starter hole at each spot marked on the horizontals. Then set the drill-press depth stop for ⅜ of an inch, and use a ⅝-inch Forstner bit to drill eight ⅜-inch-deep holes in each 1 × 2 horizontal.

STEP 6
ATTACHING SIDE PIECES TO FRONT HORIZONTALS

Apply glue to one end of a 9½-inch oak 1 × 2, butt it to the inside (drilled side) of a front horizontal, and secure it with a corner clamp. Attach another side piece, the same way, to the opposite end of the horizontal.

Attach the remaining four side pieces and two front horizontals in the same manner. Let assemblies stand with clamps in place for an hour.

STEP 7
PREPARING AND INSTALLING DOWELS

If you have a stationary or bench-type disk sander, set the miter gauge at 45 degrees, and put a slight bevel (about ¹⁄₁₆ of an inch) on each end of each dowel rod.

Clamp a pad sander upside down in a Workmate®, and lightly sand and round over the dowel-rod ends with 120-grit paper.

SIDES TO FRONTS

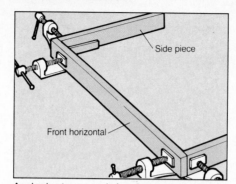

Apply glue to one end of each side piece, attach it to front horizontal, and secure the assembly with corner clamps; let it stand an hour.

ATTACHING REAR PIECES

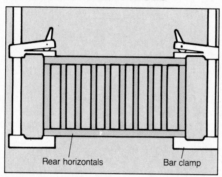

Tap rear horizontals in place, and secure corners with glue and bar clamps.

DRILLING RACK ENDS

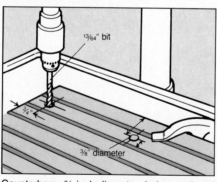

Counterbore ⅜-inch-diameter holes and drill through with a ¹³⁄₆₄-inch bit 2½ inches from front and rear edges at the center and ¾ inch from top and bottom.

DRILLING CENTER RACK

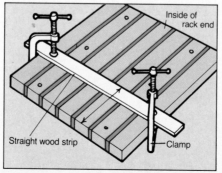

1. Clamp a straight strip of wood across the inside of each rack end, five inches from the bottom.

INSTALLING DOWELS

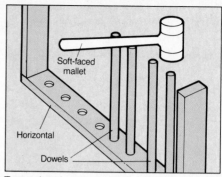

Tap a dowel rod into each hole in each front horizontal.

CUTTING RACK ENDS

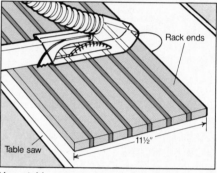

Use a table saw to cut two rack ends to 11½-inch length.

TOP AND BOTTOM RACKS

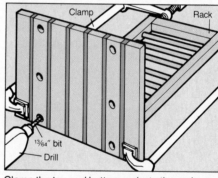

Clamp the top and bottom racks to the ends, and drill through the holes in rack ends with a ¹³⁄₆₄-inch bit.

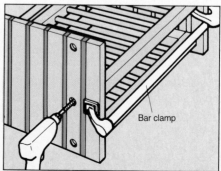

2. With center rack resting on wood strips, bar clamp ends, and drill through center holes.

Press a dowel rod into each hole in each front horizontal, and tap each with a soft-faced mallet to seat.

STEP 8
ATTACHING REAR HORIZONTALS

Stand each front-horizontal assembly with side pieces and dowel rods up. Apply glue to the ends of the side pieces. Press a rear horizontal onto the dowel-rod ends, and use a block of scrap wood and soft-faced mallet to tap back and forth along the rear horizontal until it is firmly seated on all dowel rods and butted to the end pieces.

Check alignment of the end pieces, and clamp each end of each assembly with a bar clamp. Let the racks stand for 30 minutes.

STEP 9
CUTTING RACK ENDS AND SANDING

Set the table-saw fence 23¾ inches from the blade's inside teeth, and trim one end of the oak-and-walnut slab. Reset the fence 11½ inches from the blade, and with the trimmed end of the slab against the fence, cut two rack ends to 11½ inches.

Then sand the racks and the broad surfaces of the rack ends with a pad sander and 120- and 220-grit sandpaper.

STEP 10
MARKING AND DRILLING RACK ENDS

With a steel tape rule and combination square set for 2½ inches, mark each rack end for holes 2½ inches from the front and rear edges at ¾ and 5¾ of an inch from the top and bottom edges.

Center-punch a drill-starter hole; counterbore a ⅜-inch-diameter, ⅜-inch-deep hole; and drill through with a ¹³⁄₆₄-inch bit at each spot.

STEP 11
DRILLING THE RACKS

Lay rack ends inside-surfaces up. With a combination square set for ½-inch, scribe inch-long lines parallel to front and rear edges at the center and about an inch from the top and bottom. Then clamp the bottom rack to a rack end at a right angle with two bar clamps, and

TRIMMING RACK ENDS

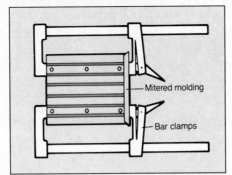

1. Miter-cut a piece of frame molding to fit the top edge of each rack end. Attach the trim piece with epoxy cement and secure it with two bar clamps.

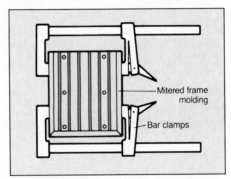

2. Cut two more pieces of molding to fit the sides of each rack end, mitered at the top and squared at the bottom, and attach them with epoxy cement and bar clamps.

ASSEMBLING WINE RACK

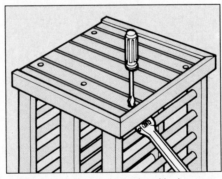

1. Attach each end to the racks with six screws, flat washers, and hex nuts.

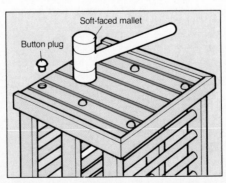

2. Tap a button plug into each hole in each rack end with a soft-faced mallet.

drill through bottom holes in the rack end with a ¹³⁄₆₄-inch bit.

Do the same at the opposite end of the rack. Then turn the rack ends upside down and drill the top rack.

Make a small mark near each edge of the inside surface of each rack end, five inches from the bottom. Then clamp a straight strip of scrap wood across each rack end, aligned with the marks.

Set the center rack atop the wood strips, and clamp rack ends in place with two bar clamps. Then drill through the center holes in the rack ends with a ¹³⁄₆₄-inch bit.

STEP 12
TRIMMING RACK ENDS

Use a miter box and backsaw to cut two pieces of frame molding at 45-degree angles to fit the top edges of the rack ends.

Mix a small amount of epoxy cement, and attach trim to each rack end with cement and two bar clamps.

Cut two more pieces of molding for each rack end, mitered at the top and squared at the bottom, and attach them with epoxy cement and bar clamps.

STEP 13
FINISHING RACK COMPONENTS

Vacuum components to remove dust, and wipe them down with a tack cloth.

Mix equal parts of Watco Natural and Medium Walnut Danish Oil Finish, apply to components and button plugs according to manufacturer's directions, and let stand for 72 hours.

Then apply two coats of Deft Clear Wood Finish to rack components.

STEP 14
ASSEMBLING RACK AND APPLYING FINAL FINISH

Insert a machine screw into each hole in a rack end and through the holes at one end of each rack. Put a flat washer and hex nut on each screw, and tighten with a screwdriver and wrench. Attach the other rack end the same way.

Tap a button plug into each hole in the rack ends with a soft-faced mallet. Then apply a final coat of Deft lacquer to the rack.

Recipe File

Many gift shops and kitchenware stores stock recipe files, but few are as attractive or spacious as the one you can build with these plans. In fact, this roomy, two-drawer design provides adequate space for coupons as well as a large collection of recipes.

One item on the bill of materials that might not be available in every home-improvement center is half-inch oak splashboard, used in the drawer construction. If you can't find it, simply substitute half-inch oak plywood.

You will find a wide variety of drawer pulls to choose from wherever you buy your supplies. Most department stores also carry 3-by-5-inch file and recipe cards and file indexes to help keep your recipe collection organized.

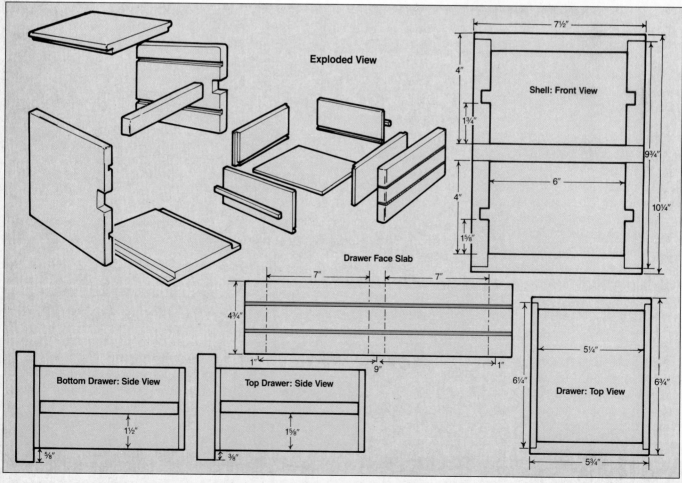

Exploded View

Shell: Front View

7½"

4"

1¾"

9¾"

6"

4"

1⅝"

10¼"

Drawer Face Slab

7"

7"

4¾"

1"

9"

1"

Bottom Drawer: Side View

1½"

⅝"

Top Drawer: Side View

1⅝"

⅜"

Drawer: Top View

5¼"

6¼"

6¾"

5¾"

PARTS LIST

Part Name	Qty	Description
Cabinet side	2	¾″ × 7¼″ × 9¾″ oak
Cabinet top and bottom	2	¾″ × 7¼″ × 7½″ oak
Cabinet-face horizontal	1	¾″ × ¾″ × 7½″ oak
Cabinet back	1	¼″ × 6¾″ × 9½″ oak plywood

Part Name	Qty	Description
Drawer front and back	4	½″ × 3½″ × 5¾″ oak or oak plywood
Drawer side	4	¼″ × 3½″ × 6¼″ oak plywood
Drawer bottom	2	⅛″ × 5½″ × 6″ hardboard

Part Name	Qty	Description
Drawer rail	4	½″ × ½″ × 6¼″ oak
Drawer-face strip	3	¾″ × 1½″ × 18″ oak
Drawer-face strip	2	⅛″ × ¾″ × 18″ walnut

BILL OF MATERIALS

Qty	Size	Material
1	¼″ × 24″ × 24″	Or larger scrap of oak plywood
1	⅛″ × 6″ × 12″	Or larger scrap of hardboard
1	1″ × 2″ × 5′	Oak
1	1″ × 8″ × 3′	Oak
1	½″ × 3½″ × 3′	Oak splashboard

Qty	Size	Material
1	⅛″ × 3″ × 24″	Walnut micro wood
1	7½″	Scrap of oak ¾″-square molding
		Carpenter's or white glue
		Five-minute epoxy cement
2	⅜″	Staples
		Drawer pulls or brass label holders with pulls
4	½″	Self-adhesive, rubber

Qty	Size	Material
		protector pads
	120-grit	Sandpaper
	220-grit	Sandpaper
		Pen-Chrome #640-11 English Oak Stain
		Shellac
		Satin-sheen polyurethane varnish
		Tack cloth

TOOLS

Steel tape rule
Combination square
Pencil
Felt-tipped pen
Claw hammer
Nail set
Center punch
Screwdriver

Miter box and backsaw
3″ C-clamps (2)
Spring clamps (2)
Corner clamps (4)
Threaded-rod clamps (3)
½″ or adjustable wrenches (2)
Staple gun
Drill press or drill-press stand

⅜″ brad-point bit
Table saw
Bandsaw (optional)
Belt sander
Pad sander
Workmate®
Paintbrush

CUTTING SCHEDULE

1. From oak 1 × 8, cut a cabinet top and a bottom to 7½ inches and two cabinet sides to 9¾ inches.

2. From ½-by-3½-inch oak splashboard or ½-inch oak plywood, cut two drawer fronts and two backs to 3½ by 5¾ inches.

3. Use a table saw or bandsaw to rip suitable scraps of ¼-inch plywood to a 3½-inch width. Cut four drawer sides to 6¼ inches. Then cut and rip a cabinet back to 6¾ by 9½ inches.

4. Rip a strip of ⅛-inch hardboard to a width of six inches. Then cut two pieces to 5½ by 6 inches.

5. Cut three pieces of oak 1 × 2 and a piece of ⅛-inch walnut micro wood to 18 inches. Then rip two strips of the ⅛-inch walnut to ¾ of an inch.

6. From a scrap of oak ¾-inch-square molding, cut a cabinet-face horizontal to 7½ inches. Either from the same stock or from ½-inch oak splashboard, cut and rip four ½-by-½-by-6¼-inch drawer rails.

STEP 1
CUTTING RABBETS, DADOES, AND NOTCHES IN CABINET PANELS

Set the table-saw fence 6¾ inches from the *near* teeth of the blade, and set the blade for a ½-inch depth. Then, with a side edge of the cabinet top against the fence, run the piece over the blade. Do likewise at the opposite end of the top and both ends of the cabinet bottom.

Move the fence to 6⅞ inches from the blade, and repeat the process. Continue making the same cuts with the fence at 7, 7⅛, 7⅜, and 7½ inches from the blade to cut a ½-by-¾-inch rabbet in each end of the cabinet top and bottom.

Set the blade for a ½-inch depth and the fence 7⅛ inches from the *near* teeth of the blade. Then run top, bottom, and side panels over the blade, with the panel faces against the fence and inside surfaces of the panels down

on the saw table. Reset the fence at seven inches from the blade, and make another pass, creating a ¼-by-½-inch rabbet along the rear edge of each panel.

Set the fence 4½ inches from the *near* teeth of the blade, and set the blade for a ¾-inch depth. Clamp the two side panels together with a pair of spring clamps. Then, with the face surface on the saw table and the panel bottoms against the fence, run the panels over the blade. Reset the fence at 4⅝ inches from the blade, and make another pass. Continue the same way with the fence set at 4¾, 4⅞, 5, 5⅛, and 5¼ inches from the blade to create a ¾-by-¾-inch notch in each side panel.

Set the blade for a ⅜-inch-deep cut and the fence 2³⁄₁₆ inches from the *near* teeth. With a side-panel top against the fence and the inside surface on the table, run the panel over the blade. Do likewise with the other side panel. Reset the fence at 2⁵/₁₆ inches from the blade, and make another pass with each side panel. Continue doing the same with the fence set at 2⁷/₁₆ and 2¾ inches to create a ⅜-by-⁹/₁₆-inch dado in each side panel.

Reset the fence 2⅛ inches from the *near* teeth of the blade, and run each side panel over the blade with the bottom edge against the fence. Make subsequent passes with the fence set at 2¼, 2⅜, 2½, 2⅝, and 2¹¹/₁₆ inches to create a second dado in each panel.

STEP 2
ASSEMBLING THE CABINET SHELL

Apply glue to the inside of each rabbet in the top panel, clamp the top panel to the side panels with four corner clamps, and let stand for two hours or overnight. Attach the bottom panel the same way, and let stand for two hours.

Apply glue to the inside of the center notches, press the ¾-by-¾-inch horizontal in place, secure it with two bar clamps, and let stand for one hour.

Lay the cabinet shell face down. Mix a small amount of epoxy cement, and apply it to the rear rabbets in the shell. Lay the cabinet back in place, put a can of paint or other heavy object on it, and let stand for five minutes.

STEP 3
MARKING AND DRILLING DRAWER-FACE STRIPS

Sort 18-inch oak 1 × 2s in a contrasting grain pattern and number one end of each with a felt-tipped pen. Turn the strips on their narrow edges, and use a combination square and pencil to scribe lines across them at one and nine inches from each end. Mark the ⅛-inch walnut strips the same way.

With a drill press and ⅜-inch bradpoint bit, drill holes through each piece centered on the lines.

STEP 4
LAMINATING AND CUTTING DRAWER FACES

Slide the first oak 1 × 2 strip onto three rod clamps. Brush a coat of glue onto a broad edge of a ⅛-inch walnut strip, and slide it onto the clamps. Apply glue to another oak strip, another walnut strip, and the third oak 1 × 2, and slide

RABBETING TOP AND BOTTOM

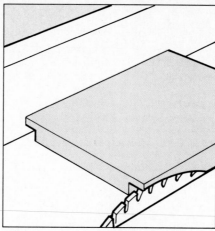

Use a table saw to cut a ½-by-¾-inch rabbet in each end of the cabinet top and bottom.

DADOES IN SIDE PANELS

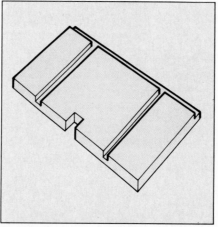

Use the table saw to cut a ⅜-by-⁹/₁₆-inch dado 1⅝ inches from the bottom and another 1¾ inches from the notch in each side panel.

DRILLING DRAWER-FACE STRIPS

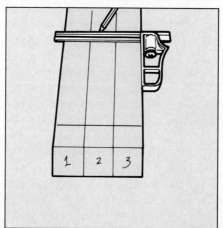

1. Scribe lines across the narrow edges of the oak 1 × 2s and broad edges of the walnut micro wood strips at one and nine inches from each end.

NOTCHING SIDE PANELS

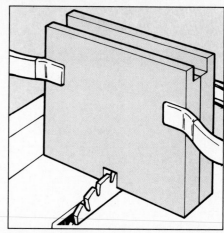

Clamp side panels together, and cut a centered ¾-by-¾-inch notch in the face surface with a table saw.

ASSEMBLING THE SHELL

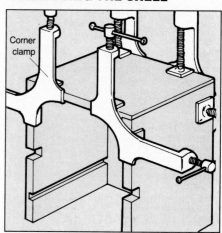

Corner clamp

Attach side panels to top and bottom with glue and corner clamps.

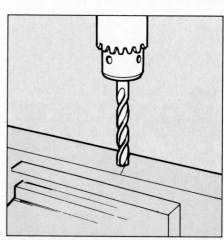

2. Then drill a ⅜-inch-diameter hole through the center of each line.

them onto the rod clamps.

Attach a cushion, flat washer, and hex nut to the end of each clamp, and tighten with two half-inch or adjustable wrenches. Wipe excess glue from the slab with a damp sponge, and let stand for two hours or overnight.

When glue has set, remove clamps, measure in 1½ inches from each end, and make a pencil mark. Use a miter box and backsaw to remove 1½ inches from each end of the slab. Then measure in seven inches from each end, and cut off two drawer faces.

STEP 5
SANDING DRAWER FACES AND SHELL
Sand front and rear surfaces of the drawer faces with a belt sander and medium belt, and round over the front side edges as you proceed. Then clamp a pad sander upside down in a Workmate®, and sand all surfaces of the drawer faces with 120- and 220-grit sandpaper. As you sand, round over the front side edges heavily, the top and bottom edges moderately, and the rear edges slightly.

Sand all exterior surfaces of the cabinet shell with a pad sander and 120- and 220-grit sandpaper. Round over all exterior corners and sharp edges as you proceed.

STEP 6
CUTTING RABBETS AND GROOVES IN DRAWER PANELS
Set the table-saw blade for a ¼-inch depth and the fence 5⅝ inches from the *near* teeth of the blade. Then run each drawer front and back over the blade, with a side edge against the fence and inside surface down on the saw table. Reset the fence at 5½ inches from the blade, and run each front and back over the blade again, creating a ¼-by-¼-inch rabbet in each side of each piece.

Set the blade for a ⅛-inch depth and set the fence ⅛ of an inch from the *near* teeth of the blade. Then run each drawer front, back, and side over the blade, with the panel bottoms against the fence and interior surfaces down on the saw table, creating a ⅛-by-⅛-inch groove in each piece.

LAMINATING STRIPS

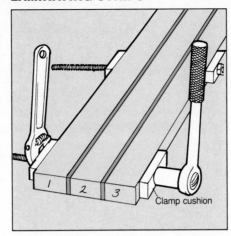

Laminate the oak and walnut strips with glue and rod clamps to create a 4¾-by-18-inch slab.

CUTTING DRAWER FACES

With a miter box and backsaw, cut 1½ inches off each end of the slab; then cut a seven-inch drawer face from each end.

RABBETING PANELS

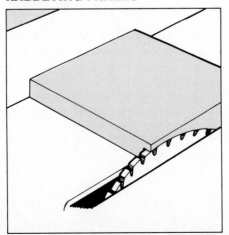

Use the table saw to cut a ¼-by-¼-inch rabbet in each end of each drawer front and rear panel.

STEP 7
ASSEMBLING THE DRAWERS
Run a bead of glue along the inside of the rabbet on one side of a drawer front and corresponding rabbet on a drawer back. Clamp a side panel in the rabbets with two corner clamps, and secure the side panel to the front and back with two staples at each end. Then tap the staples flush with a hammer.

Remove the clamps, invert the drawer assembly, and insert a drawer bottom into the grooves. Then attach the other side panel with glue and staples, and let the drawer stand with two corner clamps in place for two hours or overnight. Assemble the other drawer the same way.

STEP 8
INSTALLING DRAWER RAILS
Mark the back of one drawer T for top and the other B for bottom. Set a combination square for 1⅝ inches, and make several lines along each side panel of the top drawer 1⅝ inches from and parallel to the bottom edge. Do likewise to the bottom drawer with the square set for 1½ inches.

Mix a small amount of epoxy cement, apply a thin layer to the drawer rail, clamp it to a side panel—aligned just above the lines scribed earlier— and let stand for five minutes. Attach drawer rails to the other side panels the same way.

Drawer rails are cut slightly oversize, so they will not fit the dadoes in the shell at this point. With a stationary belt sander or portable belt sander clamped upside down in a Workmate®, carefully and gradually sand the rails down until the drawers fit snugly but move freely in the drawer channels (dadoes). Then lightly hand-sand the rails with 120-grit sandpaper.

STEP 9
ATTACHING DRAWER FACES
Mark the inside center of one drawer face T for top and the other B for bottom. Set a combination square for ⅝ of an inch, and with the square and pencil, scribe several small guide lines on the inside of each drawer face, parallel to the side edges.

With the square still set at ⅝ of an inch, mark several guide lines parallel to the bottom edge of the bottom drawer face. Reset the square for ⅜ of an inch, and make several marks parallel to the bottom inside edge of the top drawer face.

Mix a small amount of epoxy cement, and apply a thin layer to each drawer front. Lay the faces face down, and position each drawer on its respective face, inside and aligned with the guide lines. Let stand for two or three minutes, adjusting as necessary. Then clamp each drawer face to a drawer with two spring clamps, and let stand until cement sets.

STEP 10
FINISHING THE UNIT

Vacuum the cabinet shell and drawers, and wipe them down with a tack cloth. The unit is now ready for the finish of your choice.

If you wish to duplicate the finish of the cabinet shown here, first apply a liberal coat of Pen-Chrome English Oak Stain with a paintbrush. Let it penetrate for about 15 minutes, and wipe the shell and drawers dry with paper towels. Then allow the components to stand overnight.

Seal the drawers and shell with a coat of shellac, and let stand for 15 minutes, or until shellac dries. Then apply a coat of satin-sheen polyurethane varnish, and let stand overnight or until dry. If you wish to apply subsequent coats for a deeper lustre, burnish the surfaces of the cabinet shell and drawer faces with 400-grit sandpaper or #0000 steel wool after each coat except the last.

When varnish has dried, attach a ½-inch rubber protector pad inside each bottom corner of the cabinet shell. Then attach a small drawer pull (and optional pull plate) or a brass label holder with pull to the center of each drawer face.

GROOVING DRAWER PANELS

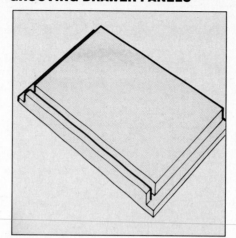

With the table-saw fence ⅛ of an inch from the blade and the blade set for a ⅛-inch depth, cut a groove along the bottom inside of each drawer panel.

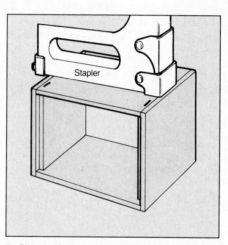

2. Slide a drawer bottom into the grooves and attach the other side panel the same way.

ATTACHING DRAWER FACES

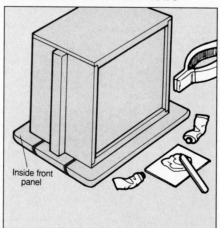

Apply epoxy cement to the drawer front panels, align drawers with the guide lines on the inside of the drawer faces, and clamp faces to drawers for five minutes.

ASSEMBLING DRAWERS

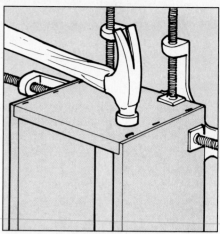

1. Glue and clamp a drawer side panel to a front and rear panel, secure with staples, and tap staples flush with a hammer.

INSTALLING DRAWER RAILS

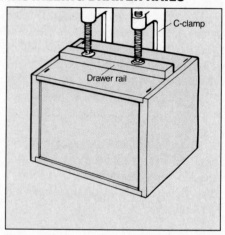

Attach drawer rails with epoxy cement and C-clamps 1⅝ inches from the bottom edge of the top drawer and 1½ inches from the bottom edge of the bottom drawer.

ATTACHING FEET

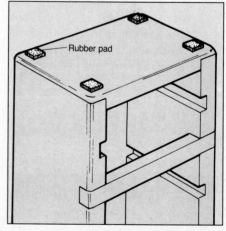

Press a ½-inch, self-adhesive, rubber protector pad to the cabinet bottom inside each corner.

Quartz Clock

Thanks to the development of miniature quartz movements, anyone can build clocks that are extremely accurate, need no winding, have no unsightly wires dangling from them, and will operate for a year on one AA-size battery.

There are special clockmaker's bits available for about $50 for drilling the cavities necessary to hold the movements. But this project provides a clock cavity without the need for such highly specialized and expensive tools.

Walnut inlays replace traditional numbers on this clock, for a clean, modern look. But don't let the idea of intricate inlay work discourage you. If you can drill holes, you can make this clock.

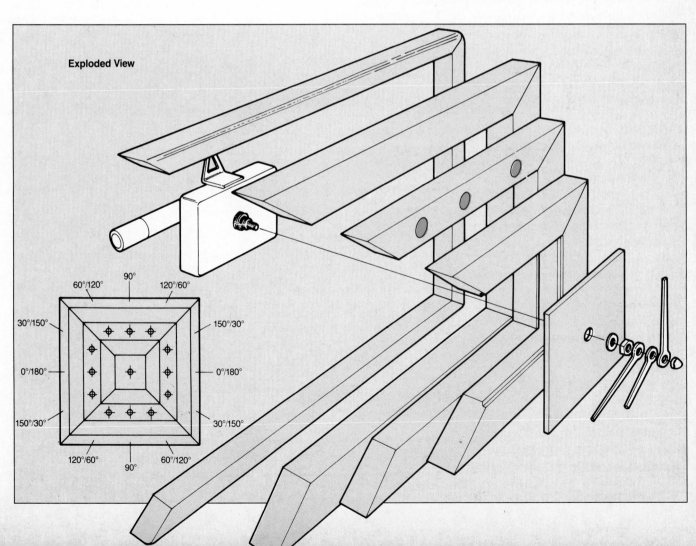

Exploded View

BILL OF MATERIALS

Qty	Size	Material	Qty	Size	Material	Qty	Size	Material
3"	⅛"•	Oak micro wood			Five-minute epoxy cement			Deft Clear Wood Finish
10'	1 × 2	Oak	1		Quartz mini-clockworks			Watco Natural Danish Oil
5'	1 × 2	Rounded oak frame molding	1	AA	Battery			Finish
12	½"	Walnut flathead tapered plugs	1		Hanger			Watco Medium Danish Oil Finish
				120-grit	Sandpaper			Tack cloth
		Carpenter's or white glue		220-grit	Sandpaper			

TOOLS

Steel tape rule	Miter box and backsaw	½" brad-point bit
Ruler or carpenter's square	Dovetail saw	Table saw
Combination square	Bar clamps (4)	Pad sander
6" protractor	Corner clamps (4)	Workmate® (optional)
Pencil	Adjustable wrench	Paintbrush
Claw hammer	Electric drill	
Center punch	⁵⁄₁₆" twist-drill bit	

STEP 1
CUTTING AND RABBETING INNER FRAME

With a miter box and backsaw, cut two pieces of oak 1 × 2 to 12 inches.

Set the table-saw fence ⅝ of an inch from the near teeth of the blade, and set the blade for a ¼-inch-deep cut. Then, with a 1 × 2 broad side against the fence, use push blocks to run each piece over the blade, creating a rabbet of ⅛-by-¼-inch dimensions.

STEP 2
MITER-CUTTING INNER FRAME

With the miter box and backsaw, cut a piece of ⅛-inch oak micro wood to three inches square.

Set the saw for a 45-degree angle, and with a rabbeted 1 × 2 positioned rabbet up, miter-cut one end. Use the piece of micro wood as a guide to mark for the opposite cut; then make the other 45-degree cut.

Use this piece as a guide to mark and cut three more identical pieces.

STEP 3
GLUING AND CLAMPING INNER FRAME

Apply glue to the ends of two inner-frame pieces, and clamp them together with a corner clamp. Do likewise with the remaining two pieces, and let stand for 30 minutes.

Remove the corner clamps, mix a

RABBETING INNER FRAME

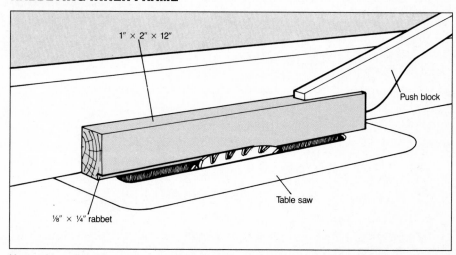

Use a table saw to cut a ⅛-by-¼-inch rabbet into two 12-inch pieces of 1 × 2. For safety's sake, use a push block.

MITER-CUTTING INNER FRAME

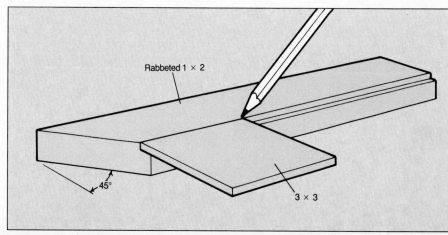

1. Cut one end of a rabbeted 1 × 2 at a 45-degree angle, and mark for second cut with the micro wood center piece.

small amount of epoxy cement, apply it to the unglued miter-cut ends of the frame halves, and secure the frame between swivel pegs in a Workmate®. Let stand for five minutes.

If you don't own a Workmate®, wrap two rubber bands diagonally from corner to corner, front and rear, and two more the same way around the remaining corners.

STEP 4
CUTTING, GLUING, AND CLAMPING SECOND AND THIRD FRAMES

Use the miter box and backsaw to cut four pieces of 1 × 2 at 45-degree angles to fit the outer edges of the inner frame.

Coat the inner edge of one piece with glue, and press it to one outer edge of the inner frame. Do likewise with the opposite piece, secure the two with two bar clamps, and let stand for at least 30 minutes.

When glue has set, attach the other two pieces the same way.

Miter-cut four more pieces of 1 × 2 to fit the outer edges of the second frame, attach them with glue and bar clamps, and let stand for 30 minutes.

STEP 5
INSTALLING CENTER PIECE

Mix a small amount of epoxy cement, and apply it to the inside lip of the rabbet in the inner frame. Press the three-inch micro wood square in place, clamp it with two bar clamps, and let stand for five minutes.

STEP 6
MARKING FOR CENTER AND INLAY HOLES

Set a combination square for 2¼ inches, measure in from each side of the clock face, and make marks in the center of the 1 × 2s in the second frame. Then use a straightedge or ruler to scribe vertical lines 2¼ inches from the left and right edges and horizontal lines 2¼ inches from the top and bottom edges, forming a square.

Scribe vertical and horizontal center lines across the clock face. Align a protractor with the center lines, and make pencil marks on the upper half of the clock face at 30, 60, 120, and 150 degrees. Rotate the protractor, and mark

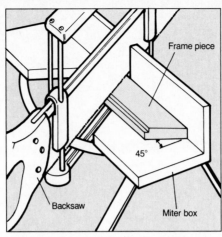

2. Cut off the opposite end of the frame piece with miter box and backsaw.

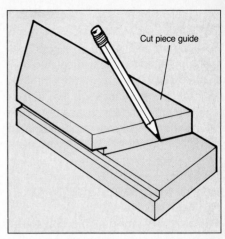

3. Use a miter-cut frame piece as a guide to mark the other three frame pieces.

ASSEMBLING INNER FRAME

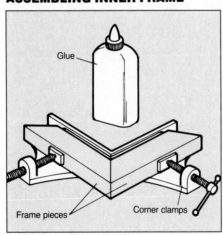

1. Glue and clamp two pairs of frame pieces with two corner clamps, and let them stand until the glue sets.

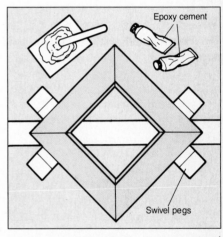

2. Join two frame halves with epoxy cement and swivel pegs in a Workmate®, or secure glued halves with rubber bands.

ASSEMBLING OTHER FRAMES

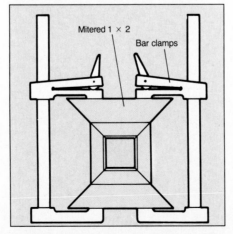

1. Miter-cut four 1 × 2 pieces to fit the outer edges of inner frame, and attach them with wood glue and bar clamps.

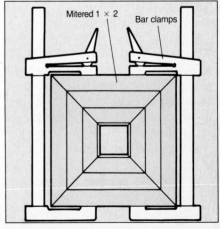

2. Similarly, cut, glue, and clamp four 1 × 2 pieces to fit the outer edges of the second frame.

the lower half of the clock face the same way.

With one end of a ruler aligned with the intersection of the vertical and horizontal center lines, move the other end to meet the protractor marks, one by one. Where the ruler crosses the lines in the center frame, mark for inlay holes.

STEP 7
PUNCHING, DRILLING, AND PLUGGING HOLES

Carefully center-punch drill-starter holes at the marks made on the center frame, as well as where the vertical and horizontal center lines intersect the lines on the center frame. Also center-punch the intersection of the center lines.

At the 12 clock-number positions, use a ½-inch brad-point bit to drill ⅜-inch-deep holes. In the center, drill through with a ⁵⁄₁₆-inch bit.

Then plug the 12 number holes with glued, ½-inch, tapered, walnut plugs, and let stand for an hour.

STEP 8
PREPARING CLOCK FACE FOR FINISHING

Fill any joint gaps in the clock face with wood filler, and let stand until it sets.

Cut off the plug heads with a dovetail saw. Then sand the clock face with a pad sander and 120- and 220-grit sandpaper.

STEP 9
CUTTING AND ASSEMBLING OUTER FRAME

Double-check horizontal and vertical measurements of the clock face.

With a miter box and backsaw set at 45 degrees, cut a piece of frame molding ¹⁄₁₆ of an inch greater than the width of the clock face. Then use that piece to mark another piece, and miter-cut that one. Mark one T for top and the other B for bottom.

Do the same with left and right frame pieces, and mark them L and R. Then hand-sand the molding, as required, with 120- and 220-grit sandpaper.

Apply glue to the miter-cut ends of the molding, assemble the frame with four corner clamps, and let stand for an hour with clamps in place.

MARKING INLAY HOLES

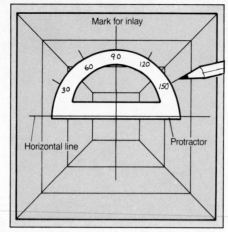

1. Use a six-inch protractor to mark the location of clock-face inlays above and below a horizontal center line.

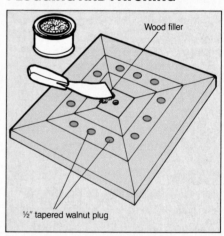

2. Use a ruler or square aligned with the protractor marks and the center to mark layout lines for the inlay holes.

DRILLING INLAY HOLES

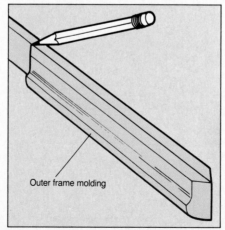

At each of the twelve inlay spots marked on the clock face, drill a ½-inch-diameter, ⅜-inch-deep hole.

PLUGGING AND PATCHING

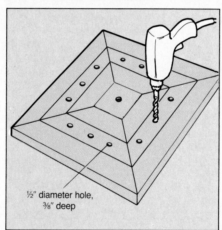

Plug the clock-face holes with ½-inch tapered walnut plugs, and fill any gaps in the joints with wood filler.

ASSEMBLING OUTER FRAME

1. Miter-cut a piece of frame molding ¹⁄₁₆ of an inch larger than the horizontal measurement of the clock face, and use it to mark a second piece. Make two vertical pieces to fit.

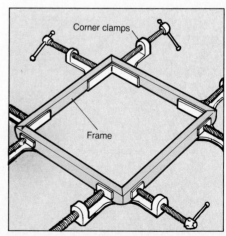

2. Apply glue to the mitered ends of the molding, and assemble the four-piece frame with four corner clamps. Let the assembly stand for at least an hour with the clamps in place.

STEP 10
GLUING THE CLOCK FACE TO THE OUTER FRAME

Mix enough epoxy cement to coat the lip of the frame. Then carefully apply a thin layer to the frame. Lay the frame face down, and press the clock face into position. Either clamp the assembly with four bar clamps near the corners, or place a heavy object on the back of the clock face, and let stand for five minutes.

STEP 11
FINISHING THE CLOCK

Vacuum the clock to remove all dust; then wipe it down with a tack cloth. It's now ready for the finish of your choice.

The clock can be finished naturally or stained. If you plan to stain, use a light stain so the walnut inlays will stand out in sharp contrast to the oak face. A half-and-half mixture of Watco Natural and Medium Walnut Danish Oil Finish is a good choice for light staining. For a natural finish, use Watco Natural to enhance the grain of the oak. Let the clock stand for 72 hours before applying three coats of Deft Clear Wood Finish.

STEP 12
INSTALLING CLOCKWORKS

Insert the clockworks into the three-by-three-inch cavity in the rear of the clock, put a flat washer and hex nut onto the clockworks spindle, and tighten the nut until it's secure, with an adjustable wrench. Do not overtighten.

Press the hour hand onto the spindle. Then secure the minute hand with a knurled nut, and press the second hand into the center of the spindle.

Install the battery, and the clock is ready for hanging.

ATTACHING FRAME TO FACE

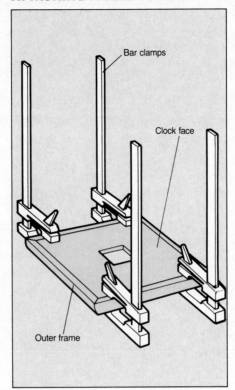

Apply epoxy cement to the inside of the frame, and clamp the clock face inside it with four bar clamps.

INSTALLING CLOCKWORKS

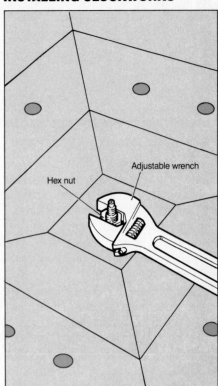

1. Install clockworks and hanger in clock's rear cavity, secure with washer and hex nut, and carefully tighten with an adjustable wrench. Do not overtighten.

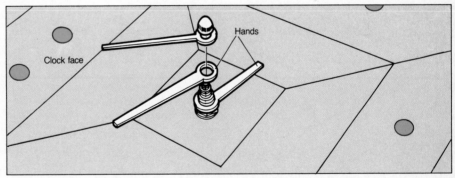

2. Attach the clock hands: the hour hand first, then the minute hand, and finally the second hand.

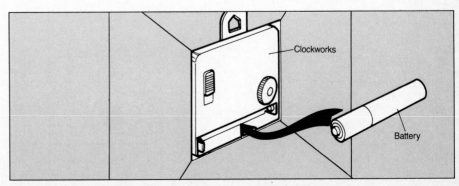

3. Slip the AA battery into position to start the clock, and set the correct time.

Spice Set

Here's a spice set that will beautifully display herbs and spices while protecting them from the effects of sunlight. You can either set the containers on a counter or in a shelf unit, or use the optional rack shown.

If you plan to stand the rack on a shelf or counter, attach four half-inch protector pads on the bottom, just inside the corners.

If you want to hang the rack, you have two options. You can install decorative picture-hanging rings near the top rear edge, or you can drill two centered holes in the back and hang the rack with ovalhead screws driven into a stud, or toggle bolts driven through a hollow wall, along with finish washers.

Decide what herbs and spices you intend to store, and have appropriate label plates engraved at a trophy shop.

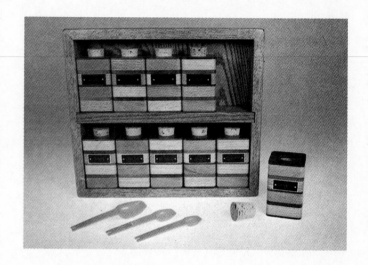

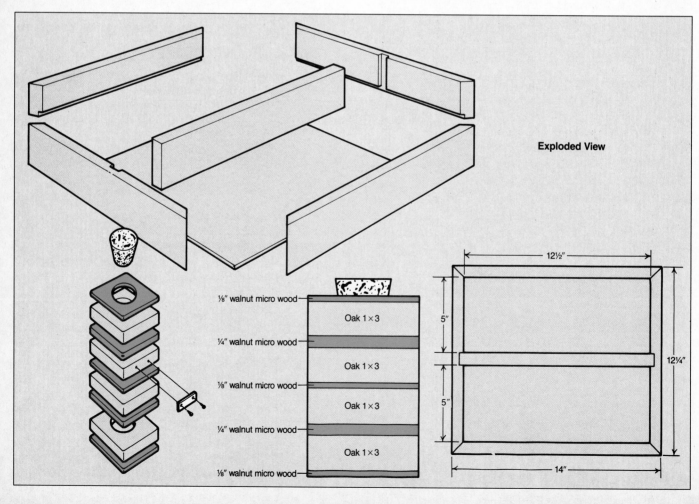

Exploded View

⅛" walnut micro wood

Oak 1 × 3

¼" walnut micro wood

Oak 1 × 3

⅛" walnut micro wood

Oak 1 × 3

¼" walnut micro wood

Oak 1 × 3

⅛" walnut micro wood

12½"

5"

5"

12¼"

14"

BILL OF MATERIALS.

Qty	Size	Material	Qty	Size	Material	Qty	Size	Material
1	¼″ × 11¼″ × 13″	Scrap G1S oak plywood			Wood filler		120-grit	Sandpaper
1	1″ × 3″ × 8′	Oak		¾″	Brads		220-grit	Sandpaper
1	1″ × 3″ × 2′	Oak		1½″	Brads		320-grit	Sandpaper
1	1″ × 4″ × 5′	Oak	40	⅛″ × 3½″	Rubber bands			Pen-Chrome 640-11
4	⅛″ × 3″ × 24″	Walnut micro wood	10	¾″ × 1¾″	Engraved label plates			English Oak Stain
3	¼″ × 3″ × 24″	Walnut micro wood	10	1¾″	Tapered corks, 1¼″ top, 1″ bottom			Deft Clear Wood Finish
		Carpenter's or white glue						Tack cloth

TOOLS

Steel tape rule	Miter box and backsaw	Table saw
Combination square	Corner clamps (4)	Bandsaw
Pencil	C-clamps (4)	Belt sander
Claw hammer	Putty knife	Pad sander
Scratch awl	Drill press or drill-press stand	Workmate®
Nail set	Electric drill	Paintbrush
Center punch	1/16″ twist-drill bit	Small dusting brush
Screw-holding screwdriver	1⅛″ and 1½″ Forstner bits	

MAKING THE RACK
STEP 1
CUTTING AND RIPPING OAK 1 × 4 RACK PIECES

Use a miter box and backsaw to cut two pieces of oak 1 × 4 to 14 inches and two to 12¼ inches, each with 45-degree angles at the ends.

Set the bandsaw fence or clamp a straight piece of wood 2¾ inches from the *near* teeth of the blade. Then rip each piece of 1 × 4 to that width.

STEP 2
RABBETING AND DADOING RACK PIECES

Set the table-saw fence 2¾ inches from the *far* teeth of the blade and the blade for a ¼-inch depth. Then run each of the miter-cut rack pieces over the blade, inside surface down. Reset the fence 2½ inches from the *near* teeth of the blade, and run each piece through the saw again, creating a ¼-by-¼-inch rabbet in the rear edge of each.

Lay a 12¼-inch rack side inside surface up. Measure down five inches from the top edge (on the inside of the miter) and make a pencil mark on the front edge. Make another mark at 5¾ inches. Do the same with the other rack side.

Remove the table-saw fence, and leave the blade set for a ¼-inch depth.

Then, with a side piece in the miter gauge and inside surface down on the saw table, run it over the blade several times to remove the material between the marks. Do likewise with the other side piece to create a ¼-by-¾-inch dado.

STEP 3
ASSEMBLING THE SPICE-RACK FRAME

Before assembling the spice-rack frame, sand the inside surfaces of all four pieces with a pad sander and 120- and 220-grit sandpaper.

Apply glue to the end of one side piece and let it soak into the grain for a

couple of minutes. Clamp the side piece to the top piece with a corner clamp. Continue gluing and clamping until all four pieces are joined.

Use a 1/16-inch bit to drill a pair of pilot holes about an inch deep at each end of the top and bottom pieces, ⅜ of an inch inside the corners. Then drive and countersink two 1½-inch brads at each corner. Let stand with the clamps in place for 30 minutes.

STEP 4
INSTALLING BACK AND SHELF

Lay the frame assembly face down, check the height and width inside the rabbets (it should be about 11¼ by 13

RIPPING OAK 1 × 4

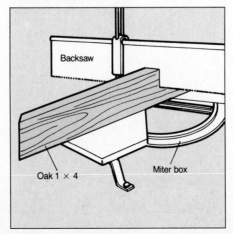

1. Miter-cut two pieces of 1 × 4 to 14 inches and two more to 12¼ inches.

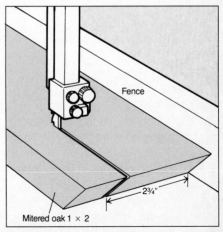

2. Use a bandsaw to rip each piece to a 2¾-inch width.

inches), and cut a piece of ¼-inch oak plywood to fit.

Sand the face of the plywood with a pad sander and 120- and 220-grit sandpaper.

Carefully apply a very thin, narrow bead of glue along the inside corner of the rabbet with a toothpick or ice-cream stick. Lay the back panel in place, and toenail ¾-inch brads through the back into the frame, and countersink the brads.

Check the width of the ·frame between the dadoes (it should be about 13 inches), and cut a piece of oak 1 × 3 to fit. Sand it with 120- and 220-grit sandpaper in a pad sander, and clean it to remove dust.

Run a thin, narrow bead of glue along the rear edge of the shelf, slide it into the dadoes, and clamp it to the back panel with a pair of C-clamps. If the back panel does not firmly contact the rear center of the shelf, drive and countersink two or three ¾-inch brads through the back into the shelf rear. Fill brad holes in the frame with wood filler, and let the rack stand for two hours.

STEP 5
SANDING AND FINISHING THE RACK

Sand the outer surfaces of the rack with a pad sander and 120- and 220-grit sandpaper. Vacuum the unit to remove dust, and wipe it down with a tack cloth.

To duplicate the finish of the rack shown, apply a coat of Pen-Chrome 640-11 English Oak Stain, let penetrate for 15 minutes, and wipe dry with paper towels. Let the rack stand for 24 hours; then apply three coats of Deft Clear Wood Finish.

MAKING THE CONTAINERS

STEP 1
RIPPING AND CUTTING OAK AND WALNUT

Set the bandsaw fence or clamp a straight piece of wood 2½ inches from the *near* teeth of the blade. Then rip four ⅛-inch and three ¼-inch walnut micro wood strips to a 2½-inch width.

Turn the strips perpendicular to the saw fence, and crosscut 30 pieces of ⅛-inch micro wood and 20 pieces of ¼-inch micro wood to 2½ inches square.

RABBETS AND DADOES

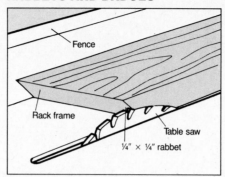

1. Use a table saw to cut a ¼-by-¼-inch rabbet in the rear edge of each piece.

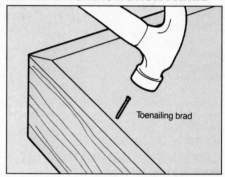

2. With the table saw, cut a ¼-by-¾-inch dado, centered across the inside surface of each 12¼-inch piece.

ASSEMBLING RACK FRAME

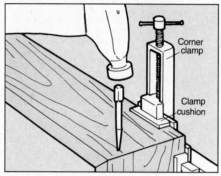

Assemble rack frame with glue and corner clamps; then drive and countersink two 1½-inch brads at each corner.

INSTALLING THE SHELF

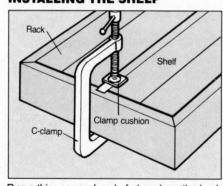

Run a thin, narrow bead of glue along the back edge of the shelf, slide it into the dadoes, and secure it with a pair of C-clamps.

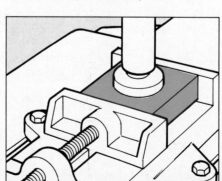

2. Bore a 1⅛-inch-diameter hole through 10 ⅛-inch walnut squares. Then bore 1½-inch holes through all other marked squares.

INSTALLING RACK BACK PANEL

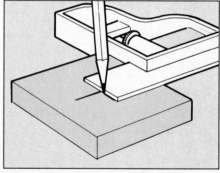

Lay back panel on glued rim of rabbet, and toenail ¾-inch brads through the back and into the frame.

DRILLING SQUARES

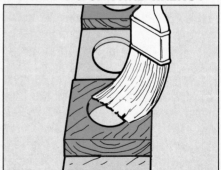

1. Set a combination square for 1¼ inches, and mark the centers of 20 ⅛-inch squares and all ¼-inch and 1 × 3 squares.

LAMINATING OAK AND WALNUT

1. Lay out squares in the order they're to be laminated, and coat them with glue, two rows at a time.

After cutting oak 1×3 into several manageable lengths, crosscut 40 pieces to 2½ inches square.

STEP 2
DRILLING OAK AND WALNUT

Set a combination square for 1¼ inches, and mark the centers of 20 pieces of ⅛-inch micro wood and all the ¼-inch micro wood and oak 1×3 for centered holes.

Put a piece of 2½-inch-wide (1×3) scrap wood in the drill-press vise, and use a 1⅛-inch Forstner bit to drill centered holes in 10 pieces of ⅛-inch walnut micro wood.

Switch to a 1½-inch Forstner bit, and drill centered holes in 10 pieces of ⅛-inch walnut micro wood, 20 pieces of ¼-inch walnut micro wood, and 40 pieces of oak 1×3.

You can save time by drilling three or four pieces of the micro wood at a time.

STEP 3
SORTING AND LAMINATING OAK AND WALNUT

Lay out oak and walnut squares in rows, each in this order: ⅛-inch undrilled walnut, oak, ¼-inch walnut, oak, ⅛-inch walnut with 1½-inch hole, oak, ¼-inch walnut, oak, and ⅛-inch walnut with 1⅛-inch hole. Arrange each walnut piece in alternating grain patterns, and do the same with the oak pieces, so the grain of each piece within the species is at right angles to the other pieces.

Brush a coat of glue onto the top surface of each piece in a row, except the ⅛-inch walnut piece with the 1⅛-inch hole. Apply glue to another row while the first row sets to slightly tacky.

Stack the pieces in the first row so that the unglued piece of ⅛-inch walnut ends up on top. Wipe the sides of the unit with a damp sponge to remove excess glue that seeps from the joints. Then secure the stack with two doubled rubber bands arranged parallel to each other and aligned with the edges of the top hole. Finally, wrap with two more rubber bands arranged perpendicular to the first two.

Wipe the sides with a sponge again, and use a finger to smooth the seepage inside the unit to an even coat that will serve to seal the wood.

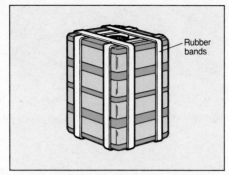

2. Stack the glued squares in order, and secure with two parallel rubber bands; then wrap two more rubber bands perpendicular to the first.

CLEANING CONTAINERS

Use a small brush to loosen dust inside the containers. Then vacuum and wipe them down with a tack cloth.

ATTACHING LABEL PLATES

2. Attach label plates with screws and a small screw-holding screwdriver.

CUTTING CORKS

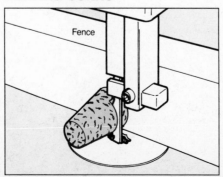

Use a bandsaw to cut ¼ inch from the top of each vacuum-bottle cork.

Assemble the second row the same way, and continue assembling the units two rows at a time. Then let stand overnight.

STEP 4
SANDING AND FINISHING

Use a belt sander and medium belt to sand the sides of the containers to a smooth and even finish. If you don't own a stationary belt sander, clamp a portable belt sander upside down in a Workmate®.

Clamp a pad sander upside down in the Workmate®, and sand all surfaces with 120- and 220-grit sandpaper. Then sand all but the bottoms with 320-grit paper.

As you sand, round over the top edges and corners and the vertical corner edges. Only slightly round over bottom edges—just enough to prevent splintering.

Use a small brush to loosen dust inside the containers. Vacuum each container and wipe it down with a tack cloth. Then apply three coats of Deft Clear Wood Finish to all surfaces.

STEP 5
ATTACHING LABEL PLATES

Arrange containers so the fronts appear in alternating grain patterns when they stand side by side. Lay each on its back, and center a label plate on the second oak square from the top, between the walnut squares.

Using the plate as a guide, mark for screw holes with the point of a scratch awl. Remove the plate, and push the scratch awl point into the container at each mark. Then tap the awl to drive a pilot hole about 3/16 of an inch deep.

Use a small screw-holding screwdriver to start each plate screw. Then carefully tighten—but don't overtighten—each screw.

STEP 6
CUTTING CORKS

Set the bandsaw fence ¼ of an inch from the *near* teeth of the blade. Then carefully cut ¼ of an inch from the top of each cork.

Brush the dust off the trimmed corks, and push one into the top of each spice container.

Canister Set

Kitchen canisters are handy for storing many kinds of staples, but most commercially made sets are impractical. Many home chefs use more than one kind of flour for cooking and baking, but store-bought sets usually include only one flour canister. Coffee stays fresher in a freezer than in the canister that comes with every commercial set. And a tea canister is a fairly useless item for both the person who uses only tea bags and the serious tea drinker who stocks several varieties of bulk tea.

With this basic set of three large canisters, you can store sugar and two kinds of flour, or whatever else you want. And you can build more to fit your needs.

When you decide what your canisters will hold, have label plates made and engraved at a local trophy shop.

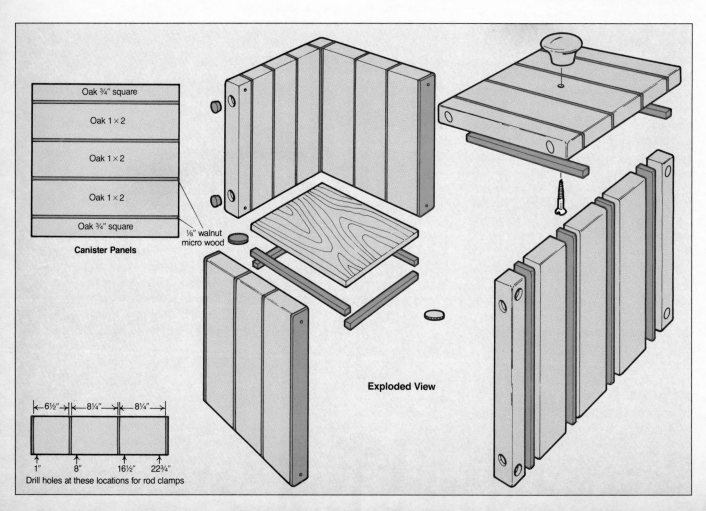

Oak ¾″ square

Oak 1 × 2

Oak 1 × 2

Oak 1 × 2

Oak ¾″ square

⅛″ walnut micro wood

Canister Panels

Exploded View

←6½″→ ←8¼″→ ←8¼″→

1″ 8″ 16½″ 22¾″

Drill holes at these locations for rod clamps

PARTS LIST

Part Name	Qty	Description	Part Name	Qty	Description	Part Name	Qty	Description
Laminating strip	18	¾″ × 1½″ × 24″ oak	Laminating strip	24	⅛″ × ¾″ × 24″ walnut	Cleat	6	¼″ × ¼″ × 4½″ walnut
Laminating strip	6	¾″ × ¾″ × 24″ oak	Cleat	12	¼″ × ¼″ × 5″ walnut	Canister bottom	3	¼″ × 5″ × 5″ oak plywood

BILL OF MATERIALS

Qty	Size	Material	Qty	Size	Material	Qty	Size	Material
1	¼″ × 5″ × 15″	Scrap G1S oak plywood			Wood filler			Watco Natural Danish Oil Finish
6	1″ × 2″ × 7′	Oak	24	1 × 8	Flathead wood screws			Watco Medium Walnut Danish Oil Finish
8	⅛″ × 3″ × 24″	Walnut micro wood	3	1¾″ × 3″	Engraved label plates			Deft Clear Wood Finish
1	¼″ × 3″ × 24″	Walnut micro wood	3		Amerock BP-846-WD pulls			Tack cloth
2	¾″ × ¾″ × 7′	Oak molding		120-grit	Sandpaper			Rubber bands
60	⅜″	Flathead walnut plugs		220-grit	Sandpaper			
		Carpenter's or white glue	12	¾″	Self-adhesive felt pads			
		Five-minute epoxy cement						

TOOLS

Steel tape rule	Screwdriver	⅜″ brad-point bit
Combination square	Screw-holding screwdriver	Table saw
Pencil	Miter box and backsaw	Bandsaw
Felt-tipped pen	Threaded-rod clamps (4–16)	Belt and pad sanders
Claw hammer	Drill press or drill-press stand	Workmate® (optional)
Scratch awl	Electric drill	Paintbrush
Center punch	3/16″ and 11/64″ twist-drill bits	Putty knife

STEP 1
SORTING, MARKING, AND DRILLING OAK

Sort 24-inch 1 × 2s into six sets of three, and sequentially mark one end 1A, 1B, and 1C through 6A, 6B, and 6C.

Stand each set on a narrow edge, and use a combination square to scribe lines across the strips at 1, 8, 16½, and 22¾ inches from the unmarked end.

Number pairs of ¾-inch molding strips 1, 2, and 3. Rotate them so sides corresponding with the narrow edges of the 1 × 2s are up, and scribe lines across them the same way.

With a drill press or drill-press stand and ⅜-inch brad-point bit, drill holes through each piece of oak, centered on the scribed lines.

STEP 2
RIPPING, MARKING, AND DRILLING WALNUT

Set the bandsaw fence or clamp a straight piece of wood ¾ of an inch from the blade. Then rip three ¾-inch-wide strips from each ⅛-inch walnut micro wood strip, for a total of 24 (eight per canister).

Sort the strips into three sets of eight, and scribe lines across the top strip in each set at 1, 8, 16½, and 22¾ inches from one end.

Align the strips in each set, and tightly wrap a rubber band around each end. Then, with a felt-tipped pen, make a mark across the end of each set corresponding with the marked ends of the oak strips.

SORTING AND MARKING OAK

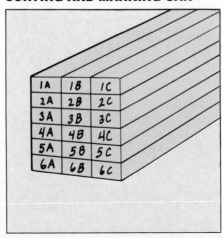

1. Sort oak 1 × 2s into six sets of three, and mark ends 1A, 1B, and 1C through 6A, 6B, and 6C.

With the drill press and ⅜-inch bit, drill holes through each set, centered on the scribed lines. When drilling end holes, remove the rubber.

STEP 3
LAMINATING OAK AND WALNUT STRIPS

Arrange oak 1 × 2s 1A, 1B, and 1C with a strip of ¾-inch molding on each side

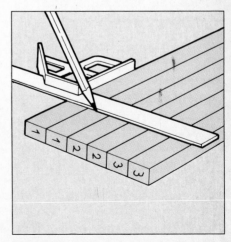

2. Rotate ¾-inch molding and 1 × 2 strips, and scribe lines across them at 1, 8, 16½, and 22¾ inches.

and a walnut strip between each oak strip. Slide the first molding strip onto four rod clamps. Brush a coat of glue onto the first walnut strip, and slide it onto the rods, down to the oak strip. Do likewise with the remaining strips, slide cushions onto the rods, followed by flat washers and nuts, and tighten the nuts with wrenches. Then assemble sets 2 and 3 the same way, and let stand for an hour.

Arrange oak 1 × 2s 4A, 4B, and 4C with a walnut strip between each and two more along the outside edges. Assemble with glue and rod clamps, and let stand an hour. Then assemble sets 5 and 6 the same way.

STEP 4
TRIMMING AND CUTTING SLABS

Set the bandsaw fence or clamp a straight strip of wood ¼ of an inch from the blade's *far* teeth, and trim the unmarked end of each slab.

Set the table-saw fence 6¾ inches from the blade's *far* teeth, and run each slab through the saw with the unmarked end against the fence. Reset the fence 8¼ inches from the *near* teeth, and run each piece through the saw again, with the unmarked end against the fence.

On one of the pieces with the marked ends, measure from the unmarked end to the center of the first hole, and set the bandsaw fence for the excess over one inch. Then trim each piece with the unmarked end against the fence.

Now run the pieces just trimmed with the bandsaw through the table saw, with the unmarked ends against the fence, to create six more 8¼-inch-long pieces.

STEP 5
MARKING AND DRILLING HOLES IN FRONT AND REAR PANELS

Three of the wide front and rear panels have holes only at one end. Mark the undrilled end of each for centered holes, one inch from the end, to correspond with the holes at the opposite end. Then use a ⅜-inch brad-point bit to drill a cosmetic ⅜-inch-deep hole at each spot.

Sort the six pieces into front and rear

DRILLING OAK

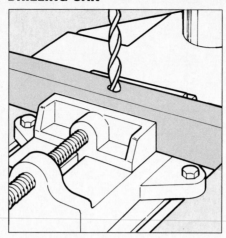

1. With a drill press and ⅜-inch brad-point bit, drill a hole centered on each line in each 1 × 2.

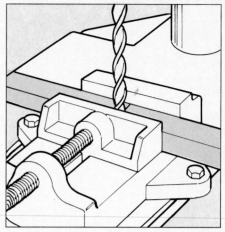

2. Then drill through each ¾-inch molding strip at each line.

DRILLING WALNUT

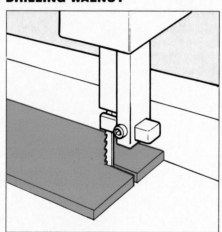

1. Set the backsaw fence ¾ of an inch from the blade, and rip 24 strips of ⅛-inch walnut micro wood.

2. Wrap a rubber band around each end of each set of eight, and mark one of the ends with a felt-tipped pen.

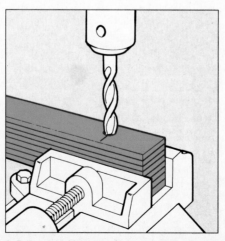

3. Drill a ⅜-inch-diameter hole through each set, centered on each line.

LAMINATING OAK AND WALNUT

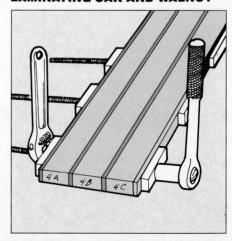

1. Use glue and rod clamps to laminate sets 1, 2, and 3 with ¾-inch molding strips on the outer edges.

panels, and mark the bottom of each to indicate inside surfaces.

Set a combination square for 1½ inches, and scribe lines across the outside surface of the ¾-inch molding on each panel, 1½ inches inside each corner. Reset the square to ⅜ of an inch; then mark the center of each scribed line.

Center-punch a drill-starter hole and drill a ⅜-inch-diameter, ⅜-inch-deep hole at each spot. Then drill through each hole with an ¹¹⁄₆₄-inch bit.

STEP 6
ASSEMBLING CANISTERS

Apply glue to one long edge of a canister side panel, butt it to a front panel, and clamp each end with a corner clamp. Then secure with two 1 × 8 flathead wood screws and power-drive bit. Let stand, with clamps in place, for 30 minutes.

Glue and clamp another side panel to the opposite end of the front panel, secure with two screws, and let stand for 30 minutes.

Apply glue to the rear edges of the side panels, clamp one side to a rear panel with two corner clamps, and drive two screws through the rear panel into the side panel. Move the clamps to the opposite side, and secure the rear panel there with two screws.

Assemble the other canisters the same way. Plug all holes with ⅜-inch walnut plugs and glue. Then let the canisters stand, with clamps in place, for two hours or overnight.

STEP 7
TRIMMING, DRILLING, AND PLUGGING LIDS

Match each of the 6½-inch-wide pieces left from Step 4 with a canister. These lids will be slightly oversize. Either trim each with a bandsaw, or sand front and rear edges with a stationary belt sander to fit.

Stand the three lids on their side edges, and use a combination square set at ¾ of an inch to scribe lines across the ends without holes. Reset the square for ⅜ of an inch, and mark the center of each line. Invert the lids, and mark the opposite sides the same way.

Center-punch a drill-starter hole at each spot marked. Then drill a ⅜-inch-

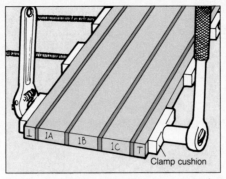

2. Laminate sets 4, 5, and 6 the same way, but without ¾-inch molding.

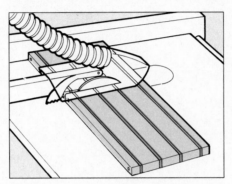

2. Use a table saw to cut a 6¾-inch and two 8¼-inch pieces from each slab.

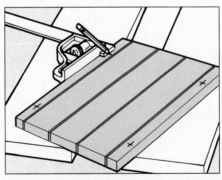

2. Use a combination square to mark front and rear panels for holes 1½ inches inside top and bottom edges and ⅜ of an inch inside the side edges.

ASSEMBLING CANISTERS

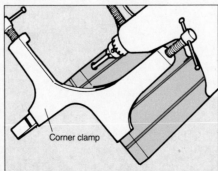

1. Glue and clamp a front panel to a side panel; then secure with two 1 × 8 screws.

CUTTING SLABS

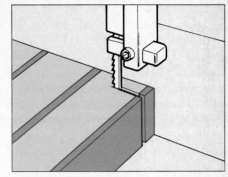

1. Use the bandsaw to trim ¼ of an inch from the unmarked end of each slab.

DRILLING PANELS

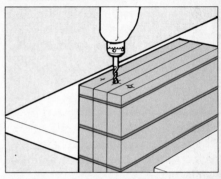

1. Mark the undrilled ends of three front and rear panels one inch from the end. Then drill a cosmetic ⅜-inch-diameter, ⅜-inch-deep hole at each spot marked.

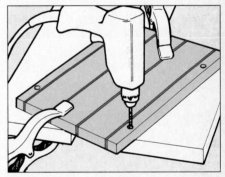

3. Counterbore a ⅜-inch-diameter, ⅜-inch-deep hole at each spot; then drill through with an ¹¹⁄₆₄-inch bit.

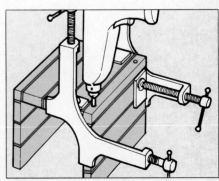

2. Attach another side panel to the front panel the same way.

diameter, ⅜-inch-deep cosmetic hole at each spot.

Set the combination square for 3¼ inches, measure in from the front edge of each lid, and scribe a line across the center 1 × 2. Then measure in from one side and mark the center of that line. If you're installing a single-screw pull, this is the mark for the screw hole. If you're installing Amerock BP-846-WD pulls, measure ⅜ of an inch from each side of the center mark and mark the center line. Then center-punch a drill-starter hole and drill a 3⁄16-inch-diameter hole at each spot (two per lid).

Insert a glued ⅜-inch, tapered, walnut plug into each hole in the lid sides, and let stand two hours or overnight.

STEP 8
SANDING CANISTERS AND LIDS

Cut plugs off with a dovetail saw; then sand plug heads smooth with a belt sander and medium belt.

Clamp lids, top side up, to overhang the edge of a work surface, and round over the front and rear edges with a belt sander and medium belt.

Sand all surfaces of lids and outside surfaces of canisters with a pad sander and 120- and 220-grit sandpaper. Round over top edges and corners of the lids and bottom edges of the canisters as you proceed. Slightly round over the vertical corners of the canisters and very slightly round over the top edges of the canisters—just enough to prevent splintering. Then sand the tops and bottoms of the canisters to a smooth, even finish.

When sanding the lids, clamp the pad sander upside down in a Workmate®.

STEP 9
CUTTING AND INSTALLING CLEATS

Set the bandsaw fence ¼ of an inch from the *near* teeth of the blade. Then rip five ¼-inch walnut strips of ¼-inch micro wood. From those strips, cut 12 cleats to five inches and six to 4½ inches.

Lay lids upside down, and position a canister upside down atop each. Then

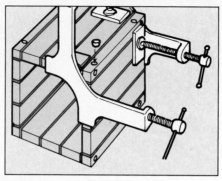

3. Attach the rear panel with glue, clamps, and screws, and plug holes with glued ⅜-inch walnut plugs.

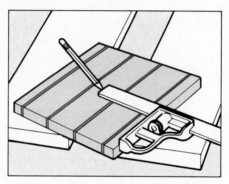

2. Set combination square for 3¼ inches and mark the center of each lid for pull-screw holes.

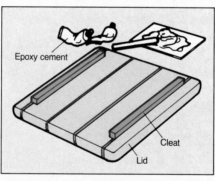

2. Attach two five-inch cleats to the underside of each lid with five-minute epoxy cement.

CUTTING CANISTER BOTTOMS

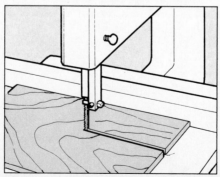

1. Set bandsaw fence five inches from blade, and rip a scrap of ¼-inch plywood to that width.

DRILLING LIDS

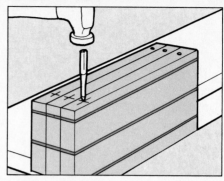

1. Mark, center-punch, and drill ⅜-inch-diameter, ⅜-inch-deep holes ¾ of an inch inside the undrilled ends of the lids.

INSTALLING CLEATS

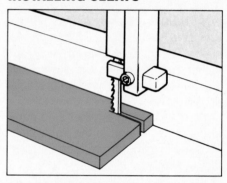

1. Use a bandsaw to rip five ¼-inch-wide strips of ¼-inch walnut micro wood.

3. Install cleats along the inside bottom edges of the canisters with epoxy cement.

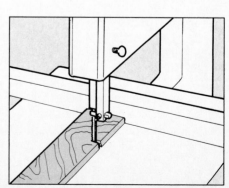

2. Then cut three five-by-five-inch squares from the plywood.

make a small pencil mark inside each corner, parallel with the front and rear edges of the lids.

Mix a small amount of epoxy cement and apply a thin, even coat to one side of six five-inch cleats. Position two on the underside of each lid, aligned with the walnut strips nearest the lid side edges and inside the guide lines.

With canisters on their sides, glue a five inch cleat along the inside edge of one side panel, flush with the bottom, and let stand five minutes. Invert the canisters, attach the remaining five-inch cleats to the opposite sides, and let stand five minutes. Similarly, attach the 4½-inch cleats along the bottom inside edges of the front and rear panels.

STEP 10
CUTTING AND INSTALLING CANISTER BOTTOMS

Set the bandsaw fence or clamp a straight strip of wood five inches from the *near* teeth of the blade, and rip a scrap of ¼-inch plywood to that width. Rotate the plywood, and crosscut three five-by-five-inch squares.

Run a bead of glue along the top edges of the cleats in the bottom of each canister. Lay a plywood bottom atop the cleats, and put a gallon can of paint or other heavy object on it.

Let the canisters stand an hour. Then turn them upside down, and fill any holes or gaps in the bottom cleats with wood filler, and let stand overnight.

ATTACHING LABEL AND PADS

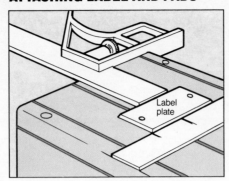

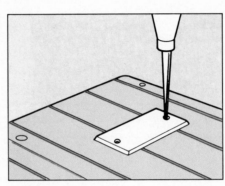

1. Center each label plate on a canister front panel, 2½ inches from the top.

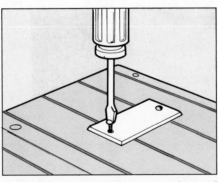

2. Mark canister fronts for screw holes with a scratch awl.

3. Attach label plates with screws and a small screw-holding screwdriver.

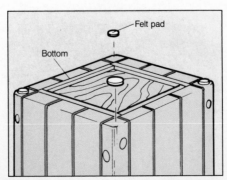

4. Attach a self-adhesive, ¾-inch felt pad inside each bottom corner of each canister.

STEP 11
FINISHING THE CANISTERS

Put the lids on the canisters and finish-sand around the corners with 220-grit sandpaper to match lids to canisters. Vacuum canisters and lids, and wipe them clean with a tack cloth.

Mix equal parts of Watco Natural and Medium Walnut Danish Oil Finish, and apply the half-and-half mixture to all components according to the manufacturer's instructions. Then let stand for 72 hours.

Attach pulls to lids with screws provided. Then apply three coats of Deft Clear Wood Finish to all surfaces of the canisters and lids.

STEP 12
ATTACHING LABEL PLATES AND FELT PADS

Set a combination square for 2½ inches. Then measure from the top of each canister, and center a label plate on the front panel.

Using the plate as a guide, mark for screw holes with the point of a scratch awl. Remove the plate, and push the awl point into the canister at each spot. Then tap the awl with a hammer to drive a pilot hole about ³⁄₁₆ of an inch deep.

Use a small screw-holding screwdriver to start each screw. Then carefully tighten each screw, but don't over-tighten.

Turn the canisters upside down, and attach a ¾-inch-diameter, self-adhesive felt pad inside each bottom corner.

Bookcase

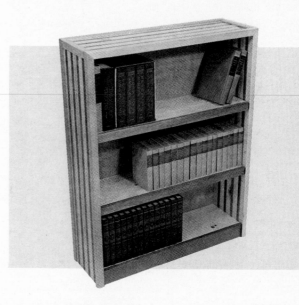

No matter what the size of the dwelling, it seldom seems to have enough shelf space. Here, then, is a versatile unit that solves this problem. Designed primarily to store books, it will also hold stereo components and display other objects.

The bookcase is made of laminated pine and redwood and is ideal for use in a kitchen, bedroom, family room, or den. It also complements two other projects in this book: the pine and redwood accent tables and the multipurpose cart.

Although the shelves are made of nominal inch-thick pine, the laminated redwood face strips add strength and rigidity as well as the appearance of thicker stock.

The shelves rest atop standard quarter-inch shelf-bracket pins that are easily adjustable.

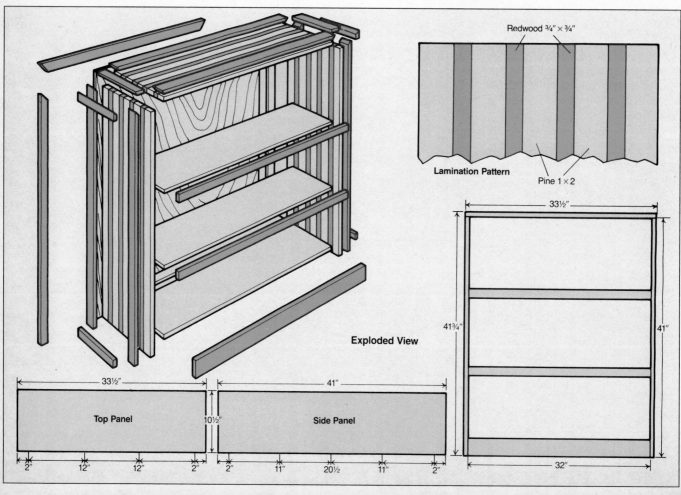

Exploded View

Lamination Pattern

Redwood ¾″ × ¾″

Pine 1 × 2

Top Panel

Side Panel

33½″

41″

10½″

2″ 12″ 12″ 2″   2″ 11″ 20½″ 11″ 2″

33½″

41¾″

41″

32″

BILL OF MATERIALS

Qty	Size	Material	Qty	Size	Material	Qty	Size	Material
1	¼" × 4' × 4'	G1S plywood or rustic pine paneling			Carpenter's or white glue	8		Shelf-bracket pins
3	1" × 6" × 8'	Kiln-dried pine			Five-minute epoxy cement		120-grit	Sandpaper
2	1" × 4" × 8'	Clear redwood			Natural wood filler		220-grit	Sandpaper
1	1" × 4" × 4'	Clear redwood			Red cedar or mahogany filler			Watco Natural Danish Oil Finish
1	1" × 12" × 8'	Kiln-dried pine		¾"	Brads			Deft Clear Wood Finish
3	1¼" × 1¼" × 8'	Outside corner molding		1¼"	Brads			Tack cloth
				1½"	Brads			

PARTS LIST

Part Name	Qty	Description	Part Name	Qty	Description	Part Name	Qty	Description
Side-panel strip	10	¾" × 1½" × 42" pine	Shelf	2	¾" × 9½" × 31¹³⁄₁₆" pine	Top trim	2	1¼" × 1¼" × 36" outside corner molding, mitered
Side-panel strip	8	¾" × ¾" × 42" redwood	Bottom face strip	1	¾" × 3" × 32¹⁄₁₆" redwood	Side trim	4	1¼" × 1¼" × 42¹⁵⁄₁₆" outside corner molding, mitered one end
Top-panel strip	5	¾" × 1½" × 34½" pine	Bottom rear strip	1	¾" × 3" × 32¹⁄₁₆" pine			
Top-panel strip	4	¾" × ¾" × 34½" redwood	Shelf face strip	2	¾" × 1½" × 31¹³⁄₁₆" redwood	Corner trim	2	1¼" × 1¼" × 8½" outside corner molding, beveled
Bottom	1	¾" × 8¾" × 32¹⁄₁₆" pine	Back panel	1	¼" × 33½" × 41¹¹⁄₁₆" plywood or paneling			

TOOLS

Steel tape rule
Carpenter's square
Combination square
Pencil
Felt pen
Claw hammer
Nail set
Center punch
Miter box and backsaw

Spring clamps (4)
Corner clamps (4)
36" bar or pipe clamp
Threaded-rod clamps (5–14)
½" or adjustable wrenches (2)
Putty knife
Drill press or drill-press stand
Electric drill
¹⁄₁₆" and ¼" twist-drill bits

⅜" brad-point bit
Circular saw and saw guide
Table saw
Belt sander
Pad sander
Workmate® (optional)
Paintbrush

CUTTING SCHEDULE (FOR TOP AND SIDE PANELS)

1. Cut two eight-foot pine 1 × 6s into four 42-inch pieces and from the other cut a 34½-inch piece.

2. Rip three 1½-inch-wide strips from each piece. Then trim two 42-inch pieces to 34½ inches, for a total of 10 42-inch and five 34½-inch pieces.

3. Cut two 42-inch pieces from an eight-foot redwood 1 × 4 and one 34½-inch piece from a four-footer.

4. Rip ⅛ of an inch from each 1 × 4 to square the edge. Then rip four ¾-by-¾-inch strips from each piece for a total of eight 42-inch pieces and four 34½-inch pieces.

STEP 1
SORTING, MARKING, AND DRILLING STRIPS

Sort 42-inch pine 1 × 2s into two sets of five, and 42-inch redwood ¾-by-¾-inch strips into two sets of four. Starting with a pine strip, arrange each set by alternating pine and redwood strips. Do the same with the five 34½-inch pine 1 × 2s and redwood ¾-inch-square strips. Then number one end of each set 1 to 9.

Rotate each set of strips so the 1 × 2s are standing on their narrow edges and

MARKING AND DRILLING STRIPS

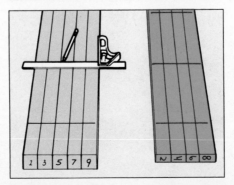

1. Mark 42-inch strips at 2½, 11½, and 21 inches and 34½-inch strips at 2½ and 12½ inches from each end.

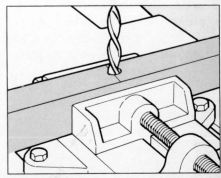

2. Drill a ⅜-inch-diameter hole centered on each line in each strip.

redwood strips are standing on corresponding edges. Then use a combination square to scribe lines across each set of 42-inch strips at 2½, 11½, and 21 inches from each end. Scribe lines across the 34½-inch strips at 2½ and 12½ inches from each end.

Use a drill press and ⅜-inch bradpoint bit to drill a hole centered on each line through each strip.

STEP 2
LAMINATING TOP AND SIDE PANELS

Arrange a set of 42-inch strips in sequential order on their broad sides. Insert five rod clamps into strip No. 1. Brush a coat of glue onto strip No. 2, and slide it onto the rod clamps, down to strip No. 1. Continue applying glue to the remaining strips until all are on the clamps. Put a cushion, flat washer, and nut on the end of each rod clamp, and tighten with two ½-inch or adjustable wrenches. Wipe excess glue from the slab with a damp sponge.

Assemble another 42-inch side panel and 34½-inch top panel the same way, and let all three stand overnight.

STEP 3
TRIMMING, DRILLING, AND SANDING TOP AND SIDE PANELS

Use a belt sander and medium belt to sand both broad surfaces of each panel to a smooth, even finish. Then use a T-square or carpenter's square to scribe a line across each panel a half-inch from one end. With a saw guide and circular saw equipped with a fine-tooth plywood blade, trim a half-inch from one end of each panel.

Then measure from the trimmed end to the opposite end, and scribe a line across each side panel at 41 inches and the top panel at 33½ inches. Then trim the panels to those finished lengths, using the circular saw.

Set a combination square for 1⅞ inches. Measuring from the bottom of each side panel, mark the inside surface for drill-starter holes at 13, 14, 15, 16, 17, 26, 27, 28, 29, and 30 inches at 1⅞ inches from the front edge and from the rear edge.

LAMINATING TOP AND SIDES

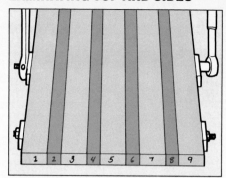

Assemble top and sides with glue and rod clamps.

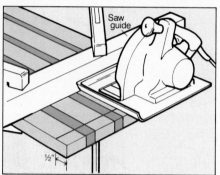

2. Trim side-panel ends with a circular saw and guide to 41 inches and top panel to 33½ inches.

DRILLING SIDES

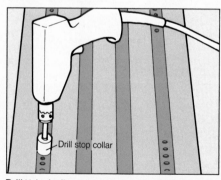

Drill ¼-inch-diameter, ⅜-inch-deep bracket holes 1⅞ inches from front and rear edges.

CUTTING BOTTOM AND SHELF

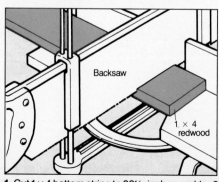

1. Cut 1 × 4 bottom strips to 32¹⁄₁₆ inches and 1 × 2 shelf-face strips to 31¹³⁄₁₆ inches.

TRIMMING TOP AND SIDES

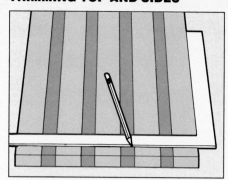

1. Use a carpenter's square to scribe a line a half-inch inside one end of each panel.

MARKING SIDES

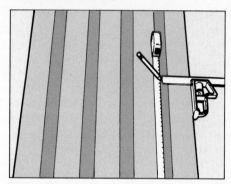

Mark the inside of each side panel for shelf-bracket holes as explained in text.

ATTACHING TOP AND SIDES

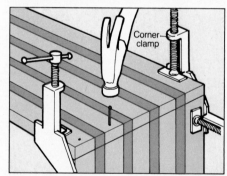

Butt the top panel to the top edges of the side panels, and clamp each end with two corner clamps. Secure with glue and 1½-inch brads.

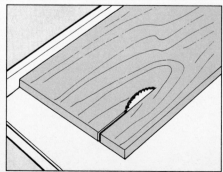

2. Rip bottom 1 × 12 to a width of 8¾ inches and 1 × 12 shelves to 9½ inches.

Center-punch a drill-starter hole at each spot marked. Then, with a ¼-inch bit and drill stop, drill ⅜-inch-deep holes in each side panel.

Set the table-saw fence 10¼ inches from the near teeth of the blade. Then run each panel through the saw with the front edge against the fence to remove a quarter-inch from the rear edge.

Finish-sand the broad surfaces of each panel with a pad sander and 120- and 220-grit sandpaper.

STEP 4
ATTACHING TOP AND SIDE PANELS

Stand side panels upright, lay the top panel atop them, and dry clamp the panels with corner clamps at front and rear corners. While leaving the top-panel clamp screws tight, loosen the side-panel clamp screws on one side only, and tilt the side panel out so the top edge is completely exposed.

Run a bead of glue along the top edge of the side panel, butt the top panel to it, and tighten the side-panel clamp screws. Do the same at the opposite side panel.

With a ¹⁄₁₆-inch bit and electric drill, drill a pilot hole through the center of each top-panel pine strip, ⅜ of an inch from the end. Then drive a 1½-inch brad through each pilot hole into the side panel, and countersink the brads. Attach the other end of the top panel to the opposite side panel the same way, with five brads. Let the assembly stand for two hours or overnight.

STEP 5
CUTTING AND RIPPING BOTTOM AND SHELF PIECES

Measure the distance between the top inside corners of the assembly; it should be about 32¹⁄₁₆ inches, depending on how much material was removed by sanding. Then cut a piece of pine 1 × 12, pine 1 × 6, and redwood 1 × 4 to that length. Cut two pieces of pine 1 × 12 and one redwood 1 × 4 a quarter-inch shorter (31¹³⁄₁₆ inches if the inside width of the bookcase is 32¹⁄₁₆ inches).

Set the table-saw fence 8¾ inches from the *near* teeth of the blade, and rip the longest 1 × 12 to that width. Reset the fence at 9½ inches, and rip the

ASSEMBLING BOTTOM

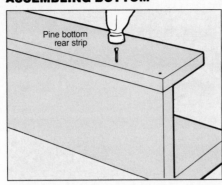

1. Attach the pine bottom rear strip to the rear edge of the bottom with glue and 1¼-inch brads.

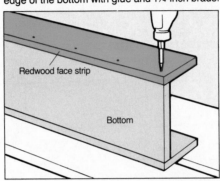

2. Attach the redwood face strip to the front edge of the bottom the same way, and countersink the brads.

ATTACHING SHELF FACES

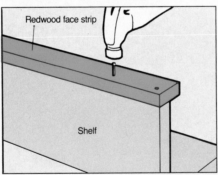

Run a bead of glue along the front edge of each shelf, attach redwood face strip with 1¼-inch brads, and countersink brads.

INSTALLING BOTTOM

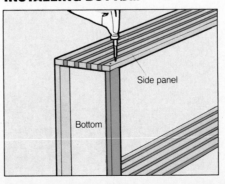

Attach each side panel to the bottom assembly with glue and two 1¼-inch brads driven into the rear strip and two more into the face strip.

other two 1 × 12s to that width.

Set the fence three inches from the *near* teeth of the blade, and rip the 32¹⁄₁₆-inch pine 1 × 6 and redwood 1 × 4 to that width. Reset the fence 1½ inches from the *near* teeth of the blade, and rip two strips from the 31¹³⁄₁₆-inch redwood 1 × 4 to that width, with a rounded edge against the fence on each pass.

STEP 6
ASSEMBLING AND SANDING BOTTOM AND SHELVES

Sand the broad surfaces of the bottom and shelves, as required, with a pad sander and 120-grit sandpaper.

Stand the bottom on its front edge, run a bead of glue down its rear edge, and butt the three-inch-wide pine strip to it. Secure the strip with five 1¼-inch brads, and countersink the brads.

Invert the bottom, and run a bead of glue along the front edge. Then attach the three-inch-wide redwood strip, rounded edge down, with five 1¼-inch brads, and countersink the brads.

Similarly, stand each shelf on its rear edge, apply glue to the front edge, attach a 1½-inch-wide redwood strip to each, square edge up, with five 1¼-inch brads, and countersink the brads.

Fill the brad holes in the redwood with mahogany or red cedar wood filler. Then fill any flaws or gaps between the pine and redwood with natural wood filler, and let bottom and shelves stand for an hour or until filler hardens.

Use a pad sander and 120-grit sandpaper to sand the bottom and shelf faces and to round over the top front edges. Then finish-sand the top and front surfaces of the shelves and bottom with 220-grit sandpaper.

STEP 7
INSTALLING THE BOOKCASE BOTTOM

Lay the laminated assembly on its side, and position the bottom assembly between the side panels. Lift the upper side panel slightly, insert the glue-bottle nozzle, and apply glue to the end of the bottom assembly.

Press the side panel back in place, and drive two 1¼-inch brads through the side panel into the three-inch-wide pine strip at the rear of the bottom.

Drive two more brads into the redwood bottom face. Then countersink the brads.

Carefully turn the assembly over so that it lies on its opposite side. Lift the upper side panel, as before, and apply glue to the end of the bottom assembly. Then attach the side panel with four 1¼-inch brads, and countersink them.

STEP 8
CUTTING AND ATTACHING THE BACK PANEL

Set the table-saw fence 14½ inches from the *far* teeth of the blade, and rip the ¼-inch plywood to a 33½-inch width.

Measure the height of the bookcase. It should be about 41¹¹⁄₁₆ inches, depending on how much material was removed from the top panel during sanding. For that height, set the table-saw fence 5⁵⁄₁₆ inches from the *far* teeth of the blade, and cut the plywood to finished dimensions of 33½ by 41¹¹⁄₁₆ inches.

Sand the face of the back panel, as required, with a pad sander and 220-grit sandpaper.

Lay the bookcase face down, and run a thin, narrow bead of glue along the rear edges of the top and side panels and a wavy bead across the bottom pine strip. Let stand for 10 to 15 minutes, until the glue gets slightly tacky. Then carefully lay the back panel in place, and secure it with ¾-inch brads at the corners and about every six to eight inches apart along the edges and across the bottom. Then countersink the brads.

STEP 9
CUTTING AND ATTACHING TRIM

With a miter box and backsaw, cut one end of a piece of corner molding at a 45-degree angle. Lay the piece along the top front edge of the bookcase, and use the opposite end of the case to mark for the second cut, and cut it at a 45-degree angle to fit. Cut another piece the same way to fit the top rear edge.

Mix a small amount of epoxy cement, and apply it to the inside of the front piece of molding, avoiding the

ATTACHING BACK PANEL

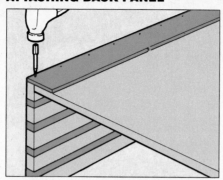

Run a bead of glue along the rear edges of the bookcase, and attach the back panel with ¾-inch brads.

ATTACHING TRIM

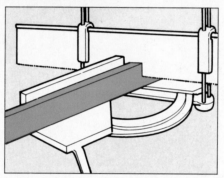

1. Use a miter box and backsaw to cut outside corner molding to fit top front and rear edges.

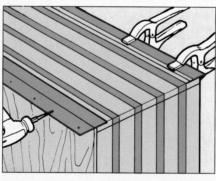

2. Attach front trim with epoxy cement and spring clamps and rear trim with glue and ¾-inch brads.

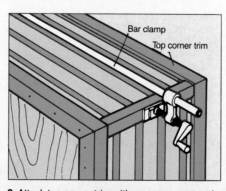

3. Attach top corner trim with epoxy cement and a 36-inch bar or pipe clamp.

outer edges to prevent seepage of excess. Position the piece along the front edge, and hold it in place with four spring clamps.

Run a thin bead of carpenter's glue along both inside surfaces of the rear piece, position it along the rear edge, and secure it with five ¾-inch brads, driven through the back. Countersink the brads.

Lay the bookcase on its side atop two scraps of 2 × 4. Cut two pieces of corner molding to fit the front and rear edges, mitred at the top ends and cut square at the bottoms. Attach the front trim with epoxy cement and clamps and the rear trim with glue and brads, as above. Turn the bookcase over, and attach trim to the opposite side the same way.

Stand the bookcase upright. Measure between the front and rear trim at the top left and right corners. Cut two pieces of corner molding to fit. Then bevel both surfaces of each end at a 45-degree angle with a bench disk or belt sander, and round over sharp edges by hand with 120-grit sandpaper. (In the absence of a bench sander, round over both surfaces of the ends by hand.) Finish-sand bevels by hand with 220-grit sandpaper.

Mix a small amount of epoxy cement, and apply it to the inside corner surfaces of the molding. Push a piece of molding in place along each top corner, secure the pieces with a 36-inch bar or pipe clamp, and let stand for five minutes.

STEP 10
FINISH-SANDING AND FINISHING

With a pad sander and 220-grit sandpaper, sand corner molding, and round over edges and corners. Then vacuum the bookcase and shelves and wipe them down with a tack cloth.

Apply a coat of Watco Natural Danish Oil Finish to the bookcase and shelves according to the manufacturer's directions. After wiping dry with paper towels, let the components stand for 72 hours. Then apply three coats of Deft Clear Wood Finish to all surfaces.

Install each shelf with four shelf brackets inserted in the holes in the side panels.

Computer Desk

As personal computers find their way into more homes and businesses, the need for attractive computer furnishings increases. This compact, trestle-style desk was designed to fill that need. But even if you don't own a computer, this unit, with or without the riser shelf, doubles as a typing desk and is built to standard height for just such purposes.

With the riser shelf standing at the rear of the desk top, there is plenty of room for a computer, keyboard, monitor, printer, and other hardware. Spanning the space between one trestle and the other is a stabilizer that serves as a spacious shelf for books, software, and supplies.

The plans call for construction with pine or fir and redwood, but you may substitute contrasting hardwoods.

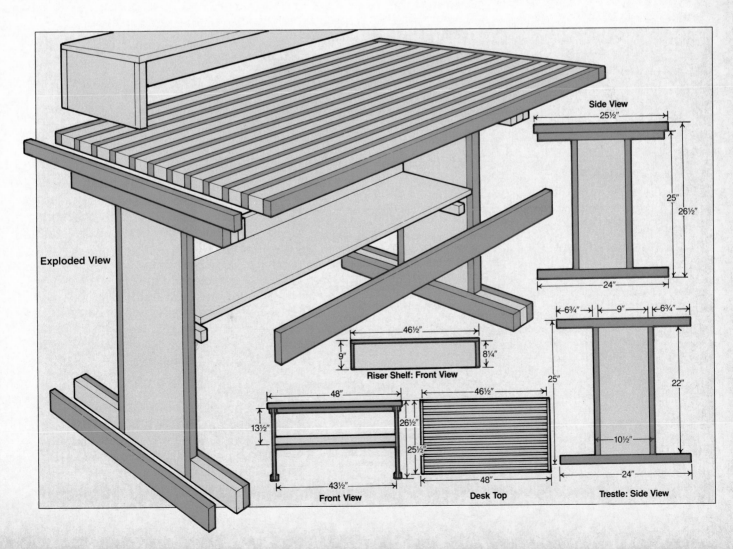

Exploded View

Side View
25½″
25″
26½″
24″

6¾″ — 9″ — 6¾″
25″
22″
10½″
24″
Trestle: Side View

Riser Shelf: Front View
46½″
9″
8¼″

Front View
48″
13½″
26½″
25½″
43½″

Desk Top
46½″
48″

PARTS LIST

Part Name	Qty	Description	Part Name	Qty	Description	Part Name	Qty	Description
Top strip	11	1½″ × 1½″ × 47½″ pine/fir	Trestle horizontal	8	¾″ × 1½″ × 24″ redwood	Trestle stabilizer	1	¾″ × 9¼″ × 43½″ redwood
Top strip	12	¾″ × 1½″ × 47½″ redwood	Trestle horizontal insert	8	¾″ × 1½″ × 6¾″ pine/fir	Riser top	1	¾″ × 9″ × 46½″ pine/fir
Top end-trim	2	¾″ × 1½″ × 25½″ redwood	Trestle shelf	1	¾″ × 9″ × 43½″ pine/fir	Riser-top trim	1	¾″ × ¾″ × 46½″ redwood
Trestle vertical	2	¾″ × 9″ × 25″ pine/fir	Trestle-shelf trim	2	¾″ × 1½″ × 43½″ redwood	Riser back	1	¾″ × 9″ × 46½″ redwood
Trestle vertical trim	4	¾″ × ¾″ × 25″ redwood	Trestle-shelf cleat	2	¾″ × ¾″ × 9″ redwood	Riser side	2	¾″ × 9″ × 8¼″ pine/fir
						Riser-side trim	2	¾″ × ¾″ × 8¼″ redwood

BILL OF MATERIALS

Qty	Size	Material	Qty	Size	Material	Qty	Size	Material
5	1″ × 4″ × 8′	Clear redwood			Natural wood filler		220-grit	Sandpaper
1	1″ × 4″ × 6′	Clear redwood		1¼″	Brads			Watco Natural Danish
1	1″ × 10″ × 8′	Clear redwood		1½″	Brads			Oil Finish
2	1″ × 10″ × 8′	Kiln-dried pine or fir	12	1½ × 8	Flathead wood screws			Deft Clear Wood
3	2″ × 4″ × 8′	Kiln-dried pine or fir	8	2 × 10	Flathead wood screws			Finish
		Carpenter's or white glue	4	½″	Self-adhesive felt cushions			Tack cloth
		Mahogany wood filler		120-grit	Sandpaper			

TOOLS

Steel tape rule
Carpenter's square
Combination square
Pencil
Felt-tipped pen
Claw hammer
Soft-faced mallet
Nail set
Center punch
Screwdriver

Miter box and backsaw
Dovetail saw
Edge clamps (2)
Spring clamps (4)
Bar clamps (4)
Threaded-rod clamps (5)
½″ or adjustable wrenches (2)
Drill press or drill-press stand
Electric drill
1/16″, 11/64″, and 13/64″ twist-drill bits

⅜″ brad-point bit
Power-drive bit
Circular saw and guide
Table saw
Belt and pad sanders
Plug cutter
Workmate®
Paintbrush
Yardstick

CUTTING SCHEDULE

1. From three eight-foot pine or fir 2 × 4s and three eight-foot redwood 1 × 4s, cut six 47½-inch pieces of each.

2. From an eight-foot redwood 1 × 4, cut one piece to 43½ inches and two to 24 inches. From another, cut two pieces to 24, one to 26½, one to 9, and one to 8¼ inches. Then cut a 25-inch and 46-inch piece from a six-foot redwood 1 × 4.

3. From an eight-foot pine or fir 1 × 10, cut two pieces to 25 inches, two to 8¼ inches, and two to 6¾ inches. From the other, cut a 43½-inch and a 46½-inch piece. Then from the eight-foot redwood 1 × 10, cut a piece to 46½ inches and another to 43½ inches.

4. Set the table-saw fence 3½ inches from the blade's *far* teeth. Then run the six 2 × 4s and all 1 × 4 redwood stock, *except the 43½-inch piece,* through the saw to square one edge.

5. Reset the blade 9¼ inches from the *far* teeth of the blade, and run all 1 × 10 stock through the saw, *except the 43½-inch redwood,* to square

one edge. Set the fence nine inches from the *near* teeth, and run the same pieces through the saw again, squaring opposite edges.

6. Set the fence 1½ inches from the *near* teeth of the blade and, with the squared edge against the fence, rip two 1½-by-1½-inch strips from each 2 × 4.

7. With squared edges against the fence, rip two ¾-by-1½-inch strips from the 47½-inch, 26½-inch, and 24-inch redwood 1 × 4s. From the two 6¾-inch pieces of pine or fir, rip eight 1½-inch-wide strips.

8. With one rounded edge of the 43½-inch redwood 1 × 4 against the fence, rip a 1½-inch-wide strip. Turn the piece over and run it through the saw again with the other rounded edge against the fence.

9. Set the fence at ¾ of an inch from the *near* teeth of the blade. Then from remaining redwood, rip one 46½-inch, four 25-inch, two 9-inch, and two 8¼-inch pieces—all ¾ by ¾ inches.

STEP 1
PRELIMINARY SANDING

Before beginning assembling, it's necessary to sand some of the desk parts that would be difficult to sand after construction.

Use a pad sander and 120-grit sandpaper to sand trestle verticals, trestle shelf, trestle stabilizer, riser top, riser back, and riser sides to a smooth, even finish. Then sand the trestle horizontals and horizontal inserts to remove the saw-blade marks.

STEP 2
SORTING, MARKING, AND DRILLING DESKTOP STRIPS

Sort 12 47½-inch redwood 1 × 2s and 11 pine or fir 2 × 2s into an alternating arrangement with 1 × 2s on the ends. Then consecutively number one end 1 to 23.

Separate 1 × 2s and 2 × 2s, but keep each set in sequential order. Rotate the 1 × 2s so their broad surfaces are up on the work surface. Divide them into sets of four, align them, and scribe lines across them at 3½, 13⅝, and 23¾ inches from each end.

Rotate the 2 × 2s so their corresponding surfaces are up, and mark them as you did the 1 × 2s.

With a drill press or drill-press stand and electric drill and ⅜-inch brad-point bit, drill holes through each strip, centered on the lines.

STEP 3
LAMINATING THE DESK TOP

Arrange all the desktop strips in numerical order. Slide five rod clamps through the holes of strip 1. Then rotate the strips so the surfaces to be glued are facing up. Brush an even coat of glue onto the strips, and slide them onto the rod clamps. When all strips are on the clamps, put a cushion, flat washer, and hex nut on each rod, and tighten the nuts with two half-inch or adjustable wrenches. Then let the slab stand overnight.

STEP 4
ROUGH-SANDING AND TRIMMING THE DESK TOP

When the glue has dried, rough-sand the top and bottom of the desktop slab to an even finish with a belt sander and medium belt.

Use a circular saw and saw guide to remove a half-inch from each end of the slab, for a finished length of 46½ inches.

Sand the top and bottom surfaces of the slab with a pad sander and 120-grit sandpaper.

STEP 5
ATTACHING END TRIM

Measure the width of the slab, and trim the two 26½-inch redwood 1 × 2s to fit. Stand each on a narrow edge atop the desk top, a few inches inside the end. Starting with the first 2 × 2 in the slab, mark the end of every other one with an X. With a yardstick lying against the redwood 1 × 2, find the center of each marked 2 × 2, and mark the corresponding spot on the redwood strip.

Use a combination square to scribe

SORTING DESKTOP STRIPS

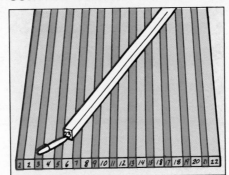

Alternate 12 redwood 1 × 2s with 11 pine or fir 2 × 2s, placing redwood on the ends, and number them from 1 to 23.

DRILLING STRIPS

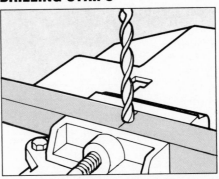

With a drill press and ⅜-inch brad-point bit, drill holes in strips centered on the lines.

ATTACHING END TRIM

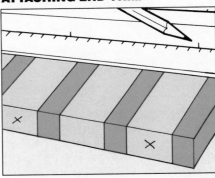

1. Starting with the one nearest the edge, mark an X on the end of every other 2 × 2 in the desk top. Then with the end-trim strip near the edge, make marks on it corresponding with the centers of the marked 2 × 2s.

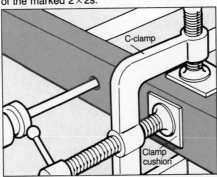

3. Attach end trim with glue and edge clamps, and secure each piece with six 1½ × 8 flathead wood screws.

MARKING STRIPS

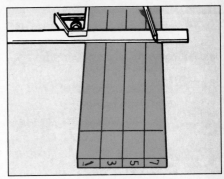

Scribe lines across the strips at 3½, 13⅝, and 23¾ inches from each end.

LAMINATING DESK TOP

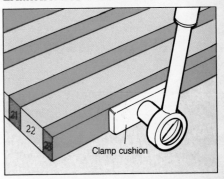

Laminate the desktop strips with glue and five threaded-rod clamps.

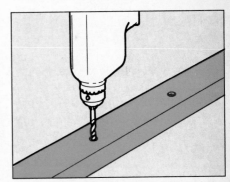

2. Counterbore a ⅜-inch-diameter, ⅜-inch-deep hole centered on each line on the end trim. Then drill through with an ¹¹⁄₆₄-inch bit.

MARKING TRESTLES

Scribe lines across the 25-inch pieces of ¾-inch-square redwood at 1, 6¾, and 12½ inches from each end.

lines across each redwood 1 × 2 at the spots marked. Set the square for ¾ of an inch, and mark the center of each line. Center-punch a drill-starter hole; counterbore a ⅜-inch-diameter, ⅜-inch-deep hole; and drill through with an ¹¹⁄₆₄-inch bit at each spot.

Dry-clamp each piece to one end of the desktop slab with a pair of edge clamps. Loosen the center clamp screws, remove the strip, and brush an even coat of glue onto its inside surface. Reposition the strip, tighten the clamp screws, and attach the strip with six 1½ × 8 flathead wood screws. Let stand for two hours.

STEP 6
SANDING END TRIM AND PLUGGING HOLES

Use a belt sander and medium belt to sand the top and bottom of the end trim flush with slab surfaces. Then sand out cross-grain scratches with a pad sander and 120-grit sandpaper.

With a drill press and ⅜-inch plug cutter, cut 22 plugs from scraps of pine or fir. Dip one end of each plug in glue, insert the plugs in the screw holes, and tap them in with a soft-faced mallet. Wipe away excess glue with a damp sponge, and let stand for an hour or until glue sets.

Cut off plug heads with a dovetail saw, and finish-sand the top with a pad sander and 120- and 220-grit sandpaper, rounding over corners and edges as you proceed.

STEP 7
ASSEMBLING TRESTLE VERTICALS

Align the four 25-inch pieces of ¾-square redwood, and use a combination square to scribe lines across them at 1, 6¾, and 12½ inches from each end. Set the square at ⅜ of an inch, and mark the center of each line for a hole. Center-punch a drill-starter hole and drill a ¹⁄₁₆-inch-diameter pilot hole at each spot.

Clamp a 9-by-25-inch piece of pine in a vise or Workmate®, and brush an even coat of glue down a 25-inch edge. Then attach a piece of redwood trim with five 1½-inch brads, and countersink the brads. Attach redwood trim the same way to the opposite edge and to

ATTACHING TRIM

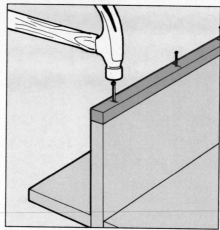

Attach trim to trestle verticals with glue and 1½-inch brads, and countersink the brads.

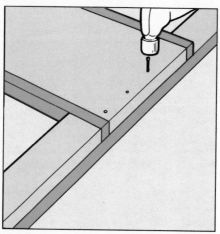

2. Attach the trestle vertical to the horizontal with glue and 1¼-inch brads, and countersink the brads.

ASSEMBLING TRESTLE SHELF

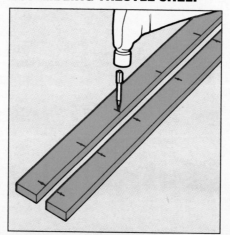

1. Mark each 43½-inch redwood 1 × 2 for holes ⅜ of an inch inside the squared edge at 1, 8, 15, and 21¾ inches from each end.

ATTACHING TRESTLES

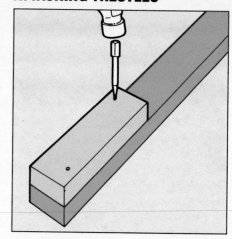

1. Attach a 6¾-inch pine or fir 1 × 2 to one end of a 24-inch redwood 1 × 2 with glue and two 1¼-inch brads, and countersink the brads.

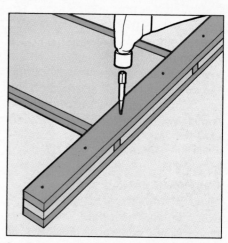

3. Attach the inside 24-inch redwood 1 × 2 with glue and five 1¼-inch brads, and countersink the brads.

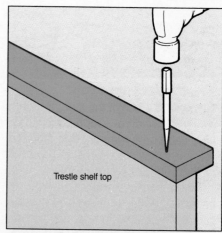

Trestle shelf top

2. Attach redwood trim to front and rear edges of the 43½-inch pine or fir trestle shelf with glue and 1½-inch brads, and countersink the brads.

the other trestle vertical.

Fill brad holes with mahogany wood filler, and when glue and filler set, sand all surfaces of the verticals with a pad sander and 120- and 220-grit sandpaper.

STEP 8
ATTACHING TRESTLE HORIZONTALS TO VERTICALS

Run a wavy bead of glue over one broad surface of a 6¾-inch pine 1 × 2, and attach it to one end of a 24-inch redwood 1 × 2 with two 1¼-inch brads, and countersink the brads.

Run a bead of glue across the outside surface of a trestle vertical, near the top, and lay it on the horizontal, with one edge against the pine insert. Attach the vertical to the horizontal with four 1¼-inch brads, and countersink the brads.

Attach another pine insert with glue and brads at the end of the horizontal opposite the first insert. Then run a wavy bead of glue along a broad surface of another horizontal, and attach it to the inserts and inside surface of the vertical, flush at the top, with five brads, and countersink the brads.

Attach the horizontals and inserts to the other end of the vertical the same way. Then build another identical assembly.

Fill brad holes with mahogany wood filler. When filler and glue set, sand the assemblies, as required, with a pad sander and 120- and 220-grit sandpaper. Then hand-sand and round over sharp corners and edges with 220-grit sandpaper.

STEP 9
ASSEMBLING THE TRESTLE SHELF

Mark each 43½-inch redwood 1 × 2 for holes ⅜ of an inch inside the squared edge at 1, 8, 15, and 21¾ inches from each end. Then center-punch a drill-starter hole and drill a 1/16-inch-diameter pilot hole at each spot.

Stand the 43½-inch pine shelf on edge and brush an even coat of glue onto the top edge. Then use seven 1½-inch brads to attach a redwood strip with the squared edge flush with the shelf top. Then countersink the brads, and attach the other redwood strip, the

ATTACHING SHELF CLEATS

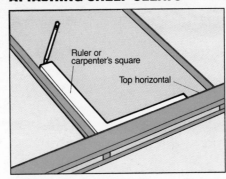

1. Make two guide marks on the inside pine or fir surface of each trestle vertical 12 inches from the top horizontal.

2. Then attach a nine-inch piece of ¾-inch-square redwood 12 inches from top horizontal.

ASSEMBLING TRESTLE

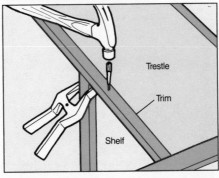

1. Clamp the shelf to a trestle with two spring clamps, and stand the assembly on end. Then attach the 43½-inch redwood 1 × 10 to the rear vertical trim with glue and three 1½-inch brads, and countersink the brads.

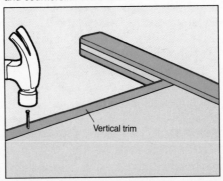

2. With the shelf glued and clamped to the cleats, drive 1½-inch brads through the vertical trim into the ends of the shelf trim.

same way, to the opposite edge.

Fill brad holes with mahogany wood filler. When filler and glue set, sand the shelf top and redwood trim with a pad sander and 120- and 220-grit sandpaper, and round over the top edges of the redwood as you sand.

STEP 10
ASSEMBLING THE TRESTLE

Lay each trestle end-assembly inside surface up, measure 12 inches down from the top horizontal, and make two guide marks on the pine surface of each vertical. Run a bead of glue down one edge of each shelf cleat, align it with the guide marks, and attach it 12 inches from the top horizontal with two 1¼-inch brads. Countersink the brads.

Stand the trestle shelf on end, and clamp a trestle end-assembly to the shelf cleat with a pair of spring clamps. Run a bead of glue down one end of the 43-inch redwood 1 × 10, butt the glued end to the inside of the rear redwood trim on the trestle vertical, and position it against the underside of the top horizontal. Attach the stabilizer by driving three 1½-inch brads through the redwood trim. Then countersink the brads.

Carefully turn the assembly over, and clamp the other end of the shelf to the other trestle end-assembly. Then attach the stabilizer with glue and brads.

Set the trestle upright, and remove the shelf. Run a bead of glue along the top of each shelf cleat. Replace the shelf, and clamp it to the cleats. Then drive a 1½-inch brad through the trestle vertical trim into the end of the front shelf trim. Do likewise at the rear and at the opposite end of the shelf.

Fill the brad holes with mahogany wood filler, and let stand until the filler and glue set. Then sand filled holes with a pad sander and 220-grit sandpaper.

STEP 11
ATTACHING THE TRESTLE TO THE DESK TOP

Turn the trestle upside down on a Workmate®, or pair of sawhorses. Set a combination square for 5¼ inches, and make a small mark across the underside of each pine insert in the horizontals, 5¼ inches from the end. Reset the square for 1½ inches, and make another mark on each insert. Reset the square for 1⅛ inches, and mark the center of each line for a drill-starter hole.

Center-punch a drill-starter hole at each spot. Counterbore two ⅜-inch-diameter, ¾-inch-deep holes in each insert, and drill through each with a ¹³⁄₆₄-inch bit.

Lay the desk top upside down, and position the trestle upside down on it. Align the top horizontals of the trestle inside the redwood edge strips of the top—at the front, rear, and on both sides.

Clamp the trestle to the top with four bar clamps or C-clamps: one at each end of each trestle horizontal. Then use an electric drill and power-drive bit to drive a 2 × 10 flathead wood screw through each inside hole in each insert into the underside of the desk top. Remove the clamps, and drive screws through the outside holes. Then tighten all screws by hand with a screwdriver.

STEP 12
ASSEMBLING THE RISER SHELF

Dry-clamp an 8¼-inch-high riser side to each end of the 46½-inch riser back with a corner clamp. Loosen the clamp screw holding the riser side, run a bead of glue down the rear edge of the riser side, clamp it to the riser back, drive three 1½-inch brads through the back into each side, and countersink the brads.

Set the riser assembly upright, and run a bead of glue along the top edges of the riser sides. Run a bead of glue along the rear edge of the riser top. Position the riser top on the riser sides, butted against the riser back. Then drive and countersink three brads through each end of the riser top into a riser side. Lay the assembly face down, and attach the riser back to the top with seven 1½-inch brads, and countersink the brads.

Lay the assembly face up. Run a bead of glue along the front edges. Then attach an 8¼-inch piece of redwood trim to the front of each riser side with two brads, and attach the 46½-inch piece of trim to the front edge of the riser top with brads. Countersink all brads, and fill the brad holes with ma-

ATTACHING TRESTLE TO TOP

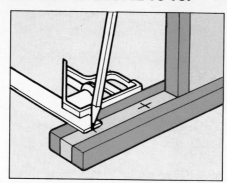

1. Mark the underside of each top horizontal for centered holes 1½ and 5¼ inches from each end.

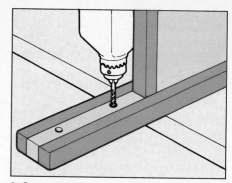

2. Counterbore a ⅜-inch-diameter, ¾-inch-deep holes, and drill through with a ¹³⁄₆₄-inch bit.

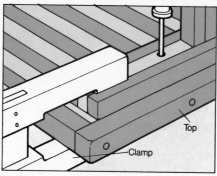

3. With trestle clamped to the desk top, drive a 2 × 10 flathead wood screw through each inside hole in the horizontals. Remove clamps, and drive screws through the outside holes.

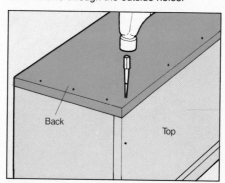

2. Apply glue to top edges of riser sides and rear edge of riser top. Drive 1½-inch brads through top into sides and through back into top; then countersink brads.

hogany wood filler.

Let the riser assembly stand until glue and filler set. Then sand the unit with a pad sander and 120- and 220-grit sandpaper, rounding over corners and edges as you proceed.

STEP 13
FINISHING THE DESK

Hand-sand the desk and riser assembly, as required, with 220-grit sandpaper. Then vacuum and wipe them with a tack cloth to remove all dust.

ASSEMBLING RISER SHELF

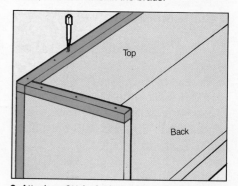

1. Attach an 8¼-inch piece of pine or fir to each end of the 46½-inch redwood riser back with glue and a corner clamp, secure with three 1½-inch brads, and countersink the brads.

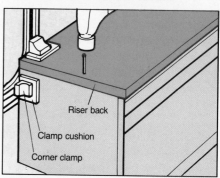

3. Attach an 8¼-inch piece of ¾-inch-square redwood to the front edge of each riser side and the 46½-inch piece to the front edge of the riser top with glue and brads. Then countersink the brads.

To duplicate the finish of the desk shown, apply a coat of Watco Natural Danish Oil Finish according to the manufacturer's directions. Let stand for 72 hours, and apply three coats of Deft Clear Wood Finish to all surfaces.

Press two half-inch, self-adhesive felt cushions onto the bottom edge of each riser side, just inside the front and rear corners. Then attach three more to the bottom edge of the riser back. Stand the riser shelf at the back of the desk top.

Multipurpose Cart

Do you need a roll-around stand big enough to hold a tabletop TV up to 28 inches wide, with room below for a video cassette recorder and TV computer game? Here's just the project for you.

Do you need an attractive cart that's substantial enough to hold a microwave oven at a comfortable height? This is the design for you to build.

Do you need a stand for stereo components, with enough room for turntable, amplifier, tuner, and tape deck? This one will fill the bill.

Yes, this cart design answers all these needs and can also function as a serving cart, or, with rubber-wheel casters, a patio cart. What's more, it coordinates with the accent tables described in the Accent Table Set project.

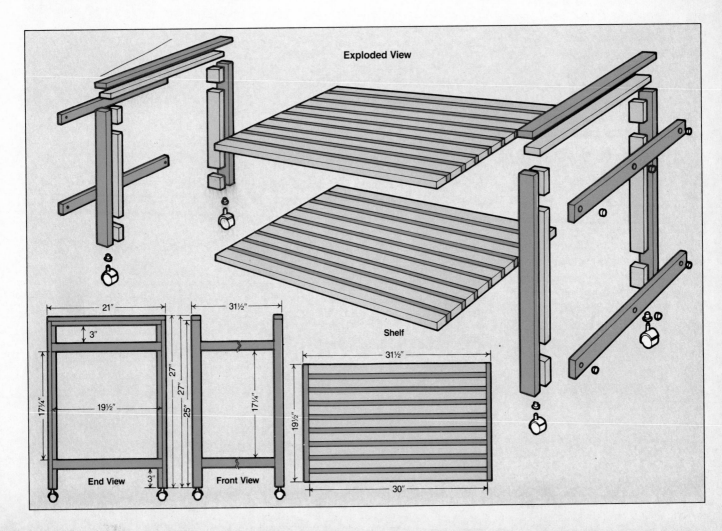

Exploded View

Shelf

End View

Front View

21″

31½″

3″

27″

27″

25″

17¼″

17¼″

19½″

3″

31½″

19½″

30″

BILL OF MATERIALS

Qty	Size	Material	Qty	Size	Material	Qty	Size	Material
1	1″ × 4″ × 6′	Kiln-dried pine			Wood filler	120-grit		Sandpaper
4	1″ × 4″ × 8′	Clear redwood		1″	Brads	220-grit		Sandpaper
3	2″ × 4″ × 8′	Kiln-dried pine	80	1 × 8	Flathead wood screws			Deft Clear Wood Finish
28	3⁄8″	Pine plugs	92	1½ × 8	Flathead wood screws			Watco Natural Danish Oil
8	3⁄8″	Redwood plugs	4	2″	Two-wheeled, barrel-type			Finish
		Carpenter's or white glue			casters			Tack cloth

TOOLS

Steel tape rule	Dovetail saw	7⁄64″ and 11⁄64″ twist-drill bits
Combination square	C-clamps (3)	Screwdriver bit
Pencil	Corner clamps (4)	3⁄8″ plug cutter
Claw hammer	Edge clamps (2)	Table saw
Nail set	Putty knife	Belt sander
Center punch	Drill press or drill-press stand	Pad sander
Screwdriver	Electric drill	Paintbrush
Miter box and backsaw	3⁄8″ brad-point bit	

CUTTING SCHEDULE

1. Cut nine 31-inch pieces from three eight-foot pine 2 × 4s.

2. Cut a six-foot pine 1 × 4 into one 20-inch and two 24-inch pieces.

3. From three eight-foot redwood 1 × 4s, cut eight pieces to 31 inches, and one to 28 inches. Then cut another eight-footer into one 28-inch piece and three 22-inch pieces.

4. Rip each 1 × 4 into two 1 × 2s and each 2 × 4 into two 2 × 2s.

STEP 1
SORTING, MARKING, AND DRILLING STRIPS

Sort two sets of nine 31-inch pine 2 × 2s and eight redwood 1 × 2s in an alternating pattern, and number them from 1 to 17. Turn the 2 × 2s on their sides, and mark all but strip 17 for centered holes at 2½ and 11 inches from each end. Turn the 1 × 2s on broad sides, and mark each at 1, 8, and 15½ inches from each end.

Center-punch a drill-starter hole at each spot. Use a 3⁄8-inch bit to counterbore holes about 3⁄8 of an inch deep in the redwood strips and about 3⁄4 of an inch deep in the pine. Then drill through each with an 11⁄64-inch bit.

STEP 2
ASSEMBLING, SANDING, AND TRIMMING SHELVES

Spread a thin, even coat of glue on the inside surface of strip 17, and attach strip 16 to it with five one-inch screws. Attach strip 15 with glue and four 1½-inch screws. Continue the same way until two shelves are assembled, and let them stand until the glue sets.

MARKING PINE AND REDWOOD

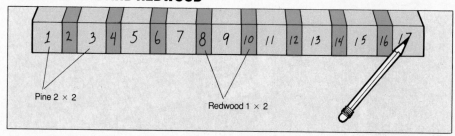

Assemble two 17-strip sets of 31-inch pine 2 × 2s alternating with redwood 1 × 2s. Number the nine pine and eight redwood strips consecutively.

DRILLING STRIPS

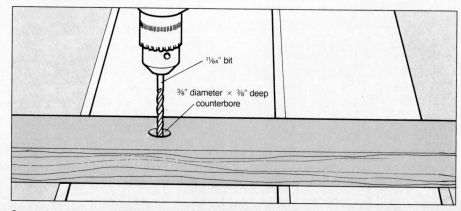

Counterbore a 3⁄8-inch-diameter, 3⁄8-inch-deep hole at each spot marked, according to instructions in the text. Then drill through with an 11⁄64-inch bit.

Fill any gaps between the strips with wood filler, and let it harden. Sand tops and bottoms of shelves with a belt sander and medium belt. Then sand with a pad sander and 120- and 220-grit sandpaper.

Set the table-saw fence a half inch from the blade's far teeth, and trim a half-inch from each end of each shelf.

STEP 3
CUTTING, DRILLING, AND ATTACHING END TRIM

Trim four 22-inch redwood 1 × 2s to fit the shelf ends. Mark a broad side of each for centered holes at 3 and 7½ inches from each end.

Center-punch a starter hole at each spot. Then counterbore ⅜-inch-diameter, ⅜-inch-deep holes, and drill through with an ¹¹⁄₆₄-inch bit.

Brush an even coat of glue onto each strip, and lightly clamp to a shelf end. Then mount with four 1½ × 8 screws, and let stand until glue sets.

STEP 4
MAKING FRAME HORIZONTALS

Trim two 22-inch redwood 1 × 2s to 21 inches and two pieces of pine 1 × 2 to 19½ inches. Lay redwood strips broad side up, and scribe a line ¾ of an inch from and parallel to each end. Turn the strips over and mark for centered holes ⅜ of an inch from each end. Center-punch starter holes; counterbore ⅜-inch-diameter, ⅜-inch-deep holes; and drill through with an ¹¹⁄₆₄-inch bit.

Prenail each pine strip with five one-inch brads. Brush a coat of glue on the opposite broad sides, and attach them to the redwood strips, aligned inside the guide lines scribed earlier. Countersink brads.

STEP 5
MAKING FRAME VERTICALS

Trim four redwood 1 × 2 verticals to 27 inches. Lay them broad side up, and scribe a line across each ¾ of an inch from the top. Turn strips over, and mark each for centered holes 4½ inches from the top and 3¾ inches from the bottom. Center-punch, counterbore, and drill, as in Step 4.

Cut eight pieces of pine 1 × 2 to three inches. Prenail each with four one-inch

ASSEMBLING SHELVES

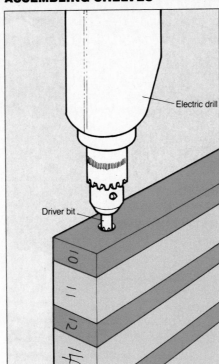

Apply glue to the strips, and assemble the shelves with screws and an electric drill with a driver bit.

ATTACHING END TRIM

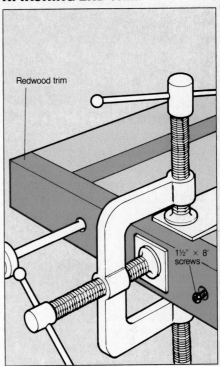

Attach the redwood end trim with glue and edge clamps, and secure it to the shelves with 1½ × 8 screws.

LAMINATING FRAME HORIZONTALS

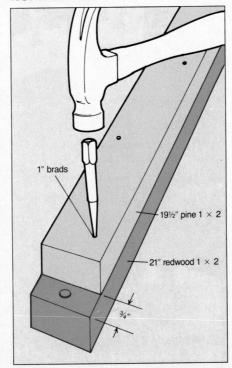

Use one-inch brads and glue to laminate two 19½-inch pine 1 × 2s to two 21-inch redwood strips, leaving ¾-inch-deep notches at the ends.

ATTACHING BLOCKS TO VERTICALS

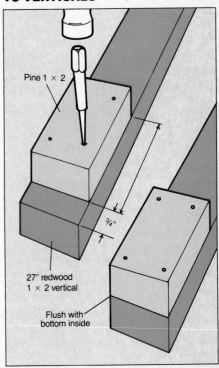

To each of four 27-inch redwood 1 × 2 verticals attach a three-inch piece of 1 × 2 pine ¾ of an inch from the top, another flush with the bottom.

brads. Coat the opposite broad sides with glue, and attach one to the top inside of each redwood 1×2, aligned with the guide lines, and another to the bottom inside, flush with the bottom.

STEP 6
ATTACHING HORIZONTALS

Apply glue to the tops of two verticals and to the notches created by the pine blocks. Clamp a horizontal between two verticals with two corner clamps.

With a 7/64-inch bit, drill a pilot hole into each vertical through each hole in the horizontal, and drive a 1½×8 screw at each spot.

Assemble another frame the same way, and fill brad holes with wood filler. When filler has dried, sand frames with 120- and 220-grit paper.

STEP 7
INSTALLING SHELVES

Stand frames upside down, 31½ inches apart. Apply glue to bottom ends of top pine blocks, lay top shelf on them, and clamp with four corner clamps.

Stand unit upright, and drill a pilot hole through each upper hole in the frame verticals with a 7/64-inch bit. Attach frames to shelf with four 1½×8 screws. Then install the bottom shelf the same way.

Measure the distance between top and bottom shelves, and cut four pieces of pine 1×2 to fit. Coat a broad side of each with glue, and clamp to inside of verticals.

STEP 8
FINISHING THE CART

Turn the unit upside down, and drill a ⅜-inch-diameter, 1½-inch-deep hole in the center of each vertical. Then tap a caster barrel into each hole.

Plug all screw holes in frames with pine plugs and holes in shelves with redwood plugs. When glue sets, cut off plug heads, and sand smooth with 120- and 220-grit paper.

Clean the cart to remove dust, apply Watco Natural Danish Oil Finish according to directions, and let stand for 72 hours. Apply three coats of Deft Clear Wood Finish; install casters.

ATTACHING FRAME HORIZONTALS TO VERTICALS

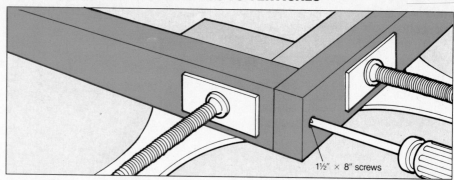

1½" × 8" screws

Apply glue to the top notches of the verticals, clamp them to the horizontals with corner clamps, and secure the assembly front and rear with 1½×8 screws.

INSTALLING SHELVES

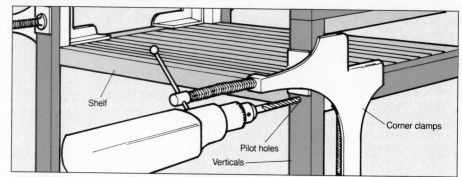

Shelf

Corner clamps

Pilot holes

Verticals

Attach the shelves to the verticals, against the pine blocks, with glue and corner clamps. Drill pilot holes, and secure the assembly with 1½×8 screws.

ATTACHING PINE 1×2 FRAME VERTICALS

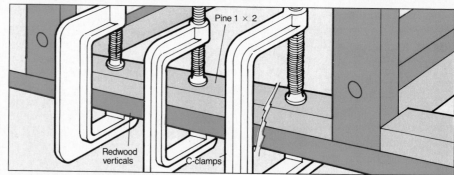

Pine 1 × 2

Redwood verticals

C-clamps

Cut four pieces of pine 1×2 to fit between the shelves, and attach the pine pieces to the redwood verticals with glue and C-clamps.

INSTALLING CASTERS

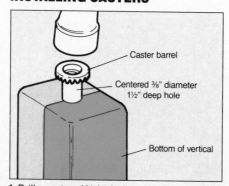

Caster barrel

Centered ⅜" diameter 1½" deep hole

Bottom of vertical

1. Drill a centered ⅜-inch-diameter 1½-inch-deep hole in the bottom of each vertical; tap a caster barrel into each.

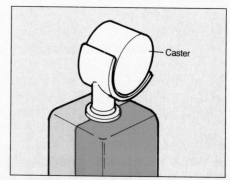

Caster

2. After finishing the cart, turn it upside down, and push a caster into each barrel.

Accent Table Set

This set of three accent tables, constructed of contrasting strips of pine and redwood, will enrich the decor of any modern den or family room.

If you prefer, you can substitute contrasting hardwoods for the specified pine and redwood. Oak and walnut, for example, or maple and cherry, or mahogany combined with either oak or maple, are all good choices. But the hardwoods are more expensive and require some extra time in the shop.

One of the advantages of working with softwoods is that you can speed up construction by driving all screws with a driver bit in an electric drill. In fact, using softwoods lets you power drive the screws without pilot holes, which must be used in hardwood construction.

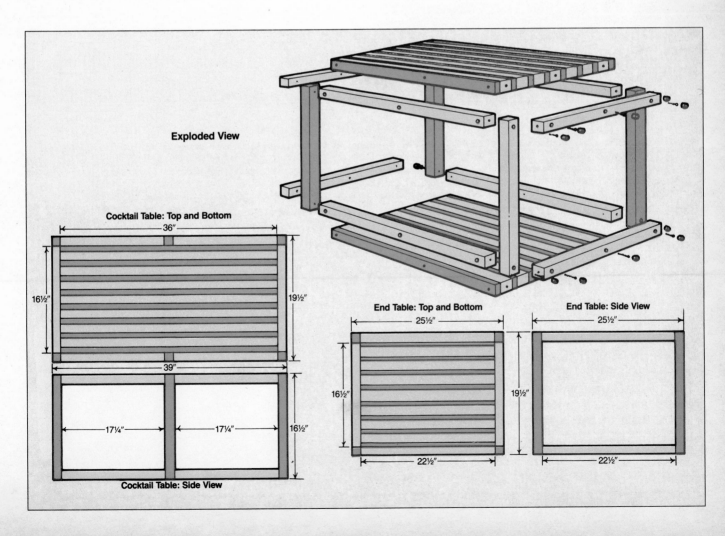

Exploded View

Cocktail Table: Top and Bottom
36″
16½″   19½″
39″
17¼″   17¼″
16½″
Cocktail Table: Side View

End Table: Top and Bottom
25½″
16½″
22½″

End Table: Side View
25½″
19½″
22½″

BILL OF MATERIALS

Qty	Size	Material	Qty	Size	Material	Qty	Size	Material
5	1″ × 4″ × 8′	Clear redwood	28	⅜″	Pine plugs	120-grit		Sandpaper
2	1″ × 4″ × 10′	Clear redwood	96	⅜″	Redwood plugs	220-grit		Sandpaper
					Carpenter's or white glue			Deft Clear Wood Finish
10	2″ × 4″ × 8′	Kiln-dried pine			Wood filler			Watco Natural Danish Oil
			212	1 × 8	Flathead wood screws			Finish
1	2″ × 4″ × 12′	Clear redwood	280	1½ × 8	Flathead wood screws			Tack cloth

PARTS LIST

Qty	Material	Size	Part	Qty	Material	Size	Part	Qty	Material	Size	Part
16	Redwood 1 × 2	37″	Cocktail-table strips	6	Redwood 2 × 2	16½″	Cocktail-table legs*	8	Pine 2 × 2	16½″	End trim
14	Pine 2 × 2	37″	Cocktail-table strips	32	Redwood 1 × 2	23½″	End-table strips	8	Redwood 2 × 2	19½″	End-table legs*
4	Pine 2 × 2	17½″	End trim	36	Pine 2 × 2	23½″	End-table strips				
8	Pine 2 × 2	18¼″	Side trim								

*Legs are cut to finished length. All other parts are cut oversize and will be trimmed to finished length during construction.

TOOLS

Steel tape rule
Combination square
Claw hammer
Center punch
Screwdriver
Miter box and backsaw
Dovetail saw

C-clamps or spring clamps (2)
Corner clamps (4)
Edge clamps (2)
Putty knife
Drill press or drill-press stand
Electric drill
⅜″ brad-point bit

7/64″ and 11/64″ twist-drill bits
Screwdriver bit
⅜″ plug cutter
Table saw
Belt sander
Pad sander
Paintbrush

CUTTING SCHEDULE

1. From five eight-foot pine 2 × 4s, cut 18 pieces to 23½ inches and one to 37 inches.

2. From one eight-foot pine 2 × 4, cut four pieces to 18¼ inches and one to 17½ inches.

3. From four eight-foot pine 2 × 4s, cut six pieces to 37 inches and five to 17½ inches.

4. From one 12-foot redwood 2 × 4, cut three pieces to 16½ inches and four to 19½ inches.

5. From five eight-foot redwood 1 × 4s, cut 16 pieces to 23½ inches and two to 37 inches.

6. From two 10-foot redwood 1 × 4s, cut six pieces to 37 inches.

7. Rip each piece of 1 × 4 into two 1 × 2s and each 2 × 4 into two 2 × 2s.

STEP 1
MARKING AND DRILLING COCKTAIL-TABLE STRIPS

Sort two sets of eight 37-inch redwood 1 × 2s and seven pine 2 × 2s in an alternating pattern. Number the ends from 1 to 15.

Turn the 1 × 2s on their broad sides, and mark all but strip 15 for centered holes at 2, 8½, and 15 inches from each end. Turn 2 × 2s on their sides, and mark them at 1, 7½, and 15½ inches from each end.

Counterbore a ⅜-inch-diameter hole about ¼ of an inch deep at each spot marked on the 1 × 2s and about ½ of an inch deep on the 2 × 2s. Then drill through each hole with an 11/64-inch bit.

STEP 2
SORTING, MARKING, AND DRILLING END-TABLE STRIPS

Sort four sets of 23½-inch pine 2 × 2s and eight redwood 1 × 2s in an alternating pattern, and then number them from 1 to 17.

Turn 2 × 2s on their sides and mark

each, except strip 17, for centered screw holes at 1½ and 11¾ inches from each end. Turn 1×2s on their broad sides, and mark each for centered screw holes one and eight inches from each end.

Counterbore and drill through each strip, as in Step 1.

STEP 3
ASSEMBLING COCKTAIL-TABLE TOP AND BOTTOM

Paint a thin, even coat of glue on the broad inside surface of strip 15, and attach strip 14 to it with six 1½×8 flathead wood screws.

Apply glue to strip 14, and attach strip 13 to it with six 1×8 flathead wood screws. Continue attaching strips this way until two slabs are assembled. Then let stand until glue sets.

STEP 4
ASSEMBLING END-TABLE TOPS AND BOTTOMS

Apply an even coat of glue to strip 17, and attach strip 16 to it with four 1×8 flathead wood screws. Apply glue to strip 16, and attach strip 15 to it with three 1½×8 screws. Continue assembling in this manner until four slabs are completed. Let stand until glue sets.

STEP 5
FILLING, SANDING, AND TRIMMING

Fill any gaps between strips on all six tops and bottoms with wood filler, and let stand until filler hardens.

Carefully sand the tops and bottoms of the slabs with a belt sander and medium belt. Then sand with a pad sander and 120- and 220-grit sandpaper.

Set the table-saw fence a half-inch from the blade's far teeth. Then remove a half-inch from each end of the cocktail-table top and bottom for a trimmed length of 36 inches. Do likewise with the end-table tops and bottoms for a trimmed length of 22½ inches.

STEP 6
MARKING AND DRILLING LEGS

Mark each redwood 2×2 leg for two centered holes ¾ of an inch from the top and bottom. Center-punch a drill-starter hole at each spot. Then counter-

SORTING AND MARKING COCKTAIL-TABLE STRIPS

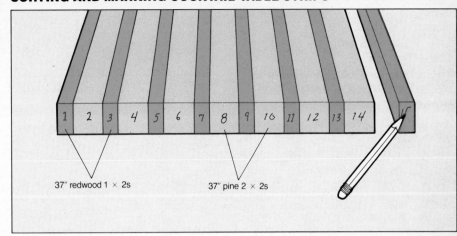

1. Sort 37-inch redwood 1×2s and pine 2×2s in an alternating pattern, and number the strips on the ends from 1 to 15.

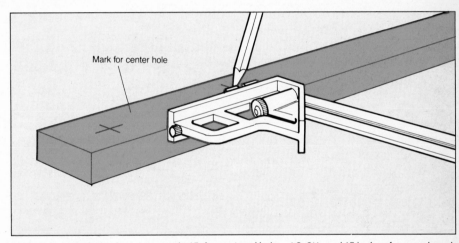

2. Mark the redwood strips, except strip 15, for centered holes at 2, 8½, and 15 inches from each end. Mark pine 2×2s at 1, 7½, and 15½ inches from each end.

ASSEMBLING COCKTAIL TABLE

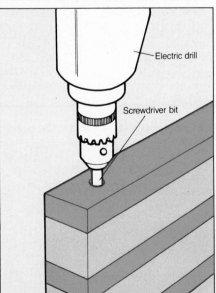

Apply glue to the sides of the strips, and assemble top and bottom with screws and screwdriver bit in an electric drill.

ASSEMBLING END TABLE

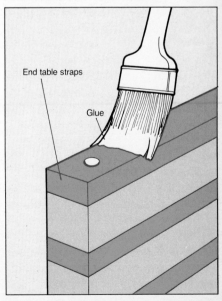

Brush an even coat of glue on the end-table strips, and assemble the tops and bottoms with screws.

bore a ⅜-inch-diameter, ¾-inch-deep hole at each spot, and drill through with an ¹¹⁄₆₄-inch bit.

STEP 7
DRILLING AND ATTACHING COCKTAIL-TABLE ENDS

Trim four 17½-inch pieces of pine 2 × 2 to fit the ends of the cocktail table top and bottom.

Mark each for centered holes at 1½ and 6 inches from each end. Center-punch and drill through, as in Step 6.

Apply a coat of glue to each piece, and attach to slab ends with two edge clamps. Secure each with four 1½ × 8 screws.

STEP 8
DRILLING AND ATTACHING END-TABLE ENDS

For each end table, trim four 17½-inch pieces of 2 × 2 pine to fit the ends of the end-table tops and bottoms, between the outside 2 × 2s; it should be about 16½ inches from the first redwood 1 × 2 to the last.

Mark, drill, and attach, as in Step 7.

STEP 9
CUTTING, DRILLING, AND ATTACHING COCKTAIL-TABLE SIDE TRIM

Cut two 18¼-inch pine 2 × 2s to 17¼ inches. Mark them for centered screw holes 1 and 8⅝ inches from each end.

Counterbore and drill through, as in previous steps. Then mount one piece to a long edge of the cocktail-table top, with the end aligned with the end of a redwood strip, creating a 1½-by-1½-inch corner notch. Mount the other piece on the corresponding part of the table bottom.

STEP 10
ATTACHING LEGS TO COCKTAIL TABLE

Apply glue to the notch, clamp a 16½-inch leg in place with a corner clamp, and attach it with one 1½ × 8 screw.

Stand table bottom up parallel to the top, and attach the leg to it the same way. Use two corner clamps to attach another leg at the center of the top and bottom, at the opposite end of the pine 2 × 2 side trim, and secure with screws.

Measure the distance from the cen-

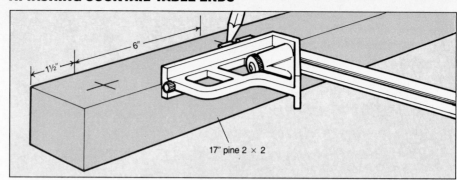

6"

1½"

17" pine 2 × 2

1. Mark four 17½-inch pieces of pine 2 × 2 for centered holes at 1½ and 6 inches from each end.

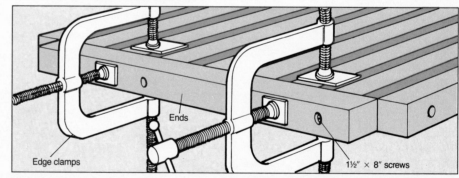

Drill and counterbore

1½" × 8" screws

2. Counterbore and drill holes at marked spots, attach ends with glue and edge clamps, and secure with 1½ × 8 screws.

ATTACHING END-TABLE ENDS

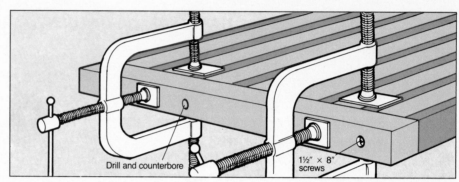

Ends

Edge clamps

1½" × 8" screws

Mark, counterbore, drill, and attach end-table ends with glue, edge clamps and 1½ × 8 screws.

ATTACHING COCKTAIL-TABLE SIDE TRIM

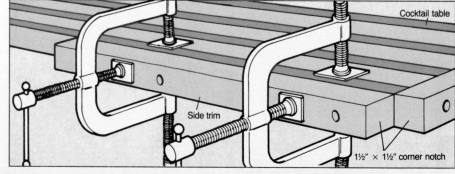

Cocktail table

Side trim

1½" × 1½" corner notch

Mark, counterbore, drill, and attach cocktail-table side trim with glue, edge clamps, and screws, creating a 1½-by-1½-inch corner notch.

ter leg to the ends of the redwood strips on the table top and bottom; it should be about 17¼ inches. Trim two more pieces of pine 2 × 2, and attach them, as in Step 9.

Then install another leg in the corner notches. Turn assembly over, and attach legs and trim to the opposite side.

STEP 11
ATTACHING END-TABLE LEGS

Apply glue to a corner notch of an end-table top, clamp a 19½-inch leg in place with a corner clamp, and secure with one screw. Attach the leg to the table bottom the same way.

Attach another leg at the opposite end. Remove the clamps from the first leg, rotate the table, and then attach another leg.

Attach the fourth leg with clamps used on the second leg, and let stand until the glue sets.

Assemble the other end table the same way.

STEP 12
DRILLING COSMETIC HOLES

One edge of each end-table top and bottom has no holes. For cosmetic purposes, mark these edges for centered holes in the middle and one inch from each end. Then drill a ⅜-inch-diameter, ⅜-inch-deep hole at each spot.

STEP 13
PLUGGING HOLES AND SANDING

Use a plug cutter to make redwood and pine plugs from available scraps. Then plug all holes in the pine with redwood plugs and all holes in the redwood with pine plugs, and let stand until glue sets.

Cut off plug heads with a dovetail saw. Then sand legs and 2 × 2 pine trim with a pad sander and 120- and 220-grit sandpaper, slightly rounding over sharp edges.

STEP 14
FINISHING TABLES

Vacuum tables and wipe them down with a tack cloth to remove dust. Then apply a coat of Watco Natural Danish Oil Finish to all surfaces, according to directions. Let tables stand for 72 hours. Then apply three coats of Deft Clear Wood Finish.

ATTACHING COCKTAIL-TABLE LEGS

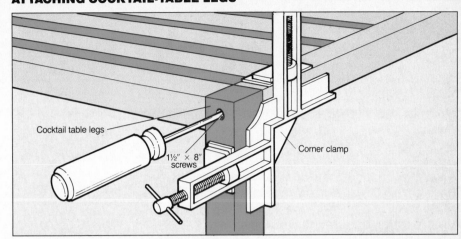

Cocktail table legs

1½" × 8" screws

Corner clamp

1. Apply glue to the corner notch, attach the leg with a corner clamp, and secure the assembly with a 1½ × 8 screw.

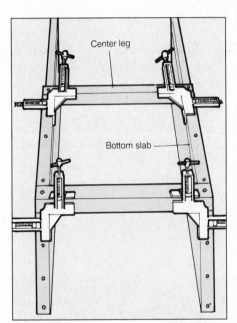

Center leg

Bottom slab

2. Attach the center leg the same way; then attach both legs to the bottom slab following the same procedure.

ATTACHING END-TABLE LEGS

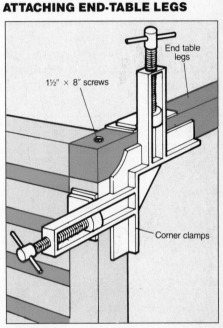

End table legs

1½" × 8" screws

Corner clamps

Apply glue to top and bottom corner notches, attach each leg with a corner clamp at each end, and secure with 1½ × 8 screws.

PLUGGING HOLES

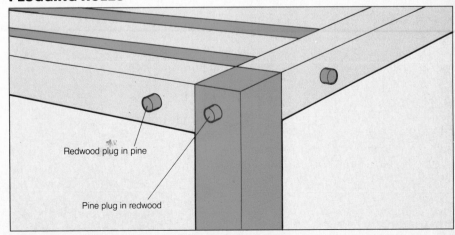

Redwood plug in pine

Pine plug in redwood

Plug the holes in pine with redwood plugs and the holes in redwood with pine plugs. When the glue sets, cut off the plug heads with a dovetail saw.

Table Lamp

A trip through a department or furniture store should convince any woodworker that with some careful attention to construction and finishing techniques, it is possible to fashion lamps that will rival anything commercially available. And they'll cost far less than comparable store-bought models.

The lamp shown here is useful almost anywhere. It's ideal as a desk lamp. A pair will prove perfect for end tables or night stands. And the three-way switch makes it great for reading or accent lighting.

Best of all, anyone who can cut wood and drill holes can build this lamp. Wiring it is even simpler. If you have never wired a lamp, don't fret. You'll learn how by following the easy directions given in this project.

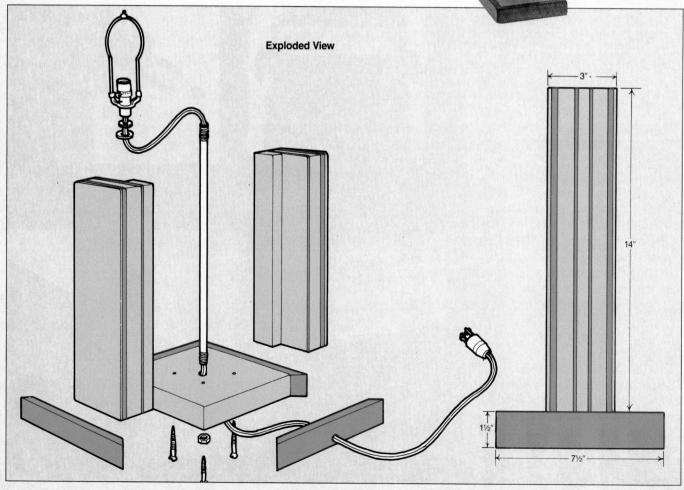

Exploded View

3″

14″

1½″

7½″

BILL OF MATERIALS

Qty	Size	Material	Qty	Size	Material	Qty	Size	Material
2	1″×2″×15″	Oak	1	⅛ IP	Brass knurled nut		320-grit	Sandpaper
4	1″×2″×7″	Oak	1	⅛ IP	Brass hex nut		#0000	Steel wool
1	1″×2″×36″	Walnut	1	⅛ IP	Brass coupler			Deft Clear Wood Finish
2	1″×4″×15″	Oak	1	⅜″	Brass lock washer			Watco Natural
2	⅛″×3″×15″	Oak micro wood	2	⅜″	Brass flat washers			Danish Oil Finish
2	⅛″×3″×15″	Walnut micro wood	1		Brass finial			Watco Medium Walnut
2	¼″×3″×15″	Walnut micro wood	1		Lamp shade			Danish Oil Finish
		Carpenter's or white glue°	6–8′	18-ga.	Two-strand electrical wire with integrally molded plug	4	½″	Round, self-adhesive felt pads
4	1¼×8	Flathead wood screws						
1	10″	Lamp harp		120-grit	Sandpaper			Tack cloth
1		Three-way lamp switch		220-grit	Sandpaper			Rubber bands
1	⅛ IP	24″ all-threaded brass tube (nipple)						

TOOLS

Steel tape rule	C-clamps (4)	Electric drill
Combination square	Bar clamps (4)	¼″, ⅜″, and ⁷⁄₁₆″ brad-point bits
Pencil	Threaded-rod clamp	⁷⁄₆₄″ and ¹¹⁄₆₄″ twist-drill bits
Claw hammer	Slip-joint pliers	Bandsaw
Center punch	Wire cutters	Hacksaw
Screwdrivers	Wire strippers	Belt and pad sanders
Miter box and backsaw	Adjustable wrench	Paintbrush

STEP 1
RIPPING WOOD STRIPS

Set bandsaw fence or clamp a straight piece of wood three inches from the blade, and rip the oak 1 × 4 to a three-inch width.

Reset the fence a half-inch from the blade, stand oak 1 × 2s on narrow edges, and trim them to ½-inch thickness.

Then, with the fence 1¼ inches from the blade, rip the 1 × 2s to ½ by 1¼ inches.

STEP 2
LAMINATING WOOD STRIPS

Lay out wood strips, broad sides up, in two sets, each consisting of a ⅛-inch oak micro wood strip, ¼-inch walnut micro wood, ripped oak 1 × 4, and ⅛-inch walnut micro wood, in that order.

Brush an even coat of glue on the broad surface of all but the ⅛-inch walnut. Then stack strips in the same order, with ⅛-inch oak and ⅛-inch walnut on the outside, and bind each set with eight doubled rubber bands.

Wipe away excess glue with a damp sponge, and let stand for 30 minutes.

RIPPING WOOD

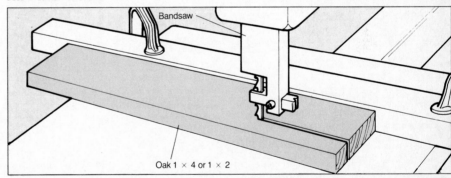

With a bandsaw, rip the oak 1 × 4 pieces to a three-inch width and the oak 1 × 2 pieces to ½-inch thickness and 1¼-inch width.

LAMINATING VERTICAL BLOCK

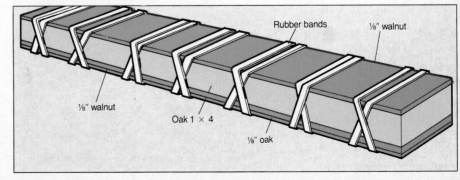

1. Glue two sets of ⅛-inch oak, ¼-inch walnut, ripped oak 1 × 4, and ⅛-inch walnut, and secure each set with eight rubber bands.

STEP 3
GLUING VERTICAL BLOCK

Remove rubber bands from the laminated strips. Brush a coat of glue onto the broad sides of two ½-by-1¼-inch oak strips, and attach each to the walnut surface of one laminated block with three or four bar clamps or C-clamps, with strips flush with the outer edges of the block, creating a ½-by-½-inch lengthwise groove. Let stand for 30 minutes.

Apply an even coat of glue to the surface of the ½-by-1¼ strips, and press the walnut surface of the other laminated block onto the glued surface. Secure with four bar clamps or C-clamps, and let stand for an hour or overnight.

STEP 4
CUTTING AND GLUING LAMP-BASE STRIPS

Cut four pieces of oak 1×2 to seven inches. Apply glue to one narrow edge of three strips, clamp the four strips with two bar clamps, and let stand for 30 minutes.

Then use a miter box and backsaw to trim a half-inch from each end, for finished dimensions of six by six inches.

STEP 5
MARKING AND DRILLING LAMP BASE

Mark the center of the base for a hole. Then set a combination square for 2¼ inches, measure in from each side, and mark for four holes 2¼ inches from the edges.

Center-punch a starter hole at each spot. Drill a ⁷⁄₁₆-inch-diameter hole through the center of the base. Then counterbore a ⅜-inch-diameter, ⅜-inch-deep hole at each remaining spot, and drill through with an ¹¹⁄₆₄-inch bit.

STEP 6
CUTTING AND ATTACHING WALNUT TRIM

With a miter box and backsaw set at 45 degrees, cut two pieces of walnut 1×2 to fit opposite edges of the base. Apply glue to the two edges of the base, clamp walnut trim in place with two bar clamps, and let stand for 30 minutes.

Then miter-cut two more pieces of walnut to fit the other two edges. Glue

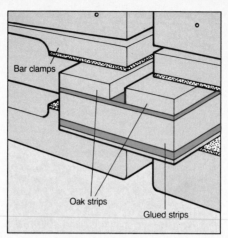

2. Apply glue to one broad surface of each ½-inch oak strip, and clamp each to an outside edge of a walnut surface of a glued set of strips, using four bar or C-clamps.

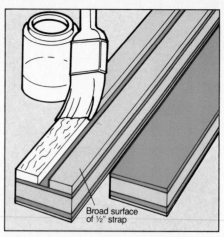

3. Brush an even coat of glue on the broad surface of each ½-inch strip.

CUTTING AND GLUING BASE

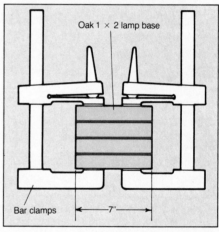

Cut four pieces of oak 1×2 to seven inches; then apply glue to the narrow edges, and clamp with two bar clamps. When the glue sets, trim the base to six by six inches.

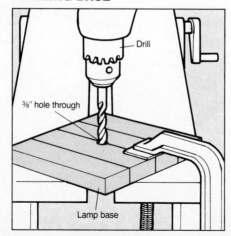

4. Clamp the remaining set of glued strips to the two ½-inch strips with four bar clamps, creating a ½-inch square center hole.

DRILLING BASE

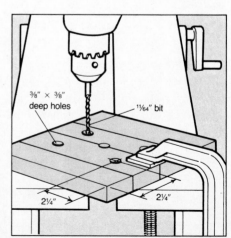

1. Drill a ⅜-inch-diameter hole through the center of the lamp base.

2. Counterbore four ⅜-inch-diameter, ⅜-inch-deep holes 2¼ inches from the base edges, and drill through with an ¹¹⁄₆₄-inch bit.

and clamp them, and let the assembly stand for an hour.

STEP 7
TRIMMING AND SANDING

Use a miter box and backsaw to trim a half-inch from each end of the laminated block, for a finished length of 14 inches.

Rough-sand the laminated edges with a belt sander and medium belt; then sand all but the bottom surfaces of the block and base with a pad sander and 120-, 220-, and 320-grit sandpaper, carefully rounding over sharp edges and corners as you sand. If necessary, sand the bottom of the walnut trim with 120-grit paper.

STEP 8
ATTACHING BASE TO BLOCK

Center the block on the base, and secure with a threaded-rod clamp with bottom cushion removed.

Drill a ⁷⁄₆₄-inch-diameter pilot hole into the block bottom through each hole in the base. Then attach the base with four 1¼ × 8 screws.

STEP 9
DRILLING WIRE HOLE IN BASE

Determine which side of the lamp will be the rear. Then mark the center of the walnut trim ⅜ of an inch from the bottom edge. Center-punch a starter hole, and drill a ¼-inch-diameter hole through the trim.

STEP 10
FINISHING LAMP BASE AND BLOCK

Hand-sand the block and base with 320-grit sandpaper; then polish with #0000 steel wool.

Vacuum the lamp to remove dust, and wipe with a tack cloth. Then mix equal portions of Watco Natural and Medium Walnut Danish Oil Finish, and apply according to the directions. Let stand for 72 hours. Then apply three coats of Deft Clear Wood Finish.

STEP 11
CUTTING AND INSTALLING THREADED TUBE

Use a hacksaw to cut the threaded brass tube to 16 inches. At one end, slide on a brass flat washer, lock

ATTACHING WALNUT TRIM

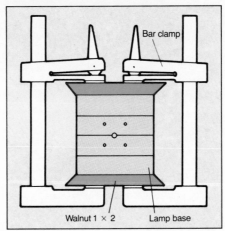

1. Cut two pieces of walnut 1 × 2, with 45-degree miters at the ends, to fit two edges of the lamp base, and attach them with glue and two bar clamps.

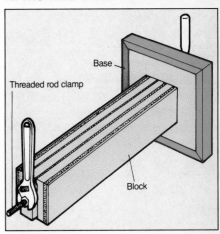

2. Cut two more pieces of walnut to fit the remaining edges, and attach them with glue and clamps.

TRIMMING AND SANDING

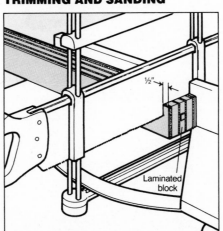

Trim a half-inch from each end of the vertical block, and rough-sand the laminated edges. Then finish-sand both the block and the base.

ATTACHING BASE TO BLOCK

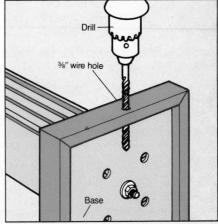

1. Secure the block to the center of the base with one threaded-rod clamp.

DRILLING BASE HOLE

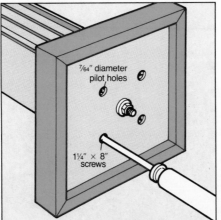

Drill a centered ¼-inch-diameter hole ⅜ of an inch from the bottom of the walnut trim on the rear side.

2. Drill ⁷⁄₆₄-inch-diameter pilot holes in the bottom of the block, and attach the base with four 1¼ × 8 screws.

washer, and twist on a hex nut flush with the end of the tube.

Slide the tube through the center hole in the bottom of the base. At the top, slide on a flat washer and twist on a knurled nut until tight.

Then carefully grip the knurled nut with pliers, and tighten the hex nut with a 9/16-inch wrench.

STEP 12
INSTALLING HARP BRACKET, SWITCH, AND HARP

Thread a brass coupler onto the top end of the threaded tube, and finger-tighten it down to the knurled nut.

Place the harp bracket on the tube, thread the switch base down to the bracket, and tighten the set screw in the base.

Insert two-strand electrical wire through the hole in the lamp base and up through the threaded tube. Separate about six inches of the two strands at the top, form a loop in each, and run the tag end of each through the loop of the other, and pull tight to form an underwriter's knot. Pull the knot down against the hole in the switch base, and trim the strands back to about 1½ inches.

Strip about a half-inch of insulation from the strand ends, twist the copper wire, and form into a hook. Then attach the two wire hooks to the switch terminals so that the hook opening faces right and will be pulled tight as you turn the screw clockwise. Snap the switch onto the switch base.

Snap the harp into the harp bracket.

STEP 13
FINISHING TOUCHES

Put a half-inch, round, self-adhesive felt pad near each bottom corner of the base, and your lamp is ready for a three-way bulb, shade, finial, and many years of service.

Since lamp shades come in a wide variety of shapes, sizes, and materials, it's a good idea to take the lamp with you when you go shopping so that you can select one that fits your hardware and looks attractive.

The shade shown in this project has a diameter of eight inches at the top and 16 inches at the bottom. Shade height is 11½ inches.

INSTALLING THREADED TUBE

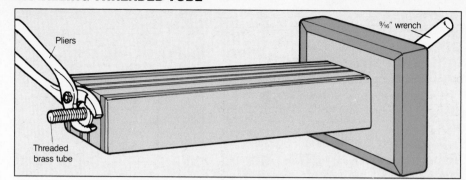

Insert 16-inch threaded tube into center hole, with a flat washer, lock washer, and hex nut at the bottom, and flat washer and knurled nut at the top. Tighten with pliers and wrench.

INSTALLING HARP BRACKET AND SWITCH

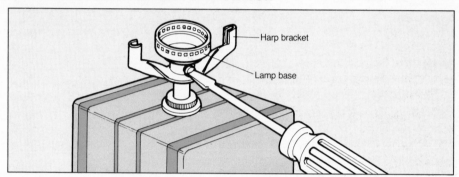

1. Thread brass coupler onto tube, followed by harp bracket and switch base. Then tighten set screw in switch base.

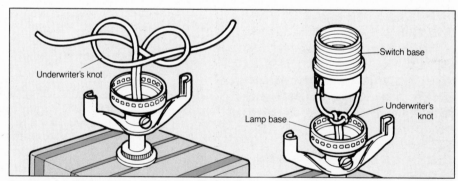

2. Tie an underwriter's knot in the cord, trim strands to 1½ inches, strip a half-inch of insulation from strand ends, and attach wire to switch terminals.

ATTACHING HARP AND BASE COVER

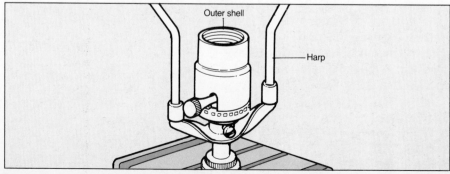

Snap the harp into its bracket. Install the switch base cover, slipping it over the switch and down into the base. Screw in a light bulb and install the shade.

Carving Board (pages 20–23). Carve, slice, and serve meats of all kinds on this laminated maple board, featuring surface V-grooves that drain juices into deep edge-gutters.

Serving Tray and Detail (pages 17–19). For tea, cocktails, or breakfast in bed, this tray, made of oak 1 × 2s, adds the warmth of wood to whatever you're serving. Oak pulls function as tray handles, and screw holes in tray ends are plugged with oak buttons.

Salt, Pepper & Picks (pages 24–26). This matching set of salt-and-pepper shakers, and toothpick holder made of laminated oak and walnut, will grace any table setting.

Candle Holders (pages 27–29). A set of three candle holders and eight matching napkin rings are slices from the same block of laminated oak and walnut.

Adjustable Bookrack and Detail (pages 37–39). To hold reference volumes or cookbooks atop desk or counter, this bookrack, made of laminated oak and walnut and oak dowel rods, suits any decor. Dowel holes in the ends of the bookrack are plugged with oak buttons.

Recipe File (pages 52–56). Store all your recipes and coupons in this spacious two-drawer filing cabinet, designed to hold three-by-five inch index cards.

Planter Box (pages 33–36). Large houseplants require large planters; this one, made of oak and walnut, accommodates pots eight inches tall and eight inches in diameter.

Wine Rack (pages 48–51). Store a full case of wine in this handsome and functional wine rack, fashioned from walnut micro wood, walnut frame molding, oak 1 × 2s, and oak dowel rods. Wine rack ends are trimmed with walnut frame molding, and screw holes are plugged with oak buttons. Bottles rest on pairs of oak dowel rods.

Coaster Set (pages 30–32). These unusual coasters are slices from a block made of laminated oak and walnut 1 × 2s. Brown felt cushions coaster bottoms; an oak rack provides storage.

Liquor Cabinet (pages 136–144). This compact liquor cabinet, designed to coordinate with the oak parquet tables, is functional as well as attractive. Supported on heavy-duty, ball-type casters, the liquor cabinet rolls to any convenient location where it doubles as a dry bar. The spacious interior houses liquor, mixers, and dozens of glasses. Although the liquor cabinet top is finished to resist the effects of water and alcohol, a vinyl place mat used for mixing drinks adds further protection.

Cutlery Block (pages 44–47). Kitchen knives should never be stored loosely in a drawer where they pose hazards and can be damaged and dulled. This large block, made of laminated oak, will store cutlery safely and attractively.

Traditional Butcher's Block and Detail (pages 113–119). A scaled-down version of the traditional butcher's block, this sturdy piece of furniture doubles as a microwave cart. It's made of laminated maple and rolls easily on dual-wheel casters.

Spice Set and Detail (pages 62–65). There's no better, more attractive way to store spices and herbs than in these containers of laminated oak and walnut, which shield contents from sunlight. The oak rack can be mounted on a wall or set atop a kitchen counter. Engraved label plates are mounted with brass-plated screws.

Canister Set (pages 66–71). Store kitchen staples in style and elegance with these oak and walnut canisters, designed to please the eye and fit any kitchen decor. Engraved label plates, available at trophy shops, are attached to canister fronts with screws.

Jewelry Chest and Details (pages 120–124). The clean, simple lines of this jewelry chest make it suitable for men or women. The chest shell is made of laminated mahogany 1 × 2s and ¼-inch oak strips. The drawer faces are ¼-inch oak. Oak and mahogany, oiled and lacquered, contrast attractively. Drawer bottoms are lined with felt to protect jewelry.

Quartz Clock and Detail (pages 57–61). This handsome cordless wall clock is made of laminated oak 1 × 2s and oak frame molding. The face shows walnut inlays instead of numbers for a clean, modern look. The miniature quartz movement, which slips into a three-by-three-inch cavity in the rear of the clock, is powered by a single AA battery.

Table Lamp and Detail (pages 92–96). This warmly attractive lamp, made of laminated oak and walnut, operates on a three-way switch. It's equally at home atop an end table, nightstand, or desk. Lamp vertical and base are finely finished with oil and lacquer.

Oak Pedestal Desk and Details (pages 145–155). This executive-size oak desk is an exquisite piece of furniture, perfect for the home, office, den, or study. The drawers, including two that are file size, glide on heavy-duty roller-bearing slides. The desk top is made of oak 1 × 2s, laminated to an oak plywood underlayment with glue and screws. Screw holes are plugged with flathead birch plugs that are sanded flush. Belwith oak pulls are a perfect match with the laminated-oak drawer faces.

Bookcase (pages 72–76). This three-shelf bookcase is both sturdy and spacious, and features adjustable shelving. The shell is made of laminated redwood and fir or pine. Pine or fir shelves are faced with redwood. Shelf brackets fit ¼-inch-diameter holes in bookcase sides and allow shelf adjustment. Bookcase shelves are faced with redwood for strength and beauty.

Multipurpose Cart and Detail (pages 83–86). Use this pine and redwood cart to house a microwave oven, stereo equipment, or a television and video accessories. For entertaining, it functions as a spacious serving cart that rolls anywhere. To enhance the visual appeal of this cart, holes in redwood surfaces are plugged with contrasting pine plugs, holes in pine surfaces with redwood plugs. Dual-wheel casters ensure effortless movement over carpets or hard floors.

Computer Desk (pages 77–82). This compact, trestle-style computer desk is made of laminated redwood, fir, and pine. A riser shelf holds the monitor at eye level, and the trestle shelf provides stability as well as storage space for books and other objects.

Chess and Checker Table (pages 131–135). This hardwood chess-and-checker table is made of four popular hardwoods. The playing surface consists of inlaid squares of walnut and maple; the borders are cherry. Top trim, legs, and rails are oak.

Oak Parquet Tables (pages 125–130). Oak parquet flooring squares are laminated to a plywood underlayment in this handsome set of tables. Cocktail table (right) and matching oak parquet end table with legs of laminated oak 2 × 2s take on the look of a traditional butcher's block, and the spacious oak parquet dining table will comfortably seat six with room to spare.

Shelf Unit (pages 40–43). There is plenty of space for books and other items in this spacious floor-to-ceiling unit. Uprights are made of clear fir 2 × 2s and 2 × 4s, shelves of laminated 1 × 2s. Laminated shelves, resting on brackets that fit ¼-inch-diameter holes in 2 × 2 verticals, are adjustable.

Accent Table Set and Details (pages 87–91). Accent tables, designed to coordinate with the multipurpose cart, are made of laminated redwood and pine. The varying grain patterns of the pine make an effective contrast with the clear redwood. Screw holes in pine surfaces plugged with redwood and those in redwood plugged with pine add an eye-catching contrast to these tables.

Traditional Butcher's Block

No book on butcher-block projects would be complete without plans for building a traditional butcher's block: that is, a heavy-duty kitchen block designed for cutting chores, with a top of laminated end-grain hardwood, preferably maple.

The block described in this project has been designed as a functional kitchen convenience, with a lean, clean appearance that makes it an attractive piece of furniture as well. Its spacious top is big enough to accommodate any cutting task or to hold a microwave oven or other kitchen appliances.

The shelf provides additional storage space, as well as stability. Dual-wheel casters let the unit roll easily over hard surfaces or carpets.

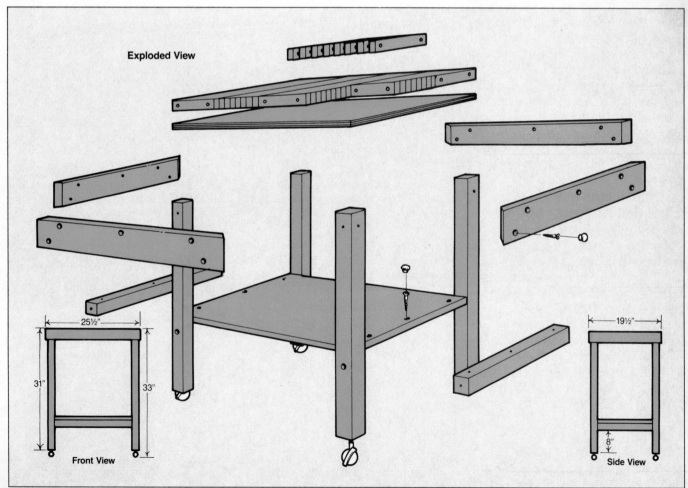

Exploded View

25½"

31"

33"

Front View

19½"

8"

Side View

BILL OF MATERIALS

Qty	Size	Material	Qty	Size	Material	Qty	Size	Material
1	½″×19″×25″	G1S hardwood plywood			Plastic resin glue	80-grit		Sandpaper
1	1″×4″×8′	Kiln-dried maple			Panel adhesive	120-grit		Sandpaper
2	1″×8″×8′	Kiln-dried maple			Natural wood filler	220-grit		Sandpaper
1	¾×5″×8′	Kiln-dried maple	14	1¼×8	Flathead wood screws			Nelsonite stabilizer with
1	¾×5″×4′	Kiln-dried maple	14	1½×8	Flathead wood screws			wax
6	⅜″	Birch button plugs	4	2×10	Flathead wood screws			Tack cloth
32	½″	Birch button plugs	4	2″	Dual-wheel, stem-type casters			
		Carpenter's or white glue						

TOOLS

Steel tape rule
Combination square
Pencil
Felt-tipped pen
Claw hammer
Soft-faced mallet
Center punch
Screwdriver
Miter box and backsaw
10″ bar clamp with double edge-clamp

attachment
12″ bar clamps (2)
36″ bar or pipe clamp
Threaded-rod clamps (6 or more)
J-roller
Notched trowel
½″ or adjustable wrenches (2)
Putty knife
Pocket knife
Drill press or drill-press stand

Electric drill
Power-drive bit
⅛″, ⁷⁄₆₄″, ¹¹⁄₆₄″, and ¹³⁄₆₄″ twist-drill bits
⅜″ and ½″ brad-point bits
Table saw
Bandsaw
Belt sander
Pad sander
Paintbrush
Workmate®

STEP 1
CUTTING PARQUET MAPLE

Cut maple 1 × 8 or other maple boards into 48-inch or smaller pieces. Then use a table saw to rip the stock to a seven-inch width.

Set the bandsaw fence or clamp a straight strip of wood 1½ inches from the *near* teeth of the blade, and crosscut 96 pieces of seven-inch-wide maple.

STEP 2
SORTING, MARKING, AND DRILLING PARQUET MAPLE

Sort the maple strips into 12 sets of eight, end grain up. Use a felt-tipped pen to run a line down one end of each set. Then make a small perpendicular mark on the end of each piece to indicate the top surface.

Set a combination square for 1½ inches, and scribe a line across each strip 1½ inches from each end. Then, with a drill press and ⅜-inch brad-point bit, drill two holes through each piece, centered on the lines.

STEP 3
LAMINATING PARQUETS

Mix about 1½ to 2 cups of plastic resin glue. If you're using Weldwood brand,

CUTTING PARQUET MAPLE

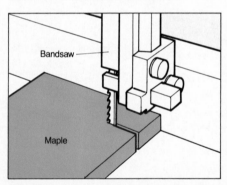

Set the bandsaw fence 1½ inches from the blade, and crosscut 96 strips from seven-inch-wide maple boards.

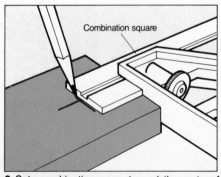

2. Set a combination square to mark the center of each piece on the broad surface, 1½ inches from each end.

DRILLING PARQUET MAPLE

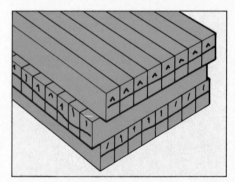

1. Sort maple strips into 12 sets of eight. Mark a line down one end of each set, and make small marks to indicate the top.

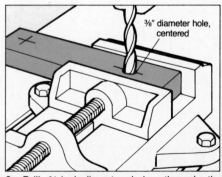

3. Drill ⅜-inch-diameter holes through the pieces, centered on the lines.

use a ¼-cup measure, and mix according to Weldwood's instructions.

With one set of parquet strips before you, end grain up, in the order they will be laminated, slide the first piece onto two threaded-rod clamps. Then rotate each remaining piece toward you so the broad surfaces to be glued are up.

Brush an even coat of glue onto all seven pieces at one time. Slide each piece onto the clamps. Then attach a cushion, flat washer, and hex nut to each clamp, and tighten the nuts with wrenches. Wipe excess glue from the parquet; let stand overnight.

Because the parquets are small, you can clamp one set at each end of the rod clamps, so that you can assemble all 12 sets with only 12 clamps, or some combination thereof.

STEP 4
ROUGH-SANDING AND TRIMMING PARQUETS

Rough-sand the top surfaces of the parquets with a belt sander (preferably stationary) and a medium belt to a smooth, even finish. Sand the bottoms even, but not uniformly smooth.

With a bandsaw or table-saw miter gauge set at zero degrees (for a right-angle cut), and the parquet strips perpendicular to the blade, trim a half-inch off the unmarked end of each parquet.

If you own a stationary belt sander, very lightly sand the cut ends to remove blade marks. Otherwise, ignore the marks and fill them later. Don't try to smooth the cut ends with a portable sander.

Measure each parquet across the strips. Because of slightly varying widths of strips and thickness of glue lines, parquet width will probably vary from about 6 to 6⅛ inches. Take the smallest measurement and set the bandsaw or table-saw fence that distance from the *near* teeth of the blade.

With parquet strips perpendicular to the blade, run each parquet through the saw with the unmarked end against the fence. As you complete each cut, rotate the parquet so strips are parallel to the blade and fence, and run the piece through the saw again to make it perfectly square.

If you own a stationary belt sander, lightly smooth the cut edges with it.

LAMINATING PARQUETS

1. Slide the first strip onto two threaded-rod clamps. Apply a coat of plastic resin glue to the remaining broad surfaces.

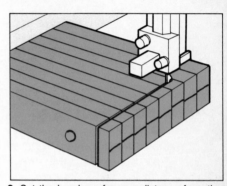

2. Slide the glued strips onto the rods; add cushions, flat washers, and hex nuts. Tighten the nuts with wrenches.

TRIMMING PARQUETS

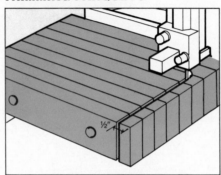

1. With the bandsaw miter gauge set at zero degrees, trim a half-inch from the unmarked end of each parquet.

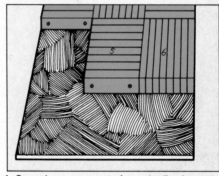

2. Set the bandsaw fence a distance from the blade equal to the width of the parquets. Then cut off the marked end.

CUTTING UNDERLAYMENT

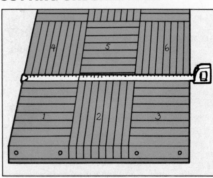

Arrange parquets and number them sequentially, measure the total width and length; cut a piece of half-inch plywood to fit.

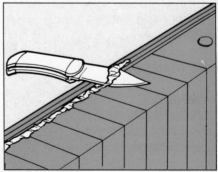

2. Firmly seat each parquet in the adhesive with a J-roller.

LAMINATING

1. Spread an even coat of panel adhesive onto the plywood underlayment with a notched trowel, and press parquets in place.

REMOVING EXCESS ADHESIVE

Use a sharp knife to cut away adhesive that has seeped from the edges of the parquets.

STEP 5
SORTING PARQUETS AND CUTTING UNDERLAYMENT

Sort parquets for the best contrast in an alternating arrangement, with strips of each parquet at right angles to those of adjacent parquets. Arrange them in a rectangle, three by four squares.

Don't despair if you find a gap or two between parquets. Move those pieces around until you achieve the best fit. Small gaps can be filled later.

When you're satisfied with the arrangement, lightly number the top of each parquet in any order that allows quence.

Measure the width and length of the arrangement. Then cut a piece of ½-inch hardwood plywood to those dimensions.

STEP 6
LAMINATING PARQUETS TO UNDERLAYMENT

Use a notched trowel to spread a liberal but even coat of panel adhesive over the surface of the plywood underlayment. Then, starting at one corner, position the parquets in sequence.

Press each parquet firmly into the adhesive, and adjust them to keep joints tight. Then use a J-roller to apply pressure to each parquet. Finally, roll the surface of the parquets from the outer edges toward the center. Adjust the parquets to eliminate gaps, and let stand for 24 hours.

STEP 7
ROUGH-SANDING THE BLOCK TOP

Use a pocket knife to trim excess adhesive from the edges of the top. Then sand the edges smooth and even with a belt sander and medium belt.

Use medium and fine belts to sand down any uneven spots on the block top. Then sand with a pad sander and 120-grit sandpaper to remove any scratches left by the sanding belts.

STEP 8
CUTTING, MARKING, AND DRILLING EDGE TRIM

Use a miter box and backsaw to cut four pieces of maple 1 × 4, with 45-degree angles at the ends, to fit each edge. Number each piece and each

SANDING BLOCK EDGES

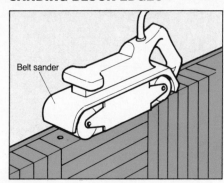

Use a belt sander and medium belt to sand block edges to a smooth, even finish.

MARKING EDGE TRIM

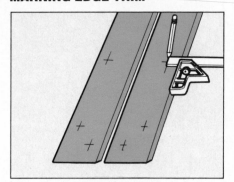

Mark the trim pieces for drill-starter holes as described in the text.

ATTACHING EDGE TRIM

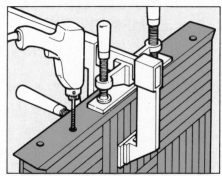

1. Attach trim to one edge with plastic resin glue and a bar clamp and edge-clamp attachment. Drive in 1¼ × 8 screws.

RIPPING STRIPS

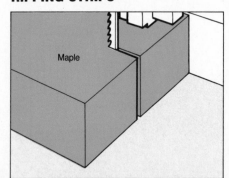

With the bandsaw fence two inches from the blade, rip the ¾ maple into legs and supports. Reset the fence one inch from the blade, and rip four shelf strips from the 26-inch piece.

CUTTING EDGE TRIM

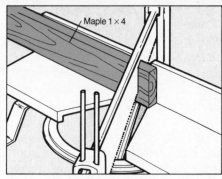

Use a miter box and backsaw to cut maple 1 × 4 to fit the edges of the block top with 45-degree miters at the ends.

DRILLING EDGE TRIM

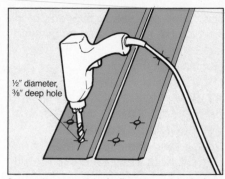

Counterbore a ½-inch-diameter, ⅜-inch-deep hole at each spot; then drill through with an 11/64-inch bit.

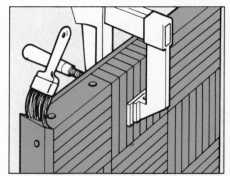

2. When attaching the remaining pieces, coat the mitered edges, as well as the block edges, with plastic resin glue.

MARKING SHELF STRIPS

Scribe lines across the narrow edges of the shelf strips at 3½ and 12¾ inches from each end.

corresponding edge with a pencil.

Lay the 1 × 4 pieces inside surface down. Measure along the outside surface near the top edge of the short pieces, and make marks at the center and at 3¾ inches from each end. Similarly, mark the long pieces at 3¾ and 9¾ inches from each end. Measure near the bottom edge and mark each piece at 1¾ inches inside each end.

Use a combination square to scribe an inch-long line perpendicular to the top edge of each piece at each spot marked. Make a similar mark at the bottom edge. Then set the square for ¾ of an inch, and mark each line for a hole ¾ of an inch from the top or bottom edge.

Center-punch a drill-starter hole and counterbore a ½-inch-diameter, ⅜-inch-deep hole at each spot. Then drill through each with an ¹¹⁄₆₄-inch bit.

STEP 9
ATTACHING TRIM TO EDGES
Clamp the top in a Workmate® with edge number one up. Dry-clamp 1 × 4 number one to it with a bar clamp and double edge clamp. Loosen the edge-clamp screws, and remove the 1 × 4.

Mix a small amount of plastic resin glue according to the manufacturer's directions. Brush an even coat onto the edge of the top, lay the trim piece in place, and tighten the edge-clamp screws. Then drive two 1¼ × 8 screws into the holes nearest the ends with an electric drill and power-drive bit. Remove the clamps, and drive screws into the other two holes.

Rotate the assembly, and attach a short piece of trim to the adjacent edge the same way. Then attach pieces three and four. When securing these three pieces, apply glue to the mitered ends as well as the edges of the top.

Wipe seeping glue away with a damp sponge, and let the top stand overnight.

STEP 10
CUTTING AND RIPPING ⁸⁄₄ MAPLE
Use a circular saw to cut two 30-inch pieces and one 26-inch piece from an eight-foot ⁸⁄₄-by-5-inch piece of maple. Then cut a four-footer into a 26-inch

DRILLING SHELF STRIPS

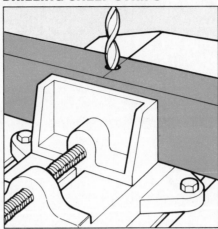

Use a drill press and ⅜-inch brad-point bit to drill holes through the shelf strips centered on the lines.

LAMINATING SHELF STRIPS

Assemble the shelf with carpenter's glue and three rod clamps.

DRILLING CASTER HOLES

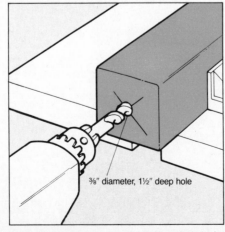

⅜" diameter, 1½" deep hole

Drill a ⅜-inch-diameter, 1½-inch-deep hole in the center of each leg bottom.

piece and a 18-inch piece.

Use a table saw or bandsaw to rip about ⅛ of an inch from one rough edge of each piece to square it.

Set the saw fence two inches from the *near* teeth of the blade, and rip two legs from each 30-inch piece and two shelf supports from the 18-inch piece.

Reset the fence one inch from the *near* teeth of the blade, and rip four shelf strips from each of the 26-inch pieces.

Use a miter box and backsaw or power miter saw to trim about a quarter-inch from one end of each leg, shelf support, and shelf strip to square it. Then trim the opposite end of each leg to a finished length of 29 inches, and the opposite end of each shelf strip to a finished length of 25½ inches.

STEP 11
MARKING, DRILLING, AND LAMINATING SHELF STRIPS
Sort the eight 25½-inch shelf strips, lay them on their broad sides, and number one end with a felt-tipped pen. Rotate them so they're standing on their narrow edges, and scribe lines across four of them at a time with a combination square at 3½ and 12¾ inches from each end.

With a drill press and ⅜-inch brad-point bit, drill holes through each strip centered on the lines.

Slide the first strip onto three threaded-rod clamps. Brush an even coat of glue onto a narrow edge of each remaining strip. Slide the strips onto the rods in numerical order. Then put a cushion, flat washer, and hex nut on each clamp rod, and tighten nuts with wrenches. Let stand overnight.

STEP 12
SANDING COMPONENTS
Sand top and bottom surfaces of the shelf to a smooth, even finish with a belt sander and medium belt. If you own a stationary belt sander, sand the sawed surfaces of each leg and shelf support with it and a medium belt. Otherwise, sand them with a portable belt sander.

Sand the parquet top and trim with a pad sander and 80-grit sandpaper. Then sand all surfaces of all components with 120-grit sandpaper, slightly rounding over sharp edges.

Fill any gaps in the parquet top and shelf with wood filler, and let stand until filler sets.

Then sand the shelf supports and top assembly with the pad sander and 220-grit sandpaper.

STEP 13
PREPARING AND MOUNTING LEGS

Mark arrows on the top of each leg to indicate the original milled surfaces; these should be perfectly parallel, whereas sawed surfaces might be slightly off.

Stand the legs upside down, and scribe a diagonal line from corner to corner and another connecting the opposite corners. Where the lines intersect, center-punch a drill-starter hole and drill a ⅜-inch-diameter, 1½-inch-deep hole.

Use the pad sander and 120-grit sandpaper to round over the bottom edges of each leg. Then sand each leg with 220-grit sandpaper, rounding over all but the top corners and edges.

Lay the top assembly upside down. Apply glue to the top of a leg, and stand it in a corner of the top assembly, with milled surfaces facing front and rear. Clamp the leg in place with a bar clamp. Then drill a 7/64-inch-diameter pilot hole through the hole in the side trim not blocked by the clamp.

Use an electric drill and power-drive bit to drive a 1½ × 8 flathead wood screw through the hole in the trim into the leg. Move the clamp to the adjacent trim piece, and secure the leg with it. Drill another pilot hole and drive another screw at a right angle to the first. Then mount the other three legs.

STEP 14
CUTTING AND ATTACHING SHELF SUPPORTS

Measure the inside distance between front and rear legs, at the bottom edge of the top-assembly trim. Use a miter box and backsaw to cut the two shelf supports to that length.

Set a combination square for eight inches and use it to mark a small guide line across the inside edge of each leg, eight inches from the bottom. Reset the square for nine inches, and mark the front edges of the front legs and rear

MOUNTING LEGS

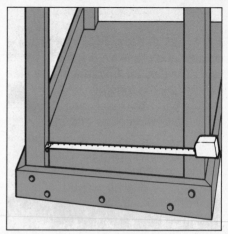

Apply carpenter's glue to the top of each leg, and clamp it to the edge trim with a bar clamp. Secure it with a 1½ × 8 screw.

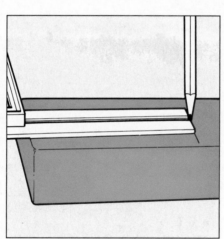

2. Mark the inside of each leg eight inches from the bottom and the outside nine inches.

4. Align the bottom of each shelf support with the lines on the inside of the legs, and attach each with a 2 × 10 screw through each hole in each leg.

ATTACHING SHELF SUPPORTS

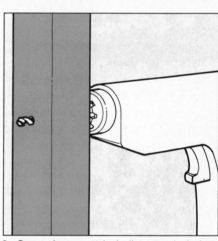

1. Measure the inside distance between front and rear legs at the edge trim, and cut two shelf supports to fit.

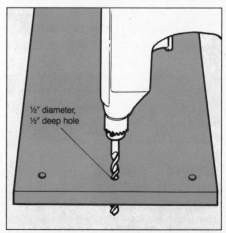

3. Counterbore a ½-inch-diameter, inch-deep hole centered on the line on the outside of each leg, and drill through with a 13/64-inch bit.

ATTACHING SHELF

½" diameter, ½" deep hole

1. Counterbore ½-inch-diameter, ½-inch-deep holes in the center and two inches inside front and rear edges; drill through with an 11/64-inch bit.

edges of the rear legs in the same way. Then mark the centers of the outside lines for screw holes.

Center-punch a drill-starter hole in the outside of each leg at each spot marked. Then counterbore a ½-inch-diameter, inch-deep hole at each spot, and drill through with a 13/64-inch bit.

With the assembly still upside down, position a shelf support between each front and rear leg, with the support bottom aligned with guide marks on the inside of the legs. If the legs slant inward, gently pull them apart to position the supports; they will then hold the supports in place on their own. If they tend outward, use a bar clamp across the bottoms of the legs to draw them together and hold the supports.

Insert a 2 × 10 flathead wood screw into each hole in each leg, and use an electric drill and power-drive bit to spin each screw with light pressure, sufficient only to make an impression in the support end. Remove supports, and drill ⅛-inch-diameter, one-inch-deep pilot holes in the ends. Replace the supports between the legs, and secure them, front and rear, with the screws.

STEP 15
PREPARING AND INSTALLING THE SHELF

Measure the distance from the outside corner of one front leg to the outside corner of the opposite front leg. Cut an equal amount from each end of the shelf so its length will match that measurement. Then rip an equal amount from each long edge of the shelf so its width will equal the shelf supports.

Sand the cut edges smooth with a belt sander and medium and fine belts. Then sand the edges with a pad sander and 120-grit sandpaper, and all surfaces except the underside with 220-grit paper, slightly rounding over edges as you sand.

Mark the top of the shelf for drill-starter holes one inch inside each end, in the center and two inches from the front and rear edges. Center-punch a drill-starter hole, and counterbore a ½-inch-diameter, ½-inch-deep hole at each spot. Then drill through with an 11/64-inch bit.

With the unit standing upright, lay the shelf on the supports. Position a front

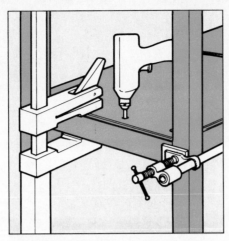

2. Clamp shelf to tops of supports, and attach with six 1½ × 8 screws. If necessary, use a bar or pipe clamps to draw legs inward.

PLUGGING HOLES

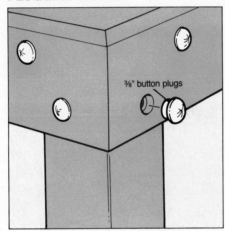

⅜" button plugs

Use a soft-faced mallet to tap a ⅜-inch button plug into each hole in the front and rear edges of the shelf and a ½-inch button plug into each remaining hole.

INSTALLING CASTERS

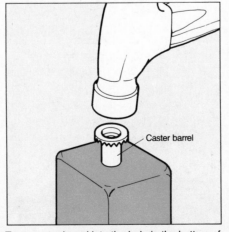

Caster barrel

Tap a caster barrel into the hole in the bottom of each leg, and push a caster into each hole.

corner of the shelf with the end flush with the outside edges of the leg and shelf support, and clamp the shelf to the support with a bar clamp or C-clamp. Then use an electric drill and power-drive bit to drive a 1½ × 8 flathead screw through the front hole in the shelf into the support.

Position the shelf against the inside edge of the other front leg. If the legs slant away from one another, use a bar or pipe clamp to draw them toward one another until the shelf edge is flush with the outside edges of the leg and support. Clamp the shelf to the support, as before, and drive another screw through the front hole of the shelf into the support.

Use the bar or pipe clamp to draw the rear legs into position, and secure the shelf to supports with screws through the rear and center holes.

STEP 16
PLUGGING HOLES, FINISHING, AND INSTALLING CASTERS

Press a ⅜-inch button plug into each hole in the front and rear edges of the shelf and a ½-inch button plug into each remaining hole. Then tap each with a soft-faced mallet to seat.

The butcher's block is now ready for the finish of your choice. If you plan to use the block as a microwave cart, simply apply whatever stain and final finish (oil, polyurethane, or lacquer) you wish. If you will be using it for food preparation, however, you must use a food-safe finish.

To duplicate the food-safe finish of the unit shown, apply a liberal coat of Nelsonite with a rag to all surfaces, and let stand overnight. Apply a second coat the following day, and let stand overnight. Note: Surfaces will be tacky after standing, but will soften with subsequent applications. Then apply a third coat, let penetrate for 30 minutes, and wipe dry with paper towels.

Let the unit stand for 24 hours; then buff with a soft cloth. Tap a caster barrel into the hole in the bottom of each leg, and push a caster into each hole.

As the top wears and shows knife marks, rejuvenate it by sanding out the scratches and cuts and reapplying Nelsonite, as described above.

Jewelry Chest

If you have shopped for a jewelry chest in recent years, you know that those worth owning carry exorbitant price tags, and those that are affordable are poorly made imports that are as ugly as they are inadequate. You have little choice but to build your own if you want top quality at a decent price.

This chest, made of carefully and finely finished hardwoods, was designed to be as practical as it is pleasant to look at. Its angular construction is gentled by rounded corners and edges that not only show off its grain and contrasting colors, but also make it equally suitable for storing men's or women's jewelry.

Although the project calls for mahogany and oak, any contrasting hardwoods are suitable.

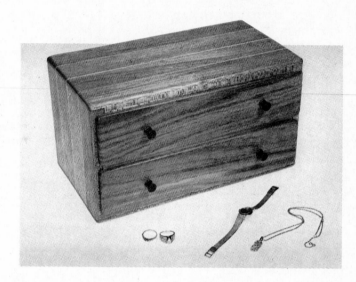

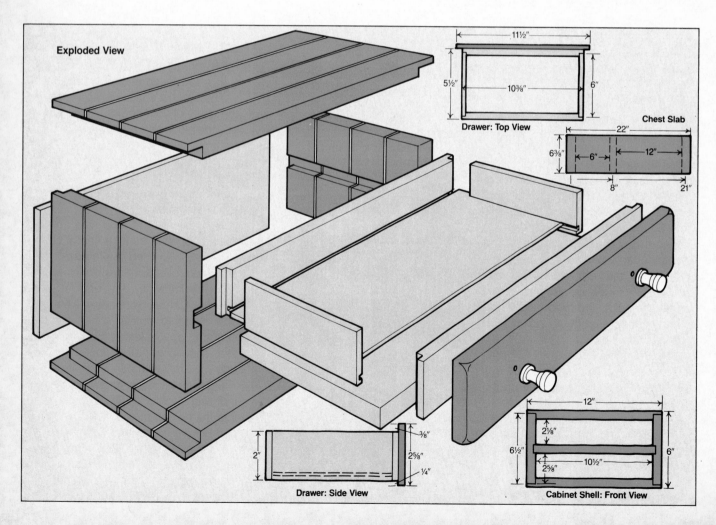

Exploded View

Drawer: Top View

Chest Slab

Drawer: Side View

Cabinet Shell: Front View

BILL OF MATERIALS

Qty	Size	Material	Qty	Size	Material	Qty	Size	Material
1	¼″ × 6″ × 11½″	Mahogany plywood			Carpenter's or white glue		320-grit	Sandpaper
1	½″ × 6″ × 24″	Mahogany plywood			Five-minute epoxy cement	2	6″ × 18″	Self-adhesive felt sheets
1	⅛″ × 12″ × 12″	Hardboard			Wood filler	4	½″	Self-adhesive felt pads
2	1″ × 2″ × 8′	Mahogany		¾″	Brads			Watco Natural Danish
1	1″ × 6″ × 12″	Mahogany	4	Small	Drawer pulls			Oil Finish
2	⅛″ × 3″ × 24″	Oak micro wood		120-grit	Sandpaper			Deft Clear Wood Finish
2	¼″ × 3″ × 24″	Oak micro wood		220-grit	Sandpaper			Tack cloth

TOOLS

Steel tape rule
Straightedge
Combination square
Pencil
Felt-tipped pen
Claw hammer
Nail set
Center punch
Screwdriver

Stubby screwdriver
Miter box and backsaw
12″ bar clamps (2)
Corner clamps (2)
Threaded-rod clamps (6)
½″ or adjustable wrenches (2)
X-Acto knife
Putty knife
Drill press or drill-press stand

Electric drill
³⁄₁₆″ twist-drill bit
⅜″ brad-point bit
Table saw
Bandsaw
Belt and pad sanders
Workmate®
Paintbrush
Rubber bands

CUTTING SCHEDULE

1. From two eight-foot mahogany 1 × 2s, cut eight pieces to 22 inches. Trim two pieces of ⅛-inch oak micro wood to 22 inches. Then trim a 12-inch scrap of mahogany 1 × 6 to 11 inches.

2. Set the bandsaw fence ¾ of an inch from the near teeth of the blade, and rip three strips from each piece of ⅛-inch oak micro wood.

3. Set the table-saw or bandsaw fence 10⅜ inches from the near teeth of the blade, and cut a nine-inch or wider scrap of ½-inch mahogany plywood to that length.

4. Set the fence 5½ inches from the near teeth of the blade, and cut a nine-inch or wider piece of ¼-inch mahogany plywood to that length.

5. Set the fence two inches from the near teeth of the blade, and rip four 2-by-10⅜ inch pieces of ½-inch mahogany plywood. Then rip four 2-by-5½-inch pieces of ¼-inch mahogany plywood.

6. Trim a scrap of ¼-inch mahogany plywood to 6 by 11½ inches.

7. Set the fence 10¹⁄₁₆ inches from the near teeth of the blade, and cut a 12-by-12-inch piece of ⅛-inch hardboard to that length. Reset the fence 5³⁄₁₆ inches from the blade, and cut two 5³⁄₁₆-by-10¹⁄₁₆-inch pieces.

8. Use a miter box and backsaw to cut two 11½-inch pieces from a strip of ¼-inch oak micro wood. Then set the bandsaw fence 2⅝ inches from the near teeth of the blade, and rip each piece to that width.

STEP 1
MARKING AND DRILLING CHEST-SHELL STRIPS

Sort 22-inch mahogany 1 × 2s into two sets of four, lay them on their broad surfaces, and number them on one end from one to four. Rotate the strips to stand on their narrow edges, and scribe lines across them at 1, 8, and 21 inches from the unmarked end.

Scribes lines on one ¾-inch-wide strip of ⅛-inch oak micro wood the same way. Then stack it on top of the other five strips, and tightly wrap a rubber band around each end. Mark across the end corresponding with the numbered ends of the mahogany with a felt-tipped pen.

Use a drill press and ⅜-inch brad-point bit to drill holes through each mahogany strip centered on the lines. Do the same with the oak strips. Note: Remove the rubber bands to drill end holes, but keep the opposite ends wrapped.

STEP 2
LAMINATING SHELL STRIPS

Brush an even coat of glue onto the inside surface of mahogany strip No. 1,

MARKING AND DRILLING CHEST-SHELL STRIPS

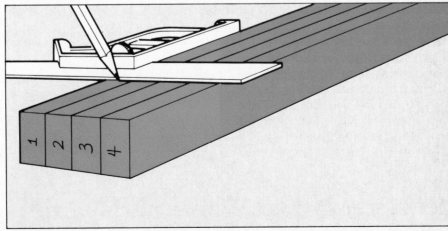

1. Scribe lines across each set of mahogany 1 × 2s and one oak strip at 1, 8, and 21 inches from the unmarked ends.

and slide it onto three rod clamps. Slide on an oak strip, brush glue onto both narrow edges of the next mahogany piece, slide it onto the rods, followed by another oak strip. Do the same with the remaining strips; then put a cushion, flat washer, and hex nut on the end of each rod, and tighten nuts.

Wipe away seeping glue with a damp sponge. Then tighten a bar clamp across each slab between the farthest separated rod clamps, and let stand overnight.

STEP 3
CUTTING AND ROUGH-SANDING COMPONENTS

Use a miter box and backsaw to cut each end off each slab, just inside the end holes. Then measure in from the end farthest from the interior holes, and cut off a 12-inch piece. Measure from the opposite end, and cut a six-inch piece.

Use a belt sander and medium belt to rough-sand the broad surfaces of each piece to a smooth, even finish.

STEP 4
CUTTING RABBETS AND DADOES IN SHELL COMPONENTS

Set the table-saw fence ¾ of an inch from the *far* teeth of the blade and set the blade for a ½-inch depth. With one end of the cabinet top against the fence and inside surface against the table, run the piece over the blade. Continue making passes to remove material between the initial cut and panel end to create a ½-inch-deep, ¾-inch-wide rabbet. Do the same at the opposite end of the panel and at each end of the bottom panel.

Set the fence 2⅝ inches from the *near* teeth and set the blade for a ¼-inch depth. With the top of a side panel against the fence and inside surface on the table, run the piece over the blade. Rotate the piece so the bottom edge is against the fence, and run it over the blade. Then do the same with the other side panel.

Move the fence away from the blade in ⅛-inch increments, while you continue to pass the panels over the blades until a ¾-inch-wide, ¼-inch-deep dado is cut in each.

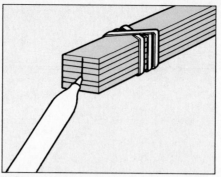

2. Stack the six ⅛-inch oak strips, and wrap a rubber band around each end. Then mark a line across the end corresponding with the numbered ends of the mahogany strips.

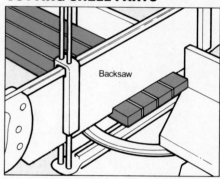

3. Drill ⅜-inch-diameter holes through all six oak strips at once, each hole centered on a guide line.

LAMINATING SHELL STRIPS

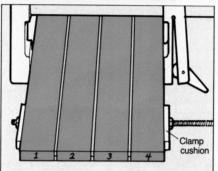

Laminate each set of four mahogany strips and three oak strips with glue and three threaded-rod clamps. Then attach a bar clamp between the most widely separated rod clamps.

CUTTING SHELL PARTS

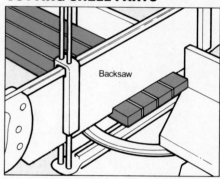

Cut the end off each slab with a miter box and backsaw. Then cut a six-inch and 12-inch piece from each slab.

RABBETS AND DADOES

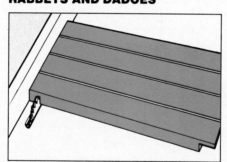

1. Use a table saw to cut ½-inch-deep, ¾-inch-wide rabbets in the ends of the top and bottom panels.

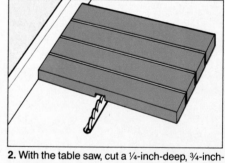

2. With the table saw, cut a ¼-inch-deep, ¾-inch-wide dado in the center inside surface of each side panel.

GROOVING DRAWER PANELS

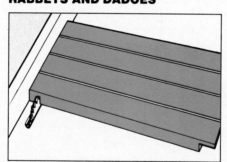

3. Then cut a ¼-inch-wide, ½-inch-deep rabbet in the rear edge of the top and bottom panel and each side panel.

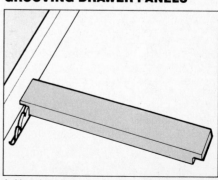

1. Use the table saw to cut a ¼-inch-by-¼-inch rabbet in the end of each drawer front and rear panel.

Set the fence ¼ of an inch from the *far* teeth of the blade and set the blade for a ½-inch depth. With the rear edge of the top panel against the fence and the inside surface down, run the piece over the blade. Then continue passing the piece over the blade until a ½-inch-deep, ¼-inch-wide rabbet is cut in the rear edge. Do likewise with the bottom and both side panels.

STEP 5
RABBETING AND GROOVING DRAWER PANELS

Set the blade for a ¼-inch depth. With the end of a drawer front or rear panel against the fence and inside surface down, run the piece over the blade; then make another pass or two to remove material from the cut to the end, making a ¼-by-¼-inch rabbet. Do the same at the opposite end and to both ends of the other front and rear panels.

Set the fence ⅛ of an inch from the *near* teeth of the blade and set the blade for a ⅛-inch depth. With a drawer panel bottom against the fence and the inside down, run it over the blade to make a ⅛-by-⅛-inch groove. Do the same with the other drawer side, front, and rear panels.

STEP 6
ASSEMBLING CHEST SHELL

Put a cabinet side panel into each rabbet of the top panel, and dry-clamp the pieces with two corner clamps at front and rear corners. Loosen the clamp screws holding the side panels, and remove the panels. Run a bead of glue along each rabbet at each end of the top panel. Replace the side panels, and secure them with the corner clamps.

Run a bead of glue along each end rabbet in the bottom panel. Push it into place at the bottom of the side panels, secure it with two corner clamps at the front and two bar clamps at the rear corners, and let stand for one hour.

Check the shell horizontal for fit in the side-panel dadoes. Sand the ends for a snug fit, as required. Run a very thin bead of glue along the inside of each dado, and gently push the horizontal into the dadoes. Tap with a mallet and block of wood until the horizontal is flush with the shell front, and let

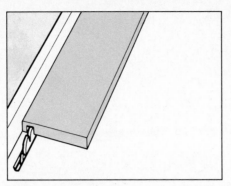

2. Then cut a ⅛-by-⅛-inch groove ⅛ of an inch from the bottom edge of each drawer panel.

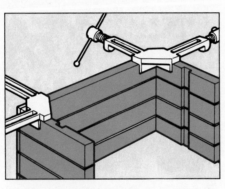

2. Then clamp a side panel into each rabbet with a corner clamp.

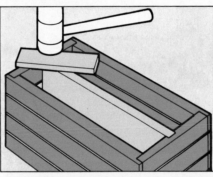

4. Run a thin bead of glue along the inside of the dado in each side panel. Then tap the shell horizontal into the dadoes with a mallet and block of wood.

ASSEMBLING DRAWERS

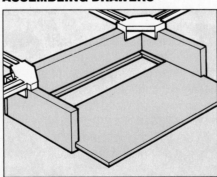

1. Glue and clamp two drawer side panels to a front panel with two corner clamps, and slide a drawer bottom into the grooves.

ASSEMBLING CHEST SHELL

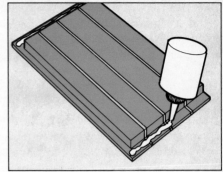

1. Run a bead of glue along each end rabbet in the top panel.

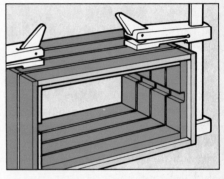

3. Attach the top panel the same way, and secure with two bar clamps near the rear corners.

5. Apply epoxy cement to the rabbets in the rear of the shell, lay shell back panel in place, and secure with two bar clamps.

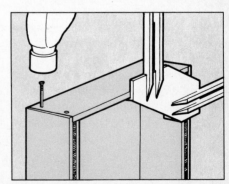

2. Glue the rear panel to the side panels, and secure side panels to rear and front panels with two ¾-inch brads at each corner.

stand for 30 minutes.

Mix a small amount of epoxy cement, and apply sparingly to the rear rabbets. Push the chest back into place, clamp front to rear with two bar clamps, and let stand for five minutes.

STEP 7
ASSEMBLING DRAWERS

Dry-clamp a drawer front to two side panels with two corner clamps. Loosen the clamp screws holding the side panels, remove panels, and run a bead of glue along the rabbets in the front panel. Replace side panels, and secure with clamps.

Slide a drawer bottom into the grooves of the side panels. Run a bead of glue along each rabbet in a rear panel, and press the panel in place against the rear edges of the side panels. Then attach each side panel to the front panel with two ¾-inch brads, and do the same at the rear panel. Countersink the brads. Assemble the other drawer and let stand for an hour.

When glue sets, sand drawers with a pad sander and 120- and 220-grit sandpaper, with sander clamped in a Workmate®.

STEP 8
ATTACHING AND DRILLING DRAWER FACES

Lay the drawer faces face down. Set a combination square for ¼ of an inch, and make several pencil marks on the inside surfaces, ¼ of an inch from the bottom edges. Reset the square, and make a mark parallel to each side of each piece.

Mix a small amount of epoxy cement, and apply it to the front panel of each drawer. Then position each drawer on a drawer face inside the guide marks. Press drawers to faces, and let stand for five minutes.

Stand the drawers face up, and mark for pull holes 1⁵⁄₁₆ inches from the top and bottom edges and 2½ inches from the ends. Center-punch a starter hole, and drill a ³⁄₁₆-inch pull hole at each spot for standard-size pull screws.

STEP 9
SANDING AND FINISHING THE CHEST

Use a pad sander and 120-, 220-, and

ATTACHING DRAWER FACES

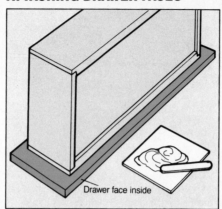

Apply epoxy cement to the front panel of each drawer. Then position the drawer on the inside of the drawer face inside the guide lines.

DRILLING PULL HOLES

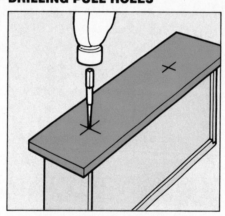

Then center-punch a drill-starter hole, and drill a ³⁄₁₆-inch-diameter hole at each spot.

320-grit sandpaper to sand the chest shell, rounding over corners and edges. Clamp the sander upside down in a Workmate®, and sand and round over drawer faces with same grades.

To duplicate the finish of the chest shown, apply Watco Natural Danish Oil Finish according to the manufacturer's directions. After 72 hours, apply three coats of Deft Clear Wood Finish.

Turn the shell upside down, and attach a one-half-inch, self-adhesive, felt pad inside each corner.

Check the inside dimensions of each drawer. Then use a straightedge and X-Acto knife to cut a piece of self-adhesive felt to fit each. Note: Cut the felt on a scrap of wood to protect workbench surface. Peel the backing from one end of the felt, press the felt in place at one end of the drawer bottom, and slowly remove the backing and position the felt as you do so.

Finally, attach two pulls to each drawer face with the screws provided.

MARKING HOLES IN FACES

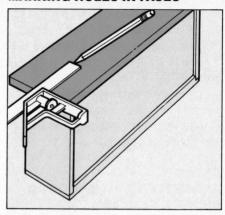

Mark each drawer face for centered pull holes 2½ inches from each end.

INSTALLING FELT

Use a straightedge and X-Acto knife to cut self-adhesive felt to fit drawer bottoms.

ATTACHING PULLS

Attach drawer pulls with screws provided and a stubby screwdriver.

Oak Parquet Tables

Here's an adaptable project that lets you build tables to fit every need, from small accent tables to large dining tables, simply by changing the top size and the leg length.

Table tops can be made any size, as long as the dimensions are divisible by six. Legs can be cut to any size. Standard leg length for dining tables is 27 inches, for cocktail tables 14½ inches, and for end tables 18 inches.

Although tops are made by laminating oak flooring parquets to a plywood underlayment, don't use flooring adhesive; it retains some resiliency even when it is fully cured. Use construction adhesive, which cures harder and is a much better choice.

For small tables, up to 36 × 36 inches, you may substitute ¾-inch plywood for the 1⅛-inch specified.

Exploded View

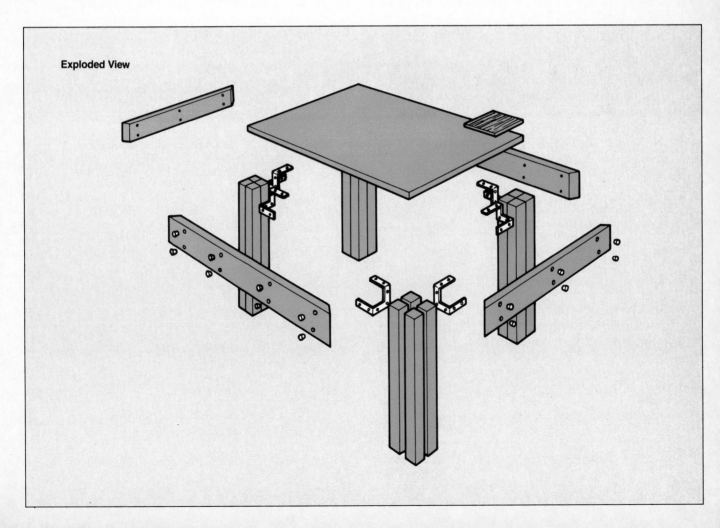

BILL OF MATERIALS

DINING TABLE

Qty	Size	Material
21	12"×12"	Bruce Cumberland III oak parquet squares
1	1⅛"×4'×8'	Shop-grade or better T&G flooring plywood
3	1"×4"×8'	Oak
5	2"×2"×8'	Oak
1	2"×2"×3'	Oak
80	½"	Flathead birch plugs
		White or carpenter's glue
2	Quarts	Panel adhesive
		Wood filler
	120-grit	Sandpaper
	220-grit	Sandpaper
	320-grit	Sandpaper
40	2×10	Flathead wood screws
40	1×8	Flathead Phillips screws
16	¾×8	Flathead Phillips screws
8	2"	Triple corner braces
		Watco Medium Walnut
		Danish Oil Finish
		Deft Clear Wood Finish

END TABLE

Qty	Size	Material
3	12"×12"	Bruce Cumberland III oak parquet squares
1	1⅛"×2'×4' or ¾"×2'×4'	Shop-grade or better plywood
1	1"×4"×8'	Oak
3	2"×2"×8'	Oak
1	2"×2"×2'	Oak
28	½"	Flathead birch plugs
		White or carpenter's glue
1	Pint	Panel adhesive
		Wood filler
	120-grit	Sandpaper
	220-grit	Sandpaper
	320-grit	Sandpaper
14	2×10	Flathead wood screws
40	1×8	Flathead Phillips screws
16	¾×8	Flathead Phillips screws
8	2"	Triple corner braces
		Watco Medium Walnut
		Danish Oil Finish
		Deft Clear Wood Finish

COCKTAIL TABLE

Qty	Size	Material
8	12"×12"	Bruce Cumberland III oak parquet squares
1	1⅛"×2'×4' or ¾"×2'×4'	Shop-grade or better plywood
2	1"×4"×7'	Oak
2	2"×2"×8'	Oak
1	2"×2"×6'	Oak
48	½"	Flathead birch plugs
		White or carpenter's glue
1	Quart	Panel adhesive
		Wood filler
	120-grit	Sandpaper
	220-grit	Sandpaper
	320-grit	Sandpaper
24	2×10	Flathead wood screws
40	1×8	Flathead Phillips screws
16	¾×8	Flathead Phillips screws
8	2"	Triple corner braces
		Watco Medium Walnut
		Danish Oil Finish
		Deft Clear Wood Finish

PARTS LIST

DINING TABLE

Part Name	Qty	Description
Underlayment	1	1⅛"×36"×84" plywood
Side rail	2	¾"×3½"×85½" mitered oak
End rail	2	¾"×3½"×37½" mitered oak
Leg piece	16	1⁵⁄₁₆"×1⁵⁄₁₆"×28" oak

END TABLE

Part Name	Qty	Description
Underlayment	1	¾" or 1⅛"×18"×24" plywood
Side rail	2	¾"×3½"×25½" mitered oak
End rail	2	¾"×3½"×19½" mitered oak
Leg piece	16	1⁵⁄₁₆"×1⁵⁄₁₆"×19" oak

COCKTAIL TABLE

Part Name	Qty	Description
Underlayment	1	¾" or 1⅛"×24"×48" plywood
Side rail	2	¾"×3½"×49½" mitered oak
End rail	2	¾"×3½"×25½" mitered oak
Leg piece	16	1⁵⁄₁₆"×1⁵⁄₁₆"×15½" oak

TOOLS

Steel tape rule
Combination square
Pencil
Claw hammer
Rubber mallet
Center punch
Screwdriver
Phillips screwdriver
Miter box and backsaw

Dovetail saw
Bar clamps or 3" C-clamps (4)
Corner clamps (4)
Putty knife
Utility or X-Acto knife
Pocket knife
Electric drill
³⁄₁₆", ⁷⁄₆₄", and ¹³⁄₆₄" twist-drill bits
½" brad-point bit

Power-driver bits
Circular saw
Saw guide
Belt sander
Pad sander
Workmate® or two sawhorses
J-roller
Notched trowel
Paintbrush

STEP 1
CUTTING THE PLYWOOD UNDERLAYMENT

With a circular saw and saw guide, rip 1½ inches off the grooved edge of the tongue-and-groove plywood to be used as the underlayment. Then trim the sheet to appropriate table dimensions.

For the large dining table, cut underlayment to 36 by 84 inches. Plywood for the cocktail table should be 24 by 48 inches. Each end-table underlayment is 18 by 24 inches.

STEP 2
LAYING PARQUET SQUARES

Use a notched trowel to spread an even coat of panel adhesive on the top of the plywood slab. Then, starting at one corner, lay parquet squares across the slab, and press them firmly into the adhesive. When the underlayment is covered with parquet squares, use a rubber mallet and block of scrap wood to tap each parquet; then roll each parquet with a J-roller to apply pressure for proper seating. Let the tabletop stand for 48 hours.

STEP 3
PREPARING TABLETOP EDGES

Use a dovetail saw to remove protruding tongues from the tongue-and-groove parquet squares. Cut away any excess adhesive that has seeped out from beneath the parquets along the edges with a pocket knife. Then carefully sand the edges smooth with a belt sander and medium belt.

During sanding, use a straight, flat strip of wood laid along the upright edge being sanded to check for any high or low spots, and sand them level accordingly.

STEP 4
ROUGH-SANDING THE TABLETOP

With a belt sander and medium belt, sand the tabletop to an even finish. Switch to a fine belt, and sand each individual parquet with the grain to remove as many cross-grain scratches as possible. Then sand the entire surface with a pad sander and 100-grit sandpaper to remove all remaining scratches.

During sanding, periodically brush

CUTTING PLYWOOD

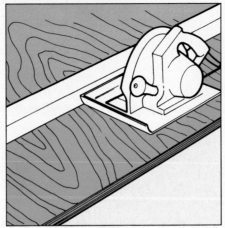

Use a circular saw and saw guide to cut underlayment to appropriate tabletop dimensions.

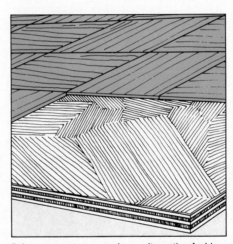

2. Lay parquet squares in an alternating fashion.

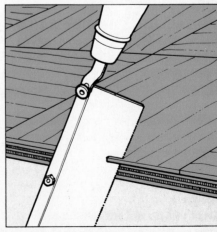

4. Roll parquet squares with a J-roller to firmly seat them in the adhesive.

LAYING PARQUET SQUARES

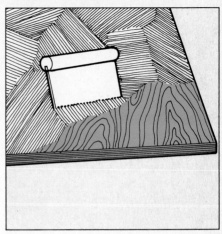

1. Spread an even coat of panel adhesive over the entire surface of the underlayment.

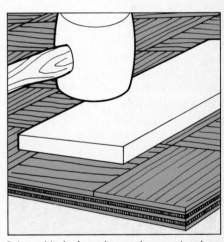

3. Lay a block of wood on each parquet and rap with a rubber mallet.

PREPARING TABLE TOP

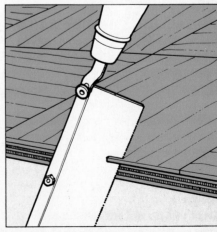

1. Cut overhanging tongues from parquet edges with a dovetail saw.

dust from the tabletop surface and carefully check for cross-grain scratches.

When all scratches have been sanded out, fill any gaps between parquets with wood filler, and let stand until filler hardens.

STEP 5
CUTTING SIDE RAILS

Lay the tabletop on two sawhorses or atop a Workmate®. Stand an oak 1 × 4 on a narrow edge in a miter box, and trim one end at a 45-degree angle. Lay the 1 × 4 broad side up along a long edge of the table top, and mark the uncut end for another miter cut. Trim that end at a 45-degree angle to fit. Then do the same with another oak 1 × 4.

STEP 6
MARKING AND DRILLING THE SIDE RAILS

Scribe lines across each dining-table side rail at 3¾, 9¾, 15¾, 21¾, 33¾, and 39¾ inches from each end; each cocktail-table side rail at 3¾, 9¾, 15¾, and 21¾ inches from each end; and each end-table side rail at 3¾ and 9¾ inches from each end.

Set a combination square for ¾ of an inch, and mark each line for holes ¾ of an inch from the top and bottom edges of the rails.

Center-punch a drill-starter hole at each spot marked. Then use a ½-inch brad-point bit to counterbore a ⅜-inch-deep hole at each spot. Switch to a 13/64-inch twist-drill bit, and drill through the center of the *top holes only*.

STEP 7
INSTALLING THE SIDE RAILS

Stand the tabletop against a Workmate® or bench with a long edge up. Apply an even coat of glue to the upright edge, and attach a side rail with 2 × 10 flathead wood screws.

Turn the table top over and rest it atop two small scraps of wood to protect the side rail just installed. Then attach the other side rail the same way.

STEP 8
CUTTING, MARKING, AND DRILLING END RAILS

Use a miter box and backsaw to cut two

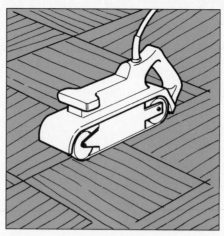

2. Rough-sand surface to an even finish with a belt sander and medium and fine belts.

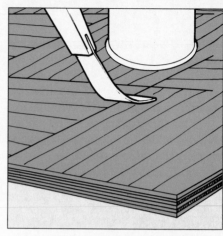

3. Fill gaps between parquets with wood filler.

MARKING RAILS

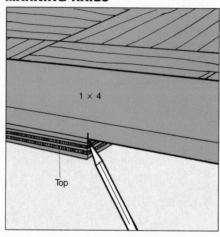

1. Lay miter-cut 1 × 4 along a side edge of the table top and mark for second cut.

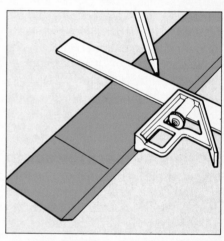

2. Scribe lines across rails 3¾ inches from each end and at six-inch intervals between.

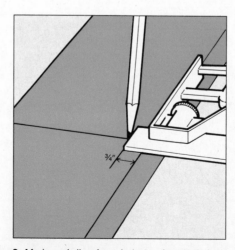

3. Mark each line for a hole ¾ of an inch from each end.

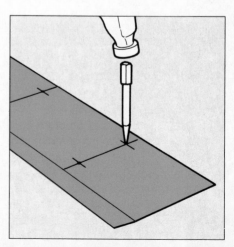

4. Center-punch a drill-starter hole at each spot marked.

pieces of oak 1 × 4 to fit the tabletop ends. Then mark each dining-table end rail for paired holes at 3¾, 9¾, and 15¾ inches from each end; and each cocktail-table or end-table end rail at 3¾ and 9¾ inches from each end.

Center-punch, counterbore, and drill through the end rails as you did the side rails.

STEP 9
INSTALLING THE END RAILS
Lay the tabletop upright atop a Workmate® or pair of sawhorses. Attach the end rails to the side rails with corner clamps.

Loosen the clamp screws holding the end rails, remove the end rails, apply glue to the tabletop ends and the mitred ends of the side rails, clamp the end rails in place, and attach with 2 × 10 flathead wood screws.

STEP 10
PLUGGING, PATCHING, AND SANDING THE TABLETOP
Plug all holes in the side and end rails with glued, tapered, ½-inch wood plugs. Then fill any gaps between the parquets and rails with wood filler, and let stand for two hours.

Cut plug heads off flush with a dovetail saw. Then sand all surfaces with a pad sander and 120-, 220-, and 320-grit sandpaper, rounding over edges and corners as you proceed.

STEP 11
LAMINATING, TRIMMING, AND SANDING LEGS
Sort 2 × 2 leg pieces into four sets of four each, and arrange so grain contrasts in the juxtaposed pieces. Then number one end of each set 1 to 4.

Brush a coat of glue onto one edge of each No. 1 piece and clamp it to a No. 2 piece with three or four bar clamps or C-clamps to form a 2 × 4. Do likewise with pieces 3 and 4, for a total of eight 2 × 4s. Let stand for two hours or overnight; then sand the broad surfaces with a belt sander and medium belt.

Brush a coat of glue onto one broad edge of piece No. 1–2, and clamp it to piece No. 3–4 to form a 4 × 4. Assemble three more 4 × 4s the same way, and let them stand overnight.

Use a miter box and backsaw to trim

INSTALLING SIDE AND END RAILS

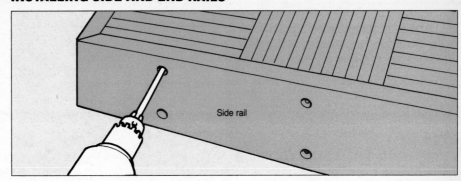

1. Attach side rails to side edges with glue and 2 × 10 flathead screws.

2. Attach end rails to side rails with corner clamps, and secure with glue and 2 × 10 flathead screws.

PLUGGING SCREW HOLES

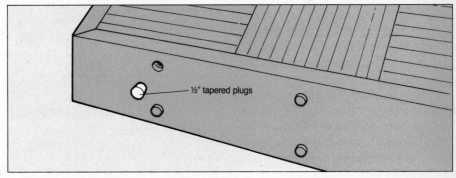

Dip ½-inch tapered plugs in glue, and plug all holes.

LAMINATING TABLE LEGS

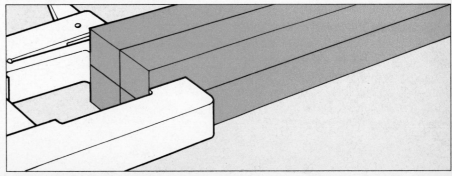

Clamp glued pieces No. 1–2 to pieces No. 3–4 to form four 4 × 4s.

a half-inch from each end of each 4 × 4. Sand the vertical surfaces of each leg with a belt sander and medium and fine belts. Then sand all surfaces with a pad sander and 120-grit sandpaper and vertical surfaces with 220- and 320-grit sandpaper, slightly rounding over vertical and bottom edges as you proceed.

STEP 12
ATTACHING THE LEGS TO THE TABLETOP

Stand each table leg upside down on a work surface, and lay another leg against one of its outside surfaces for support. Position a triple corner brace against an inside surface of the upright leg, and mark for screw holes. Mark the other inside surface the same way.

Center-punch a drill-starter hole and drill a 7/64-inch-diameter, 3/4-inch-deep pilot hole at each spot marked. Then mount two triple corner braces at the top of each leg with six 1 × 8 flathead Phillips screws.

Turn the tabletop upside down, and stand a leg in place at each corner. Mark the bottom of the tabletop and the inside of the side and end rails for screw holes, and drill 3/4-inch-deep pilot holes in the underlayment and 1/2-inch-deep holes in the side and end rails.

At each leg, drive four 1 × 8 flathead Phillips screws into the underlayment and four 3/4 × 8 screws into the side and end rails.

Note: You may prefer to finish the dining-table top and legs before assembly, then assemble the unit in the dining room. This will make moving the heavy, awkward table much easier.

STEP 13
FINISHING THE TABLES

Vacuum the tables and wipe them down with a tack cloth to remove all dust.

To duplicate the finish of the tables shown, apply Watco Medium Walnut Danish Oil Finish to all surfaces, according to the manufacturer's instructions, and let stand for 72 hours. Then apply three coats of Deft Clear Wood Finish to all surfaces of the tables.

ATTACHING BRACES TO LEGS

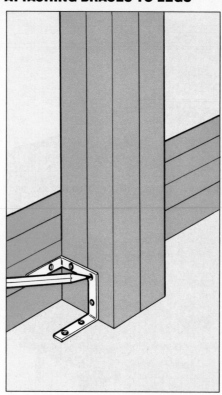
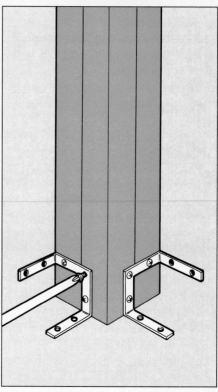

1. Use triple corner braces to mark inside surfaces of legs for screw holes.

2. Mount each triple corner brace with three 1 × 8 flathead Phillips screws.

ATTACHING LEGS TO TOP

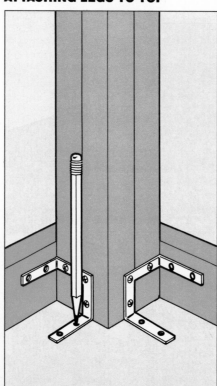
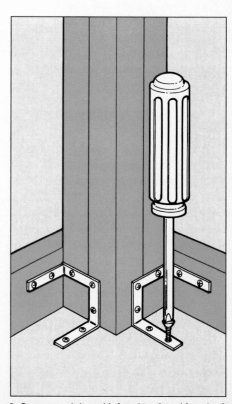

1. Stand a table leg upside down at each corner, and mark for screw holes.

2. Secure each leg with four 3/4 × 8 and four 1 × 8 flathead Phillips screws.

Chess and Checker Table

If chess or checkers is your game, here's your table. In fact, even if you don't play either game, this table is attractive enough to use anywhere an accent table is appropriate. If you wish, build a pair for use as end tables.

The table is made of four popular and beautiful hardwoods that work well together. The playing surface consists of inlaid squares of walnut and maple. The border is cherry. The legs, leg rails, and corner molding used for trimming the top are all oak.

Although the slender legs give this table an appearance of delicacy, it is actually a very sturdy unit. Of course, hardwood construction accounts for much of its strength and durability, but so do the undercarriage design and the use of corner braces.

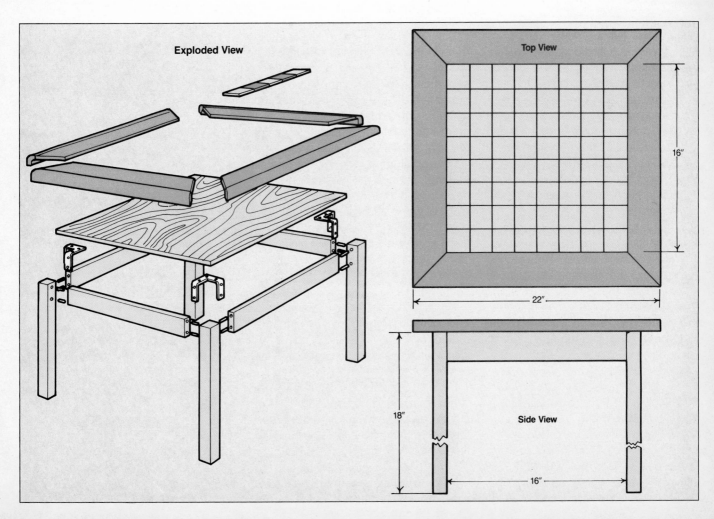

Exploded View

Top View

16"

22"

18"

Side View

16"

PARTS LIST

Part Name	Qty	Description	Part Name	Qty	Description	Part Name	Qty	Description
Leg	4	1 5/16″ × 1 5/16″ × 18″ oak	Face square	32	1/4″ × 2″ × 2″ walnut micro wood	Face border	4	1/4″ × 3″ × 22″ mitered cherry micro wood
Rail	4	3/4″ × 2 1/2″ × 16″ oak	Face square	32	1/4″ × 2″ × 2″ maple micro wood	Top trim	4	1″ × 1″ × 22 1/2″ oak outside corner molding
Underlayment	1	1/2″ × 22″ × 22″ hardwood plywood						

BILL OF MATERIALS

Qty	Size	Material	Qty	Size	Material	Qty	Size	Material
1	1/2″ × 22″ × 22″	Hardwood plywood	16	5/16″	Fluted dowel pins		120-grit	Sandpaper
3	1/4″ × 3″ × 24″	Walnut micro wood			Carpenter's or white glue		220-grit	Sandpaper
3	1/4″ × 3″ × 24″	Maple micro wood	3		Five-minute epoxy cement kits		320-grit	Sandpaper
4	1/4″ × 3″ × 24″	Cherry micro wood			Natural wood filler			Watco Natural Danish Oil Finish
1	1″ × 3″ × 6′	Oak			Red cedar wood filler			Deft Clear Wood Finish
1	2″ × 2″ × 7′	Oak	28	3/4 × 8	Flathead Phillips screws			Tack cloth
1	1″ × 1″ × 8′	Oak outside corner molding	4	2″	Triple corner braces			

TOOLS

Steel tape rule
Combination square
Claw hammer
Center punch
Phillips screwdriver
Miter box and backsaw

Spring clamps (4)
Strap clamps (2)
Putty knife
Dowel jig
Electric drill
7/64″ and 5/16″ twist-drill bits

Circular saw and guide
Bandsaw
Pad sander
Soft-faced mallet
Workmate® (optional)
Paintbrush

STEP 1
CUTTING, MARKING, AND DRILLING RAILS AND LEGS

With a miter box and backsaw, cut four oak 2 × 2 legs to 18 inches and four oak 1 × 3 rails to 16 inches.

Set a combination square for a half-inch, and make marks at each end of each rail perpendicular to the ends and a half-inch inside the top and bottom edges. Then align a dowel jig with the marks and drill two 5/16-inch-diameter holes into each end of each rail about 1 1/4 inches deep.

Measuring from the top of each leg, make marks a half-inch and two inches on two adjacent sides. Then scribe lines across the two sides at those marks. Align the dowel jig with the lines, and drill two 5/16-inch-diameter, 1/2-inch-deep holes on each adjacent side of each leg, making four holes in each leg.

STEP 2
SANDING AND ASSEMBLING RAILS AND LEGS

Erase the layout lines from the rails and legs. Then sand all surfaces of each leg with a pad sander and 120- and 220-grit sandpaper, slightly rounding over bottom and vertical edges as you pro-

ceed. Sand the rails the same way, but round over the bottom edges only.

Dip two dowel pins in glue, insert them in the side holes of one leg, and tap them in with a soft-faced mallet to seat them. Do the same with the opposite leg. Then squirt glue into the holes in one end of a rail, and run a narrow bead of glue along the end. Let the glue penetrate the end grain for a couple of minutes, and apply more as needed. Then push the rail onto the dowel pins of one leg, and tap it with a block of wood and soft-faced mallet to seat it. Make sure the vacant holes in both legs of the assembly are facing the same direction. Then attach another leg at the opposite end of the rail the same way.

If you can't get tight joints at both ends of the rail by tapping the legs with a block of wood and mallet, use a bar clamp and cushions to press the assembly together.

Build another leg assembly the same as the first. Then wrap a strap clamp around each assembly and tighten the clamps with a wrench. Let the assemblies stand for two hours or overnight.

When glue has set, tap glued dowel pins into the remaining holes in the

DRILLING RAILS

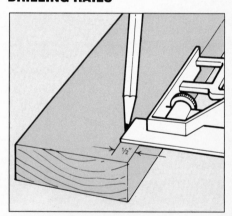

1. Mark both ends of rails a half-inch inside top and bottom edges.

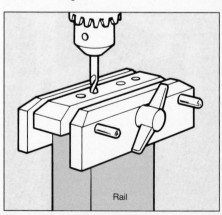

2. Align a dowel jig with the guide lines and drill two 5/16-inch-diameter, 1 1/4-inch-deep holes in each end of each rail.

legs. Then attach two more rails to one set, as above. Squeeze glue into the remaining holes in the rails and apply glue to the rail ends, as before. Then attach the other leg set by tapping it onto the dowel pins with a block of wood and mallet.

Use bar clamps to tighten the joints if necessary. Then wrap a strap clamp around the top of the leg assembly, tighten it, and let the unit stand overnight.

STEP 3
CUTTING SQUARES AND BORDERS

Set the bandsaw fence or clamp a straight piece of wood to the bandsaw table two inches from the *near* teeth of the blade. Rip three 24-inch walnut and three 24-inch maple micro wood strips to that width. Then turn each strip perpendicular to the blade, and cut 11 two-inch squares from each, to make a total of 33 walnut and 33 maple, including one extra square of each wood.

Lightly hand-sand the undersides of the squares to remove small splinters and smooth the edges.

Theoretically, the border pieces should be 22 inches long, but it's best to cut them slightly oversize, because the fit of the squares probably won't be perfect. So measure from one end of each 3-by-24-inch piece of cherry micro wood, and make a mark at 22¹⁄₁₆ inches. Use a miter box and backsaw to cut each piece at a 45-degree angle at the mark and at the opposite end.

STEP 4
CHECKING FOR FIT

Before laminating, make a dry run to determine if everything fits properly. Start by clamping two adjacent border pieces to the 22-by-22-inch plywood underlayment with four spring or C-clamps.

If you face the board, there should be one border strip across the bottom edge and another along the left edge. Start at the lower left corner with a walnut square, and arrange squares alternately across the board. Run another row up the left border strip.

If the last square in each row aligns with the inside corner of the border strip, you can proceed without further

DRILLING LEGS

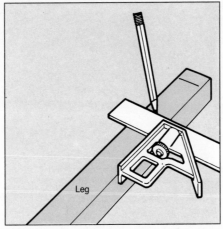

1. Scribe lines across two adjacent sides of each leg a half-inch and two inches from the top.

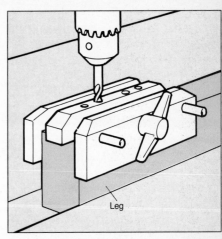

2. Align the dowel jig with each guide line, and drill a ⁵⁄₁₆-inch-diameter, ½-inch-deep hole through the center of each line.

ASSEMBLING RAILS AND LEGS

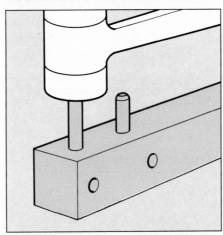

1. Tap glued dowel pins into leg holes with a soft-faced mallet.

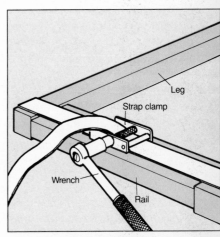

2. Tighten a strap clamp around the top of a leg-rail assembly and let stand for at least two hours.

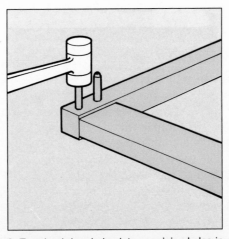

3. Tap glued dowel pins into remaining holes in legs with a soft-faced mallet.

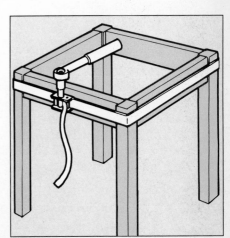

4. Tighten a strap clamp around the assembly and let stand overnight.

alterations. If the row of squares comes up short, trim or sand the border miters to fit. If the squares extend beyond the inside corners of the border strips, you'll have to slightly trim two adjacent sides of each square with the bandsaw. Be sure to use a push stick for this close work.

When you're sure everything fits, clamp the other two border pieces in place. Then start at the lower left corner with a walnut square, and lay squares in an alternating walnut-maple pattern. For the best effect, also alternate the grain patterns, so that all walnut grains run horizontally and all maple grains run vertically, or vice versa.

After you put the last square in place, starting at the lower left corner and proceeding to the right, lightly number the squares in pencil, from 1 to 64. Number the top border piece 1, the right 2, the bottom 3, and the left 4.

Keep borders 3 and 4 clamped to the underlayment, and carefully remove borders 1 and 2. Then stack each row of eight squares, with the lowest numbered square on top of each stack: 1, 9, 17, 25, 33, 41, 49, and 57. Clamp borders 1 and 2 back in place, and you're ready to laminate.

STEP 5
LAMINATING THE TABLETOP

Mix only as much epoxy cement as you can use in about three minutes. As much as you can mix on a 3-by-5-inch file card is about right and will be enough for two rows of squares. Spread a thin half-dollar-size dollop of cement on the underside of each square, and lay each in place. As the cement sets, firmly press each square to seat it.

Apply a thin, even coat of epoxy to the underside of each border strip, and clamp each in place with two spring clamps. As the cement sets, press the surface of each piece firmly onto the underlayment. Note: It's not necessary to cover the entire surface of the squares or the border pieces with cement.

STEP 6
FILLING, SANDING, AND TRIMMING THE TABLETOP

Sand the tabletop edges smooth and

CUTTING SQUARES AND BORDERS

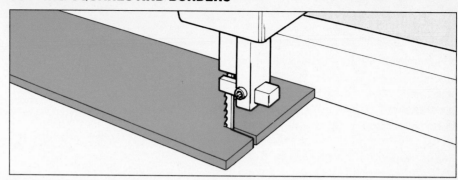

1. Use a bandsaw to rip three 24-inch walnut and three 24-inch maple micro wood strips to a two-inch width.

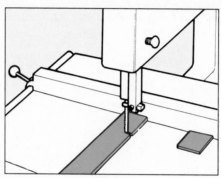

2. Turn each strip perpendicular to the blade, and cut 11 two-inch squares from each.

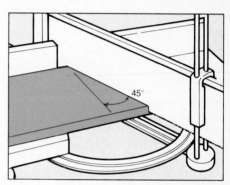

3. Use a miter box and backsaw to cut four 22¹⁄₁₆-inch border strips from ¼-inch cherry micro wood strips.

LAMINATING THE TOP

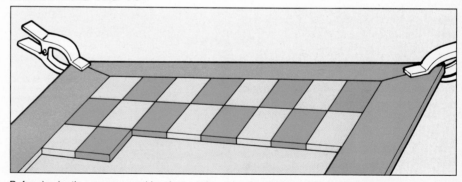

Before laminating squares and borders, make a dry run to check for proper fit. Attach squares and border pieces to the underlayment with five-minute epoxy cement.

even with a belt sander and medium belt.

Fill any gaps between walnut and maple squares with natural wood filler. Fill any gaps in the border miter joints and between the cherry border and squares with red cedar wood filler.

Let the assembly stand until the filler hardens. Then sand the top with a pad sander and 120-, 220-, and 320-grit sandpaper.

Use a miter box and backsaw to cut a

piece of oak corner molding, with a 45-degree angle at each end, to fit one edge of the table top. Temporarily clamp it in place with two spring clamps. Miter-cut one end of another piece of molding. Fit it to an adjacent edge of the tabletop, and mark the opposite end for the second cut, using the table top as a guide. Continue cutting and clamping molding until all four pieces are cut to fit.

Sand the outer surfaces of the molding with a pad sander and 120-, 220-, and 320-grit sandpaper.

Mix a small amount of epoxy cement, and coat the inside of each molding strip. Avoid putting cement on the top front edge of the molding in order to prevent seepage onto the visible portion of the table top.

Press the molding in place, and secure it with a spring clamp at each corner. Let the assembly stand for five minutes, while you continue pressing the molding to the tabletop as the cement cures.

STEP 7
ATTACHING THE LEG ASSEMBLY TO THE TOP

Lay the leg assembly on its side. Position a triple-corner brace inside each corner of the assembly, and mark for screw holes on the inside of the rails.

Center-punch a drill-starter hole and drill a $\frac{7}{64}$-inch-diameter, $\frac{1}{2}$-inch-deep pilot hole at each spot marked. Then mount a corner brace at each corner with four $\frac{3}{4} \times 8$ Phillips screws.

Turn the tabletop upside down and stand the leg assembly upside down on top of it. Use a combination square to *exactly* center the leg assembly on the underside of the table top. It should be about $2\frac{3}{16}$ inches inside each edge. Hold the assembly in place and scribe a light pencil line onto the tabletop underside along each rail.

At each corner brace, mark for three screw holes in the tabletop, while keeping the assembly aligned with the guide lines. Remove the assembly, and center-punch a drill-starter hole at each spot marked. Drill pilot holes, as before, and attach the assembly to the top with 12 $\frac{3}{4} \times 8$ Phillips screws.

STEP 8
FINISHING THE TABLE

Vacuum the table to remove dust, and wipe down all surfaces with a tack cloth.

Apply a coat of Watco Natural Danish Oil Finish according to the manufacturer's directions, and let the table stand for 72 hours. Then apply three coats of Deft Clear Wood Finish to all surfaces.

TRIMMING THE TOP

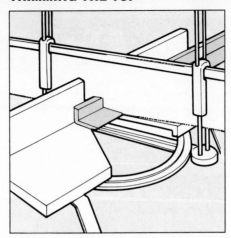

1. Use a miter box and backsaw to cut corner molding at 45-degree angles to fit tabletop edges.

2. Attach molding to table top with five-minute epoxy cement and a spring clamp at each corner.

ATTACHING LEG TO TOP

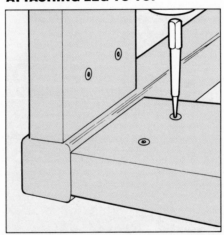

1. Center-punch drill-starter holes for corner braces inside each corner of the leg assembly.

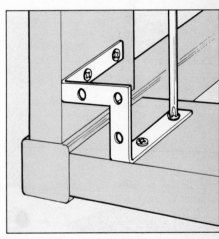

2. Attach each triple corner brace to the rails with four $\frac{3}{4} \times 8$ Phillips screws.

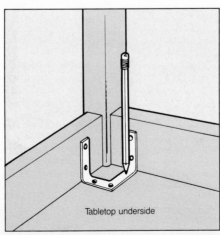

Tabletop underside

3. With the leg assembly centered upside down on the tabletop underside, mark for screw holes, using braces as guides.

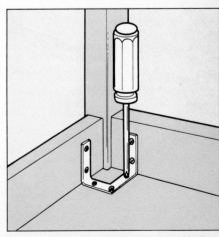

4. Attach leg assembly to table top with three $\frac{3}{4} \times 8$ Phillips screws at each corner brace.

Liquor Cabinet

This liquor cabinet was designed and finished to coordinate with the oak parquet tables and to double as a dry bar that rolls on heavy-duty, ball-type casters to wherever you happen to need it.

The cabinet's compact appearance is deceptive: its doors of laminated oak 1 × 2s enclose plenty of storage space. The cabinet floor will hold an ample supply of liquor, mixers, and cordials. The shelf is large enough to store dozens of glasses, as well as bar accessories and supplies.

The top is made of oak parquet flooring laminated to a plywood underlayment and trimmed with oak 1 × 4. It is finished for both beauty and durability and will resist the effects of water and alcohol.

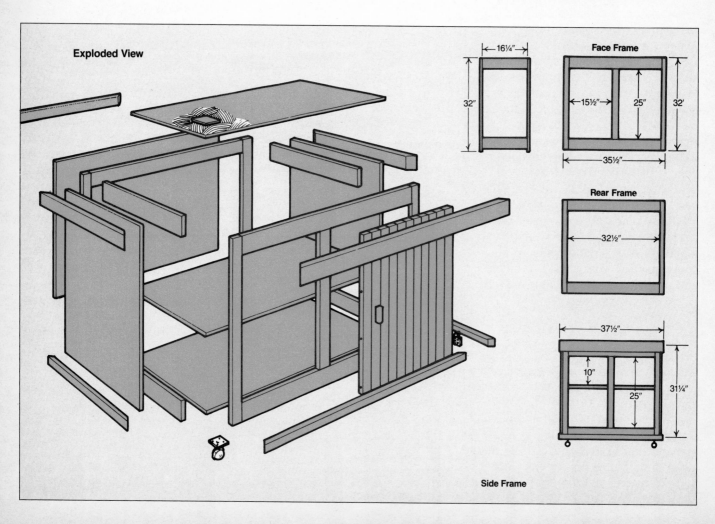

Exploded View

16¼″
32″

Face Frame
15½″   25″
32′
35½″

Rear Frame
32½″

37½″
10″
25″
31¼″

Side Frame

BILL OF MATERIALS

Qty	Size	Material	Qty	Size	Material	Qty	Size	Material
1	¼″ × 4′ × 8′	G1S oak plywood	5	12″ × 12″	Bruce Cumberland III oak parquet squares	2		Belwith P676UW door pulls
1	¾″ × 4′ × 4′	G1S oak plywood			Carpenter's or white glue	4		Metal shelf-bracket pins
1	1⅛″ × 2′ × 4′	Shop-grade T&G flooring plywood			Wood filler	4	2″	Plate-type ball casters
10	1″ × 2″ × 8′	Oak	1	Quart	Panel adhesive		120-grit	Sandpaper
1	1″ × 2″ × 6′	Kiln-dried pine		¾″	Brads		220-grit	Sandpaper
2	1″ × 4″ × 8′	Oak		1½″	Brads		320-grit	Sandpaper
1	1″ × 4″ × 12′	Kiln-dried pine	32	¾ × 8	Flathead Phillips screws			Watco Medium Walnut
1	36″	¾″-square molding	14	1¼ × 8	Flathead wood screws			Danish Oil Finish
2	1″ × 1″ × 5′	Oak outside corner molding	8	1½ × 8	Flathead wood screws			Deft Clear Wood Finish
16	⅜″	Flathead birch plugs	22	2 × 10	Flathead wood screws			Self-adhesive felt cushions
42	½″	Flathead birch plugs	4	2″	Corner braces			Tack cloth
18	5⁄16″	Fluted dowel pins	4		Self-closing cabinet hinges			

PARTS LIST

Part Name	Qty	Description	Part Name	Qty	Description	Part Name	Qty	Description
Top underlayment	1	1⅛″ × 18″ × 36″ plywood	Top trim	2	¾″ × 3½″ × 19½″ mitered oak	Bottom trim	2	¾″ × 1½″ × 37½″ mitered oak
Shelf and bottom	2	¾″ × 16¼″ × 36″ oak plywood	Front-frame horizontal	2	¾″ × 3½″ × 32½″ oak	Door strips	28	¾″ × 1½″ × 28″ oak
Side panel	2	¼″ × 18″ × 32″ oak plywood	Front-frame vertical	1	¾″ × 3½″ × 25″ oak	Rear-frame horizontal	2	¾″ × 3½″ × 32½″ kiln-dried pine
Rear panel	1	¼″ × 32″ × 35½″ oak plywood	Front-frame vertical	2	¾″ × 3½″ × 32″ oak	Side-frame horizontal	4	¾″ × 3½″ × 16¼″ kiln-dried pine
Top trim	2	¾″ × 3½″ × 37½″ mitered oak	Bottom trim	2	¾″ × 1½″ × 19½″ mitered oak	Rear-frame vertical	2	¾″ × 1½″ × 32″ kiln-dried pine

TOOLS

Steel tape rule
Combination square
Pencil
Claw hammer
Soft-faced mallet
Rubber mallet
Nail set
Center punch
Screwdriver
Phillips screwdriver
Miter box and backsaw
Dovetail saw

Spring clamps (2)
24″ bar clamps (2)
48″ bar or pipe clamps (2)
Strap clamps (3)
Corner clamps (4)
Rod clamps (4–8)
7⁄16″ or adjustable wrench
½″ or adjustable wrenches (2)
Putty knife
Utility or X-Acto knife
Pocket knife
Drill press or drill-press stand

Electric drill
1⁄16″, 5⁄64″, 3⁄16″, 7⁄64″, ¼″, 5⁄16″, and 11⁄64″ twist-drill bits
⅜″ and ½″ brad-point bits
1⁄16″ and 5⁄16″ drill collars or stops
Circular saw
Saw guide
Table saw
Belt and pad sanders
Workmate
J-roller
Paintbrush

STEP 1
LAMINATING PARQUET TOP

Use a utility or X-Acto knife to cut down the center of the backing on two parquet squares, and separating them into four 6-by-12 inch pieces.

Spread an even coat of panel adhesive onto the plywood underlayment with a notched trowel. Set three 12″ × 12″ parquet squares onto the underlayment along one long edge. Then set three 6″ × 12″ pieces along the opposite long edges, with parquets

LAMINATING PARQUET TOP

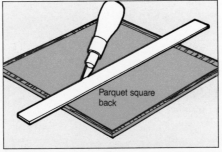

1. Use a knife to halve two parquet squares.

2. Spread panel adhesive onto the plywood underlayment, set the parquets on the adhesive one at a time, and press each firmly.

running in an alternating pattern. Tap parquets with a mallet and block of scrap wood; then use a J-roller to firmly set them in the adhesive.

Let the top stand for 48 hours. Then use a sharp knife to trim away any adhesive that has seeped out from beneath the parquet squares. Cut the protruding parquet tongues off with a dovetail saw. Then rough-sand the top and edges with a belt sander and medium and fine belts.

STEP 2
CUTTING, DRILLING, AND ATTACHING TOP TRIM

Use a miter box and backsaw to cut two pieces of oak 1 × 4 to fit the long edges of the top with 45-degree miters at the ends. Scribe lines across each at 1½ and 13 inches from each end. Mark each line ¾ of an inch from the top and bottom edges. Center-punch a drill-starter hole and counterbore a ½-inch-diameter, ⅜-inch-deep hole at each spot; then drill through the *top holes only* with a ³⁄₁₆-inch bit.

Brush an even coat of glue down one long edge of the top, and attach a piece of trim with four 2 × 10 flathead wood screws. Attach the opposite piece the same way.

Cut two pieces of oak 1 × 4 to fit the ends, and scribe lines across each in the center and 1½ inches from each end. Mark, center-punch, counterbore, and drill as above, and attach with glue and screws.

Plug all holes with ½-inch tapered wood plugs, and let stand overnight. Then cut the plug heads off flush with a dovetail saw.

STEP 3
FILLING AND FINISH-SANDING THE TOP

Sand all exterior surfaces of the top with a pad sander and 120-grit sandpaper to remove all belt-sander scratches. Then fill any gaps between parquet strips and other flaws with wood filler, and let stand for two hours or overnight.

Finish-sand with a pad sander and 120-, 220-, and 320-grit sandpaper, rounding over corners and edges as you sand.

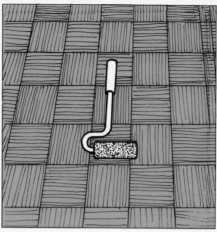

3. Use a J-roller to firmly set parquets in adhesive.

4. Trim adhesive seepage at the edges with a sharp knife.

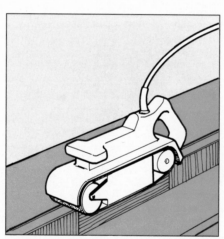

5. Rough-sand top and edges to a smooth finish with a belt sander.

ATTACHING TOP TRIM

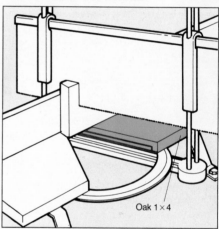

Oak 1 × 4

1. Use a miter box and backsaw to cut oak 1 × 4 to fit the long edges of top.

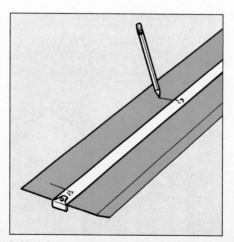

2. Mark for screw holes 1½ and 13 inches from each end.

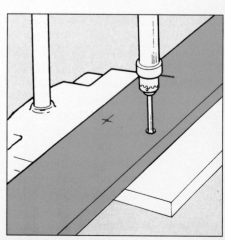

3. Counterbore ½-inch-diameter, ⅜-inch-deep holes.

STEP 4
MARKING AND DRILLING FRAME HORIZONTALS

Lay 1 × 4 oak face-frame horizontals face up and use a combination square to mark each end of each piece ¾ of an inch from the top and bottom edges. Mark the pine rear-frame horizontals the same way. Then make a mark at the bottom center of the top face-frame horizontal.

Align a dowel jig with each mark, and drill a ⁵⁄₁₆-inch-diameter, ⅞-inch-deep hole at each spot.

STEP 5
MARKING AND DRILLING FRAME VERTICALS

With the 25-inch face-frame center vertical face up, use a combination square set for ¾ of an inch to mark the center at each end. Then mark the faces of the 32-inch verticals near the inside edges at ¾ and 2¾ inches from the tops and bottoms to correspond with the end holes in the horizontals.

Align the dowel jig with each mark on the verticals, and drill a ⁵⁄₁₆-inch-diameter, ⅞-inch-deep hole at each spot.

STEP 6
ASSEMBLING FACE AND REAR FRAMES

Dip one end of two fluted dowel pins in glue, and tap them into the center holes of the face-frame horizontals with a soft-faced mallet. Apply glue to the other ends of the dowel pins, insert them into the holes in the ends of the center face-frame vertical, and tap the assembly together with the mallet and a block of scrap wood. Clamp the frame, and let stand for 30 minutes.

Glue and tap dowel pins into the holes in the 32-inch oak verticals. Apply glue to the ends of the face-frame horizontals and the dowel holes, and tap the verticals into place with the mallet and block of wood. Attach bar or pipe clamps top and bottom, and let stand for 30 minutes. Assemble the pine rear frame the same way.

STEP 7
DRILLING FACE AND REAR FRAMES

Measure down the inside of the face frame 13½ inches from the top, and

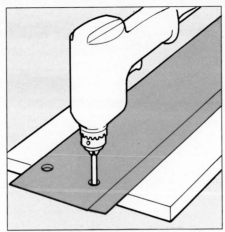

4. Drill through *top holes only* with a ³⁄₁₆-inch bit.

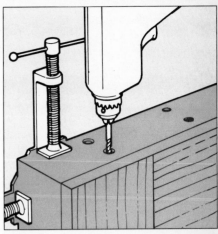

5. Attach 1 × 4 trim to the edges of the top with glue and 2 × 10 screws.

DRILLING HORIZONTALS

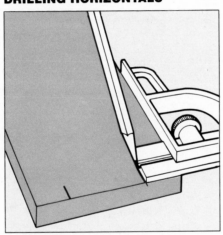

1. Mark each end of the face-frame horizontals ¾ of an inch from the top and bottom.

2. Mark the bottom center of the top horizontal and top center of the bottom horizontal.

DRILLING VERTICALS

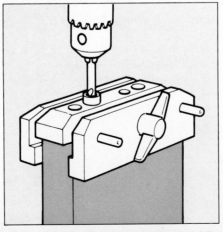

Align a dowel jig with the end marks, and drill a ⁵⁄₁₆-inch-diameter, ⅞-inch-deep hole.

ASSEMBLING FACE AND REAR

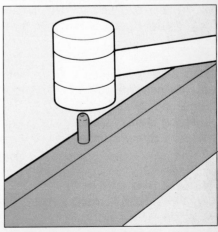

1. Tap glued dowel pins into center holes in face frame horizontals.

mark each 32-inch vertical for a centered hole. Do the same on the rear frame. Then drill a ¼-inch-diameter, ⅜-inch-deep shelf-support hole at each spot.

Set a combination square at ⅜ of an inch. Then measure along the bottom outside of the bottom horizontal on each frame, and mark for holes ⅜ of an inch from the bottom edge and 4, 10, and 17¾ inches from each end.

Counterbore a ⅜-inch-diameter, ⅜-inch-deep hole at each spot. Then drill through each hole with a ³⁄₁₆-inch bit.

Set the combination square for ¼ of an inch, and mark the face frame for holes ¼ of an inch inside the left and right edges, ¾ and 2¾ inches from the top and 1½ and 3½ inches from the bottom. Then drill a hole at each spot with a ¹⁄₁₆-inch bit.

STEP 8
ATTACHING FACE AND REAR FRAMES

Run a bead of glue down one end of a side-frame horizontal, butt it to the top left inside surface of the rear frame, secure it with a corner clamp, attach it with three 1½-inch brads, and countersink the brads. Attach another side-frame horizontal, the same way, to the right side of the frame.

Clamp a strip of ¾-inch square molding to the inside bottom edge of the rear frame with two spring clamps. Then attach two more side-frame horizontals with glue and brads, ¾ of an inch from the frame bottom, butted against the molding strip.

Remove the molding strip from the rear frame, and clamp it along the bottom inside of the face frame. Apply glue to the ends of the side frame horizontals, and secure the top horizontals to the face frame with corner clamps. Then drive a 1½-inch brad through each ¹⁄₁₆-inch-diameter hole in the face frame, and countersink the brads.

Let the frame assembly stand one hour with corner clamps in place.

STEP 9
INSTALLING CABINET BOTTOM, REAR, AND SIDE PANELS

Use a combination square and steel tape rule to mark each end of the bot-

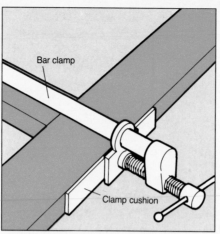

2. Glue and clamp horizontals to center vertical.

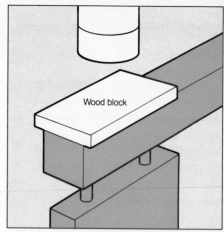

3. Use a mallet and block of wood to tap verticals into the holes of the horizontals.

DRILLING FACE AND REAR

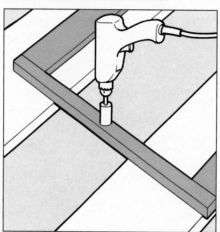

1. Drill a ¼-inch-diameter, ⅜-inch-deep hole on the inside of each 32-inch vertical, 13½ inches from the top.

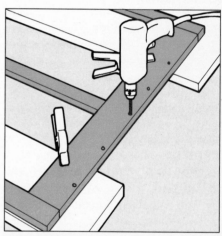

2. Counterbore a ⅜-inch-diameter, ⅜-inch-deep hole at each spot; then drill through with a ³⁄₁₆-inch bit.

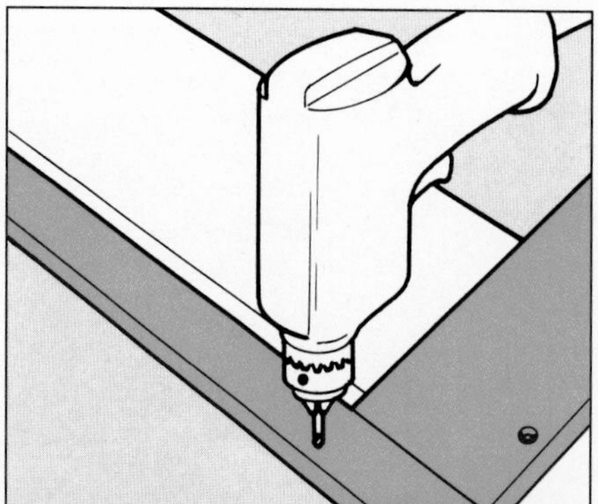

ATTACHING FACE AND REAR

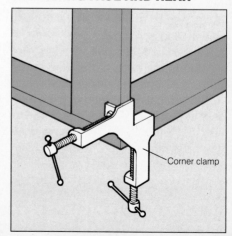

3. With a ¹⁄₁₆-inch bit, drill face frame ¾ and 2¾ inches from the top and bottom.

1. Secure glued side-frame horizontal to rear frame with a corner clamp.

tom panel ⅜ of an inch from the edge and one and six inches from each end. Then counterbore a ⅜-inch-diameter, ⅜-inch-deep hole at each spot, and drill through with an ¹¹⁄₆₄-inch bit.

Turn the frame assembly upside down, and run a bead of glue along the bottom edge of each bottom side-frame horizontal. Lay the cabinet bottom on the horizontals, and drive eight 1½ × 8 screws through each hole in the lower face-frame and rear-frame horizontals.

Lay the cabinet face down, and run a wavy bead of glue along the rear-frame horizontals and verticals. Lay the rear panel in place, and secure it with ¾-inch brads, spaced about 10 inches apart and ⅜ of an inch inside the panel edges. Countersink the brads.

Attach side panels the same way. Sand the face frame with a pad sander and 120-grit sandpaper. Then sand the face-frame, rear panel, and side panels with 220- and 320-grit sandpaper.

STEP 10
ATTACHING AND SANDING BOTTOM TRIM

With a miter box and backsaw, cut two pieces of oak 1 × 2, with 45-degree miters at the ends, to fit front and rear bottom edges of the cabinet (about 36 inches inside dimension).

Scribe lines across each strip at 1½ and 13 inches from each end. Mark the center of each line; center-punch a drill-starter hole; counterbore a ½-inch-diameter, ⅜-inch-deep hole; and drill through with an ¹¹⁄₆₄-inch bit at each spot.

Run a bead of glue across the bottom face-frame horizontal, about a ¼ of an inch from the bottom. Clamp the trim piece in place with a pair of bar clamps, and drill a pilot hole through each hole in the trim with a ⁷⁄₆₄-inch bit. Then secure the trim with four 1¼ × 8 screws. Mount the rear trim the same way.

Cut two pieces of oak 1 × 2 trim to fit the cabinet ends. Scribe lines across them in the center and 1½ inches from each end, and mark the centers for drill-starter holes. Then center-punch, counterbore, drill, and mount the trim as explained above.

Erase layout lines, and plug all holes in the trim with glued ½-inch plugs.

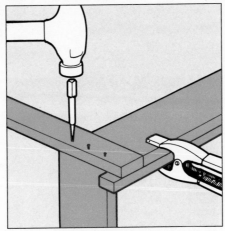

2. Clamp ¾-inch-square molding strip to the inside bottom edge of the frame before attaching side-frame horizontals.

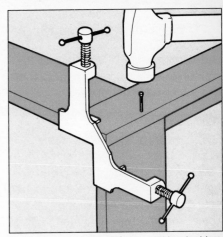

3. Attach face frame with glue and brads driven through ¹⁄₁₆-inch pilot holes.

INSTALLING PANELS

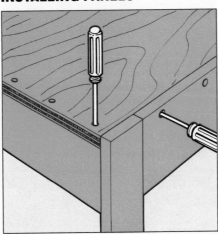

1. Attach bottom to side-frame horizontals with eight 1½ × 8 screws. Then drive a 2 × 10 screw through each hole in the lower face- and rear-frame horizontals.

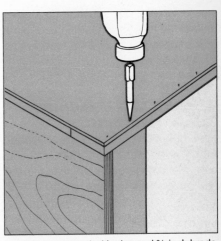

2. Attach rear panel with glue and ¾-inch brads, and countersink brads.

ATTACHING BOTTOM TRIM

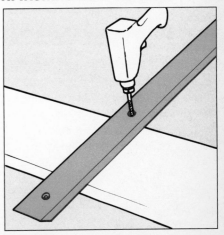

3. Apply glue to the side frame before attaching side panel with brads.

1. Counterbore and drill front and rear 1 × 2 trim at 1½ and 13 inches from each end.

When the glue has set, cut off the plug heads with a dovetail saw, and sand the plugs flush with a belt sander and medium belt. Then sand the trim with a pad sander and 120-, 220-, and 320-grit sandpaper, rounding over corners and edges as you proceed.

STEP 11
INSTALLING THE CABINET TOP

Measure along the top side-panel horizontals, and make marks four inches from the front and rear of the cabinet. Then mount two two-inch corner braces on the inside of each horizontal with two $3/4 \times 8$ flathead Phillips screws each, four inches from the front and rear of the cabinet.

Lay the cabinet top upside down on a protected surface. Turn the cabinet upside down and position it on the underside of the top. Then fasten the cabinet to the top with eight $3/4 \times 8$ screws and corner braces.

STEP 12
CUTTING AND ATTACHING CORNER MOLDING

Measure each cabinet corner between the 1×4 top and 1×2 bottom trim, and cut a piece of corner molding to fit each corner. Hand-sand the molding with 120-, 220-, and 320-grit sandpaper.

Run a thin bead of glue down each inside surface of each piece of molding, and press the molding in place at the cabinet corners. Then secure all four strips with three strap clamps wrapped at the top, bottom, and middle of the cabinet. Let stand for an hour.

STEP 13
DRILLING AND GLUING DOOR STRIPS

Sort the 28-inch door strips into two sets of 11, and number the ends sequentially. Rotate the strips to stand on their narrow edges, and use a combination square to scribe lines across them at 2 and 10 inches from each end. Then use a drill press or drill-press stand and electric drill equipped with a $3/8$-inch brad-point bit to drill a centered hole through each strip at each spot marked.

Slide strip No. 1 onto four threaded-rod clamps. Brush an even coat of glue

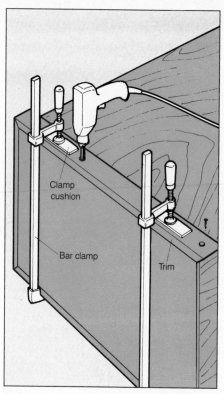

2. Clamp trim in place with bar clamps, and secure with $1\frac{1}{4} \times 8$ screws.

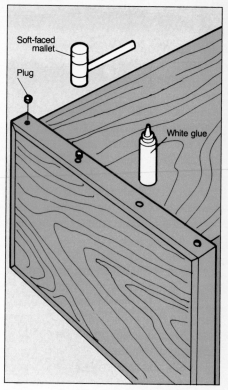

3. Use a soft-faced mallet to tap a glued $\frac{1}{2}$-inch plug into each hole.

INSTALLING TOP

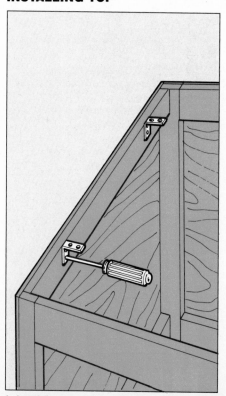

1. Attach four two-inch corner braces four inches inside front and rear corners.

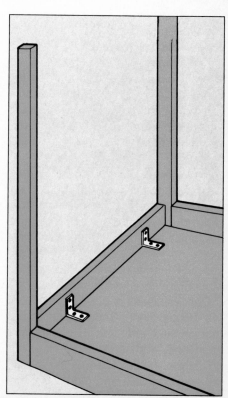

2. With cabinet top upside down, position inverted cabinet on it, and attach frame to the underside of the top with eight $3/4 \times 8$ Phillips screws.

onto a narrow edge of strip No. 2, and slide it onto the clamps down to the first strip. Continue gluing this way until all 11 strips are on the clamps. Put a clamp cushion, flat washer, and hex nut on the end of each clamp rod, and tighten the nuts with wrenches; wipe away excess glue with a damp sponge. Assemble the other door in the same way. Then let the doors stand overnight.

STEP 14
SANDING, TRIMMING, AND DRILLING THE DOORS

Rough-sand the front and rear surfaces of each door to a smooth, even finish with a belt sander and medium and fine belts.

Set the table-saw fence one inch from the *far* teeth of the blade, and trim an inch from the top and bottom edge of each door. Reset the fence 16¼ inches from the *near* teeth of the blade, and rip one side of each door. Reset the fence at 16 inches from the *near* teeth, and rip the opposite side, for finished dimensions of 16 by 26 inches. Then plug the holes with glued ⅜-inch plugs, and let stand until the glue sets.

Set a combination square for two inches. Then use a steel tape rule and square to mark each door for pull-screw holes at 8½ and 12¼ inches from the top, two inches from the inside edge. Center-punch a drill-starter hole, and drill a ³⁄₁₆-inch-diameter hole at each spot.

Cut off plug heads with a dovetail saw. Then round over top and bottom door-face edges with a belt sander and medium and fine belts. Then sand all surfaces with a pad sander and 120-, 220-, and 320-grit sandpaper, rounding over top and bottom edges and slightly rounding over side edges as you proceed.

STEP 15
FINISHING CABINET COMPONENTS

Finish-sand the cabinet shelf, and vacuum all components to remove dust. Wipe everything down with a tack cloth, and all components are ready for the finish of your choice.

To duplicate the finish of the cabinet shown, apply Watco Medium Walnut Danish Oil Finish to all surfaces, ac-

ATTACHING CORNER MOLDING

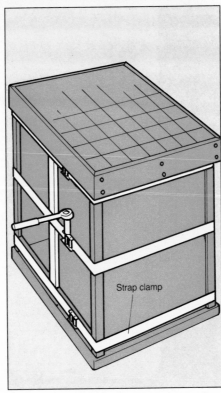

Attach corner molding with glue between top and bottom trim, and secure with three strap clamps.

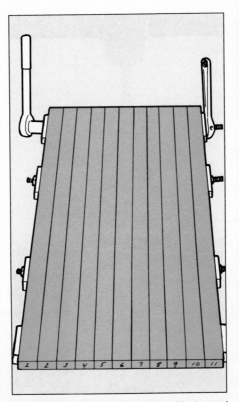

2. Laminate each set of door strips with glue and four rod clamps.

GLUING DOOR STRIPS

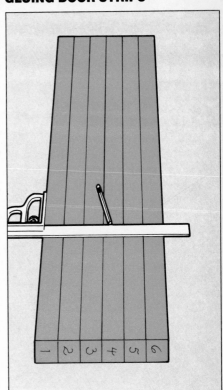

1. Use a combination square to scribe lines across narrow edges of 1 × 2s at 2 and 10 inches from each end.

DRILLING DOORS

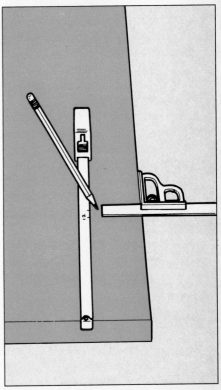

1. Use a combination square and steel tape rule to mark each door for pull holes 8½ and 12¼ inches from the top and two inches inside the edge.

cording to the manufacturer's directions, and let stand for 72 hours. Then apply three coats of Deft Clear Wood Finish to all surfaces, and two more coats to the top.

STEP 16
INSTALLING HARDWARE, SHELF, AND DOORS

Turn the cabinet upside down on a protected surface, and put the casters in position to mark for mounting holes. Place front caster plates 1¾ inches inside the front and side bottom trim pieces. Place rear caster plates in corresponding positions. Center-punch drill-starter holes, and drill ½-inch-deep pilot holes with a ⁷⁄₆₄-inch bit at the spots marked, and mount each caster with four ¾ × 8 flathead Phillips screws.

Set a combination square for three inches and use it to position the hinges three inches from the top and bottom on the inside surface of each door. Use the hinges to mark for screw holes. Then center-punch a drill-starter hole and drill a ⁵⁄₆₄-inch-diameter, ½-inch-deep hole at each spot. Mount hinges and pulls with the screws provided.

Lay the cabinet face up, and lay the doors in place. Adjust doors so the hinges are against the corner molding and tops are one inch from the 1 × 4 top trim. Mark the face frame for hinge holes; then center-punch and drill ⁵⁄₆₄-inch-diameter pilot holes.

Move the cabinet to the room where it will be kept, and lay it on its back. Attach the doors with the screws provided, and stand the cabinet upright.

Press self-adhesive felt cushions in place on the face-frame horizontals near the inside corners of the door openings.

Install four metal shelf-bracket pins in the holes in the inside frame verticals, and lay the shelf atop them.

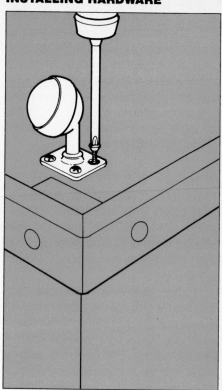

1. Install a caster 1¾ inches inside each bottom corner with four ¾ × 8 flathead Phillips screws.

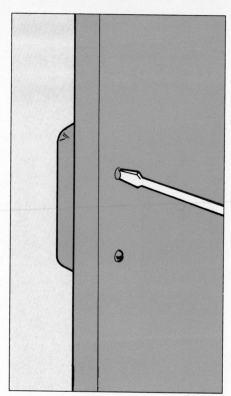

2. Attach pulls to doors with screws provided in the holes drilled earlier.

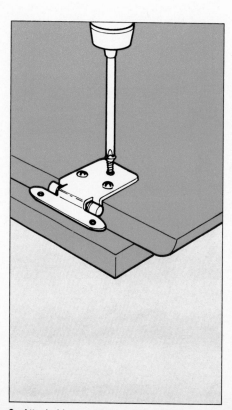

2. Attach hinges with screws provided, three inches from tops and bottoms of doors.

3. Position doors one inch from top trim, and mark for hinge holes in face frames.

Oak Pedestal Desk

Whether you need a desk for home or business, here's one that will fit anywhere. It's a finely finished piece of oak furniture as well as a spacious and efficient work station.

This is an executive-size desk; its broad top has more than 15 square feet of work surface. The top is made of oak 1 × 2s laminated to an oak plywood underlayment.

The pedestals are made of solid oak and oak plywood. There are four drawers, two of which are file size, and all glide effortlessly on heavy-duty, suspension-type, roller-bearing slides.

Drawer faces are made of laminated oak 1 × 2s and are fitted with handsome oak pulls.

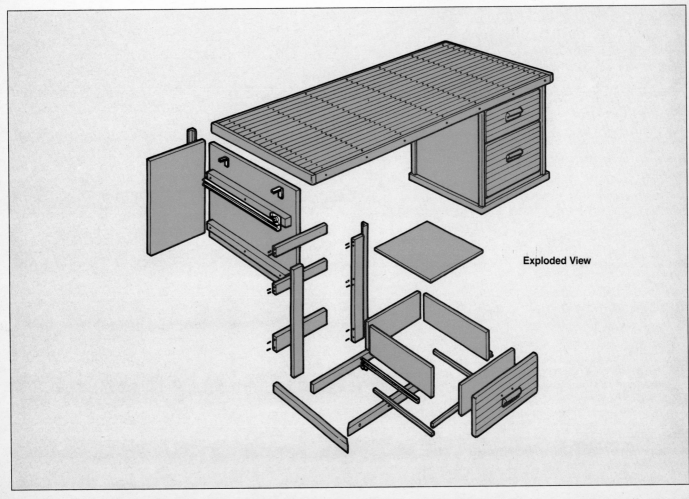

Exploded View

BILL OF MATERIALS

Qty	Size	Material	Qty	Size	Material	Qty	Size	Material
1	½″ × 4′ × 8′	Mahogany plywood			Wood filler	4		Belwith P676-UW drawer pulls
2	¾″ × 4′ × 8′	Oak plywood, G1S		¾″	Brads			
1	¼″ × 4′ × 4′	Tempered hardboard		1″	Brads	4	20″	Knape & Vogt #1300 drawer-slide sets
27	1″ × 2″ × 8′	Oak		1¼″	Brads			
1	1″ × 3″ × 6′	Oak	16	¾ × 8	Flathead Phillips or square-recessed screws		120-grit	Sandpaper
1	1″ × 4″ × 3′	Oak					220-grit	Sandpaper
2	2″ × 2″ × 8′	Kiln-dried pine or fir					320-grit	Sandpaper
3	½″ × ¾″ × 8′	Parting bead	200	1 × 8	Flathead Phillips or square-recessed screws		#0000	Steel wool
1	½″ × ¾″ × 3′	Parting bead						Watco Medium Walnut Danish Oil Finish
2	1″ × 1″ × 9′	Oak outside corner molding	40	1¼ × 8	Flathead Phillips or square-recessed screws			Deft Clear Wood Finish
203	⅜″	Tapered birch plugs						Self-adhesive felt cushions
20	5⁄16″	Fluted dowel pins	8	2½″	Corner braces			Tack cloth
		Carpenter's or white glue						
		Five-minute epoxy cement						

PARTS LIST

Part Name	Qty	Description	Part Name	Qty	Description	Part Name	Qty	Description
Top strip	19	¾″ × 1½″ × 72″ oak	Pedestal-base molding	4	¾″ × 1½″ × 21″ mitered oak	Drawer-bottom cleat	8	½″ × ¾″ × 18½″ parting bead
Edge trim	2	¾″ × 1½″ × 70″ oak	Pedestal-base molding	4	¾″ × 1½″ × 24½″ mitered oak	Cleat/front strip	12	½″ × ¾″ × 13″ parting bead
Edge trim	2	¾″ × 1½″ × 30″ oak	Pedestal corner mold	8	1″ × 1″ × 25½″ oak outside corner molding	Drawer side	4	½″ × 11½″ × 20″ mahogany plywood
Drawer-face strip	30	¾″ × 1½″ × 17″ oak	Underlayment	1	¾″ × 31″ × 72″ oak plywood	Drawer rear	2	½″ × 11½″ × 13″ mahogany plywood
Face-frame vertical	4	¾″ × 1½″ × 27″ oak	Pedestal side	4	¾″ × 23″ × 27″ oak plywood	Drawer side	4	½″ × 7″ × 20″ mahogany plywood
Face-frame horizontal	2	¾″ × 1½″ × 15″ oak	Pedestal rear	2	¾″ × 18″ × 27″ oak plywood	Drawer rear	2	½″ × 7″ × 13″ mahogany plywood
Face-frame horizontal	2	¾″ × 2½″ × 15″ oak	Drawer-channel strip	8	1½″ × 1½″ × 20¾″ fir or pine	Drawer bottom	4	¼″ × 12 5⁄16″ × 19 7⁄16″ hardboard
Face-frame horizontal	2	¾″ × 3½″ × 15″ oak						
Pedestal-front base insert	2	¾″ × 2½″ × 18″ oak						

TOOLS

Steel tape rule	Strap clamps (2)	Electric drill
Yardstick	Edge clamps (2)	11⁄64″, 13⁄64″, and 5⁄16″ twist-drill bits
Combination square	Spring clamps (2)	⅜″ brad-point bit
Felt-tipped pen	24″ bar clamps (3)	#8 countersink bit
Claw hammer	36″ bar or pipe clamps (2)	Power-drive bit
Soft-faced mallet	Corner clamps (4)	Circular saw and guide
Scratch awl	Threaded-rod clamps (3–12)	Table saw
Nail set	7⁄16″ wrench	Belt and pad sanders
Center punch	½″ or adjustable wrenches (2)	Workmate® or two sawhorses
Phillips screwdriver	Dowel jig	Paintbrush
Miter box and backsaw	Drill press or drill-press stand	Putty knife

CUTTING SCHEDULE

1. Cut 19 eight-foot oak 1 × 2s to 72 inches. Then trim the leftovers to 17 inches.

2. From two eight-foot oak 1 × 2s, cut two 70-inch pieces and two 17-inch pieces.

3. From two more eight-footers, cut nine 17-inch pieces and one 27-inch piece.

4. Then cut two 27-inch and two 15-inch pieces from one eight-footer and one 27-inch piece from another eight-footer. Put 69-inch leftovers aside for later use.

5. Cut two pieces of oak 1 × 3 to 15 inches and two to 18 inches. Then cut two pieces of oak 1 × 4 to 15 inches.

6. From two eight-foot clear fir or kiln-dried pine 2 × 2s, cut eight pieces to 20¾ inches.

7. From three eight-foot parting-bead strips, cut eight pieces to 18½ inches and 10 to 13 inches. Cut two more 13-inch pieces from the three-footer.

8. From a sheet of ¾-inch oak plywood, cross-cut three 27-by-48-inch pieces. From those, rip four 23-inch pieces and two 18-inch pieces. Trim the other sheet of oak plywood to a 72-inch length.

9. Crosscut two 20-by-48-inch pieces and one 13-by-48-inch piece of ½-inch mahogany plywood. From each of those, rip two 11½-inch and two seven-inch pieces.

10. Cut two pieces of ¼-inch hardboard to 12 15⁄16 by 48 inches. Then from those cut four pieces to 19 7⁄16 inches.

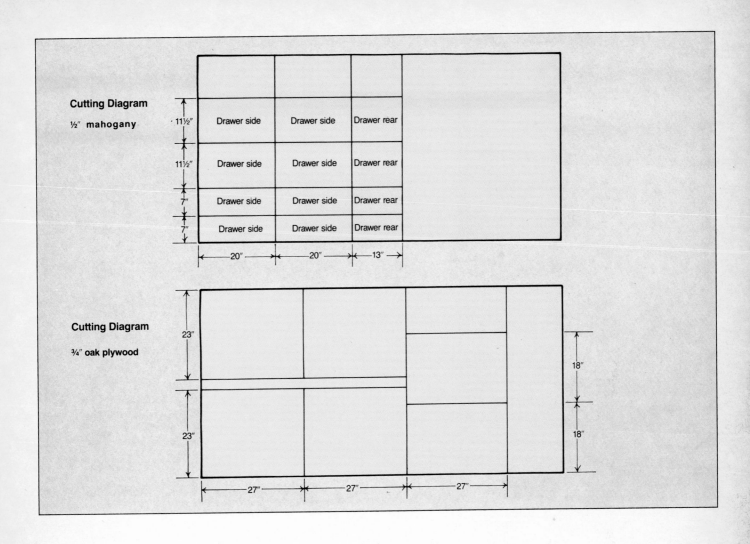

Cutting Diagram

½″ mahogany

11½″ — Drawer side | Drawer side | Drawer rear
11½″ — Drawer side | Drawer side | Drawer rear
7″ — Drawer side | Drawer side | Drawer rear
7″ — Drawer side | Drawer side | Drawer rear

20″ — 20″ — 13″

Cutting Diagram

¾″ oak plywood

23″ — 23″ — 18″ — 18″

27″ — 27″ — 27″

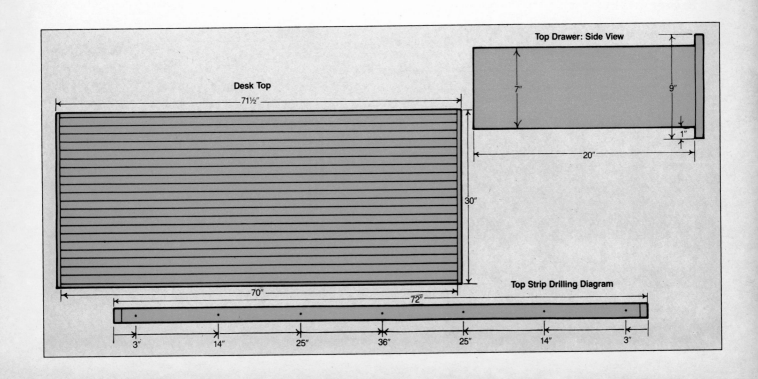

Top Drawer: Side View

7″ — 9″ — 1″ — 20″

Desk Top

71½″

30″

70″ — 72″

Top Strip Drilling Diagram

3″ — 14″ — 25″ — 36″ — 25″ — 14″ — 3″

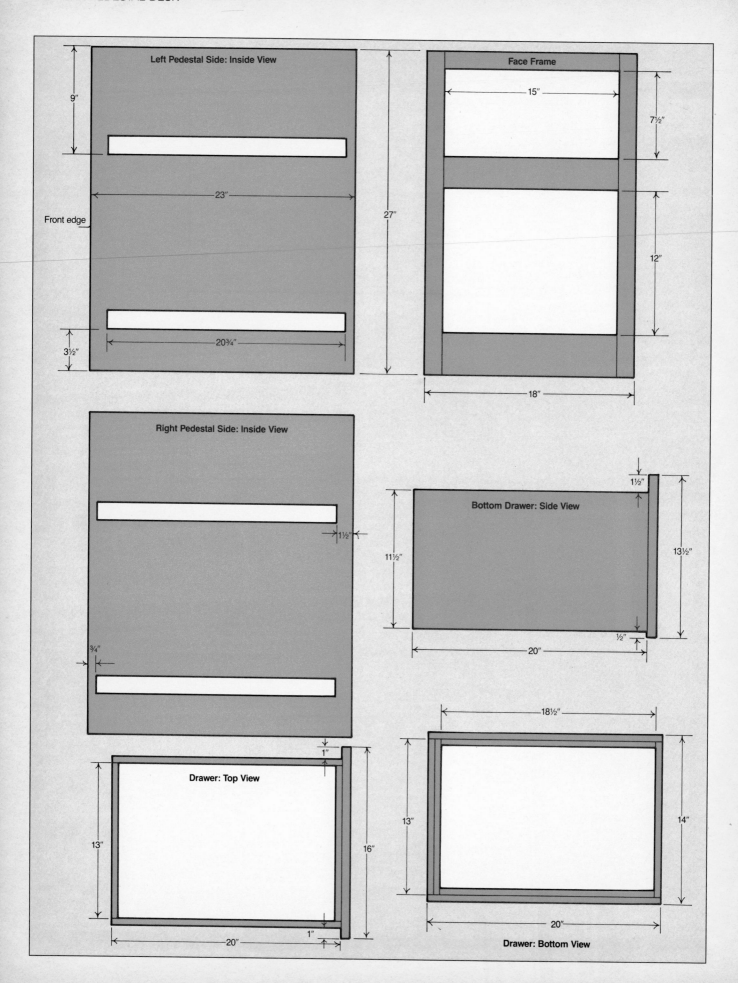

Left Pedestal Side: Inside View

9"

Front edge

23"

27"

20¾"

3½"

Face Frame

15"

7½"

12"

18"

Right Pedestal Side: Inside View

1½"

¾"

Bottom Drawer: Side View

1½"

11½"

13½"

½"

20"

18½"

Drawer: Top View

1"

13"

16"

1"

20"

13"

14"

20"

Drawer: Bottom View

STEP 1
MARKING AND DRILLING FACE-FRAME COMPONENTS

Mark arrows on ends of face-frame horizontals to indicate front and top surfaces. Mark tops of verticals to indicate inside surfaces.

Scribe small pencil lines at 1 × 2 horizontal ends, parallel to and centered between top and bottom edges. Make marks at ends of 1 × 3 and 1 × 4 horizontals ¾ of an inch from top and bottom edges.

Lay face-frame verticals face up, measure along each, near the inside edge, and make marks perpendicular to the edge at ¾ and 2¾ inches from the bottom and ¾, 9¾, and 10¾ inches from the top.

Align a dowel jig with the marks on the verticals, and drill ⁵⁄₁₆-inch-diameter, ¾-inch-deep holes in the inside edges. Drill inch-deep holes in the ends of the horizontals.

STEP 2
ASSEMBLING FACE FRAMES

Stand face-frame verticals holes up, insert glued dowel pins in holes, and tap them in with a soft-faced mallet.

Squeeze glue into the holes in one end of a 1 × 2, 1 × 3, and 1 × 4 horizontal, and apply a small amount to the ends. Tap the 1 × 2 onto the top dowel pin, the 1 × 3 onto the center pins, and the 1 × 4 onto the bottom pins with a block of wood and mallet. Clamp the assembly with three bar clamps, and let stand for an hour. Assemble another frame the same way. When glue has set, sand faces with a pad sander and 120- and 220-grit sandpaper.

STEP 3
ATTACHING DRAWER-CHANNEL STRIPS

Scribe lines across drawer-channel strips in the center and one inch from each end. Then counterbore three ⅜-inch-diameter, ¾-inch-deep holes in each strip, and drill through with an ¹¹⁄₆₄-inch bit.

Mark the top edge of each pedestal side panel with arrows to indicate front and outside surfaces. Lay panels inside surface up. With a combination square, scribe several short lines across each panel 3½ inches from the

MARKING FACE FRAME COMPONENTS

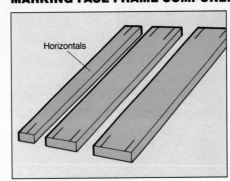

1. Use a combination square to mark the horizontals as described in the text.

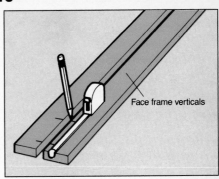

2. Mark the face-frame verticals as described in the text.

DRILLING DOWEL HOLES

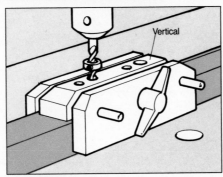

1. Align dowel jig with marks on verticals; use depth-stop on ⁵⁄₁₆-inch bit to drill ¾-inch-deep dowel-pin holes.

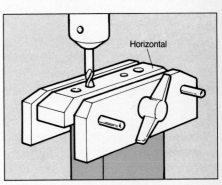

2. Use the dowel jig and ⁵⁄₁₆-inch bit to drill inch-deep holes in the ends of the horizontals.

ASSEMBLING FACE FRAMES

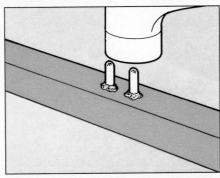

1. Dip one end of the fluted dowel pins in glue, and tap them into the holes in the verticals with a soft-faced mallet.

2. Use an applicator bottle to squeeze glue into the holes in one end of each horizontal.

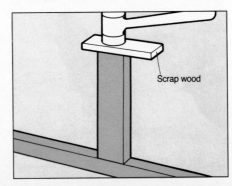

3. With a scrap of wood and mallet, tap each horizontal onto the dowel pins in a vertical.

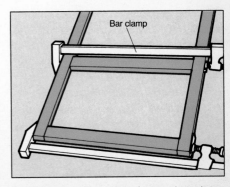

4. After assembling a face frame, clamp it top, bottom, and across the 1 × 3 with bar clamps.

bottom and nine inches from the top. Then scribe a short line ¾ of an inch from the rear edge, perpendicular to and just above the lines scribed earlier.

Run a wavy bead of glue along the underside of two channel strips. Position the bottom edge of each along the horizontal guide lines and ¾ of an inch inside the rear edge. Clamp ends with spring clamps, and use an electric drill and power-drive bit to drive a 1¼ × 8 screw through each hole. Then install strips on the remaining panels in the same way.

STEP 4
ASSEMBLING PEDESTALS

Stand a side panel upright, butt a rear panel to it against the rear ends of the channel strips, and secure the top corner with a corner clamp. Clamp the opposite side panel the same way. Lay the assembly on its front edges, and secure bottom corners with clamps.

Loosen clamp screws on one side holding the side panel. Tilt the assembly away from the side panel. Then run a bead of glue down the side edge of the rear panel, and apply glue to the rear ends of the channel strips. Reposition and clamp the side panel; then drive and countersink five 1¼-inch brads through the side panel into the rear panel.

Attach the opposite side panel the same way. Then assemble another pedestal to this point, and let stand, clamped, for one hour.

Remove bottom clamps, and lay each unit on its back. Apply glue to the front ends of the channel strips, and lay a face frame in place. Drive a 1¼-inch brad through each side panel, near the bottom, into each side of the frame. Do the same near the top, countersink the brads, and fill top holes with wood filler.

Attach a bar clamp to each side of each unit, level with top channel strips, and let stand an hour.

Sand the front and top of each 18-inch oak 1 × 3 with a pad sander and 120- and 220-grit paper. Mix a small amount of epoxy cement, and apply it to the back of each piece. Lay each in place on a face frame, flush with the bottom, and clamp with two spring clamps for five minutes.

MARKING AND DRILLING DRAWER-CHANNEL STRIPS

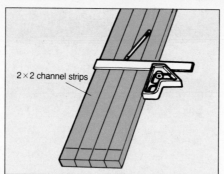

1. Scribe lines across the 2 × 2 channel strips one inch from each end and in the center.

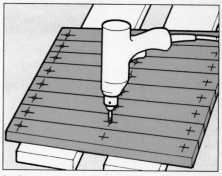

2. Counterbore ⅜-inch-diameter, ¾-inch-deep holes centered on the lines; then drill through with an ¹¹/₆₄-inch bit.

ATTACHING CHANNEL STRIPS TO SIDE

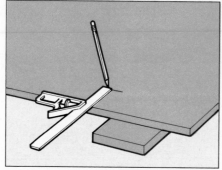

1. Scribe guide lines on the inside of each pedestal side panel 3½ inches from the bottom and nine inches from the top.

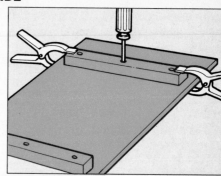

2. Glue channel strips to side panels with bottom edges set on guide lines and ¾ inch from rear edge of panel. Clamp and secure with 1¼ × 8 screws.

ASSEMBLING PEDESTALS

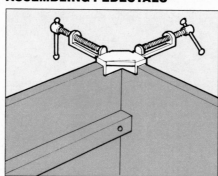

1. Apply glue to one edge of a rear panel and to rear ends of channel strips on one side panel. Clamp the panels together.

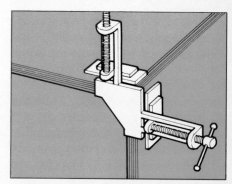

2. Attach the other side panel to the opposite edge of the rear panel with glue and corner clamps.

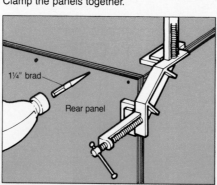

3. Drive five 1¼-inch brads through each side panel into the rear panel, and countersink the brads.

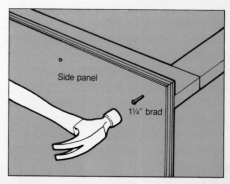

4. Drive a 1¼-inch brad through each side panel into the face frame near the top and near the bottom.

STEP 5
SANDING PEDESTALS AND ATTACHING TRIM

Sand side and rear panels with a pad sander and 120- and 220-grit paper. Sand top, front, and bottom edges with 120-grit paper until smooth.

With each pedestal on its back, measure from one bottom corner to the other, and miter-cut a piece of oak 1 × 2 to fit. Mark the outside of the piece for centered holes in the middle and two inches from each end. Then counterbore a ⅜-inch-diameter, ⅜-inch-deep hole at each spot, and drill through with an ¹¹⁄₆₄-inch bit.

Run a bead of glue along the underside of the strip, and clamp it flush along the bottom front of the pedestal. Then attach it with three 1 × 8 flathead screws, and tap a glued plug into each hole. Continue attaching the base molding, and trim the other pedestal.

Cut eight pieces of corner molding to fit the corners of the pedestals. Run a bead of glue down the inside of each strip, press four pieces in place along the vertical corners of each pedestal, secure with three strap clamps, and let stand for an hour.

Sand plug heads flush with a belt sander and fine belt. Then sand base trim with a pad sander and 120- and 220-grit paper, rounding over corners and slightly rounding over edges.

STEP 6
SORTING, MARKING, AND DRILLING TOP STRIPS

Sort 1 × 2 top strips for best grain contrast, and number one end of each. Then scribe lines across the tops at 3, 14, 25, and 36 inches from each end.

Counterbore ⅜-inch-diameter, ⅜-inch-deep holes, centered on the lines. Then drill through with an ¹¹⁄₆₄-inch bit.

STEP 7
LAMINATING TOP STRIPS TO UNDERLAYMENT

Lay the plywood underlayment good face down. Brush an even coat of glue onto the broad underside of top strip 19, and lay it along one long edge of the plywood. Clamp it at one corner with a spring clamp, and put another clamp between the first two holes. Drive a 1 × 8 screw into the first hole, move the

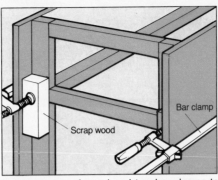

5. Use scraps of wood and two bar clamps to press the face frame against the channel strips, and let stand one hour.

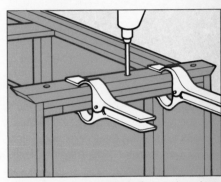

6. Apply epoxy cement to the rear surface of each 18-inch oak 1 × 3. Clamp each in place to a face frame flush with bottom.

ATTACHING PEDESTAL TRIM

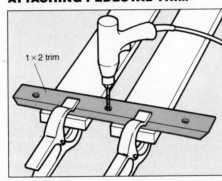

1. Counterbore centered ⅜-inch-diameter, ⅜-inch-deep holes in 1 × 2 trim, and drill through with an ¹¹⁄₆₄-inch bit.

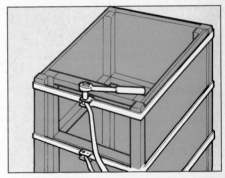

2. Apply glue to rear surface of trim strips, clamp along the pedestal bottom, and attach with three 1 × 8 screws.

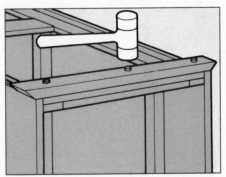

3. Squirt glue into screw holes, and tap ⅜-inch tapered plugs into the holes with a soft-faced mallet.

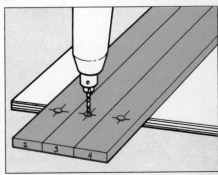

4. Press glued corner molding in place at the pedestal corners, and attach three strap clamps.

MARKING AND DRILLING TOP STRIPS

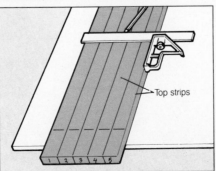

1. Scribe lines across the 72-inch top strips at 3, 14, 25, and 36 inches from each end.

2. Counterbore ⅜-inch-diameter, ⅜-inch-deep holes, centered on the lines; then drill through with an ¹¹⁄₆₄-inch bit.

end clamp to a spot between the second and third holes, and drive a screw through the second hole. Continue leapfrogging the clamps and driving screws through the remaining holes.

Brush glue onto the underside of strip 18 and onto the edge that will join strip 19. Position the strip, and secure with a bar clamp between the first two holes. Clamp the numbered ends of the strips, and drive a screw through the first hole. Then leapfrog the clamps as you drive each additional screw.

Wipe excess glue away with a damp sponge, and continue attaching strips.

STEP 8
CUTTING THE TOP AND PLUGGING HOLES

Lay the top upside down. Then use a circular saw and saw guide to rip excess plywood away along the edge of strip No. 1. Then cut one inch from each end, for a finished length of 70 inches.

Rough-sand the top to an even finish with a belt sander and medium belt. Then tap a glued plug into each hole, and let stand for an hour or more.

When glue has set, sand plug heads flush with a belt sander and medium and fine belts.

STEP 9
ATTACHING EDGE TRIM TO TOP

Cut two pieces of 1 × 2 to fit the 70-inch edges of the top. Then mark a broad surface of each for centered holes at 2, 13, 24, and 35 inches from each end. Counterbore a ⅜-inch-diameter, ⅜-inch-deep hole at each spot; then drill through with an ¹¹⁄₆₄-inch bit.

Brush a coat of glue onto the underside of the 1 × 2, and clamp it to the edge with two edge clamps, centered about a foot apart. Clamp one end with bar clamps at the end and between the first two holes. Drive a 1 × 8 screw into the end hole. Move the end clamp to a spot between the second and third holes, and drive another screw. Continue leapfrogging clamps as you drive remaining screws. Attach the opposite strip the same way.

Cut a piece of oak 1 × 2 to fit each end, and mark each for centered holes at 1½ and 10½ inches from each end. Counterbore and drill through, and at-

LAMINATING STRIPS TO UNDERLAYMENT

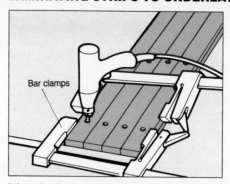

1. Lay glued strips atop underlayment, attach bar clamps and drive a 1 × 8 screw through first hole.

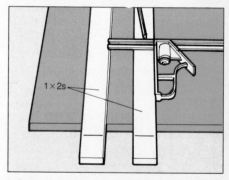

2. Reposition the end clamp between the second and third row of holes, and drive a screw into the second hole.

CUTTING THE TOP

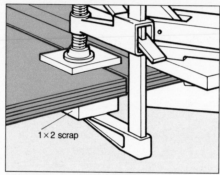

1. When ripping excess plywood, use a scrap of 1 × 2 and bar clamps to support the plywood at leading edge of kerf.

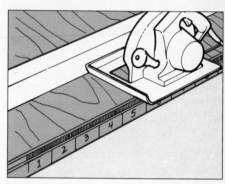

2. Use a circular saw and guide to trim one inch from each end of the top.

PLUGGING HOLES

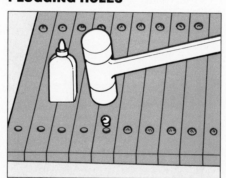

Squirt a small amount of glue into each hole in one row; then tap a tapered plug into each hole with a soft-faced mallet.

ATTACHING EDGE TRIM

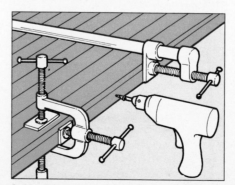

1. Scribe lines across two 70-inch 1 × 2s at 2, 13, 24, and 35 inches from each end.

2. Attach glued strip to long edge of top with edge clamps and bar or pipe clamps; secure with screws in the first two holes.

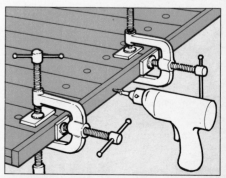

3. Clamp glued strip to the end of the top with four edge clamps; then secure with four 1 × 8 screws.

tach with glue, four edge clamps, and screws.

Plug all holes in the edge trim with glued plugs, and let stand for an hour.

STEP 10
SANDING THE TOP

When the glue sets, sand the plug heads flush with a belt sander and medium and fine belts. Then sand all surfaces with a pad sander and 120-grit sandpaper, rounding over corners and edges as you sand. Then sand the top with 220- and 320-grit paper, and polish with #0000 steel wool.

STEP 11
MARKING, DRILLING, AND LAMINATING DRAWER-FACE STRIPS

Sort 1 × 2 drawer-face strips into two sets of nine and two sets of six; then number one end of each set.

Stand strips in each set on narrow edges, and scribe lines across them at 1½ and 8½ inches from each end. Then drill ⅜-inch-diameter holes in each, centered on the lines.

Slide the first strip onto three threaded-rod clamps. Brush an even coat of glue onto a narrow edge of each remaining strip in the set, and slide them onto the rods in sequential order. Put a cushion, flat washer, and hex nut on the end of each rod, and tighten nuts.

Assemble the other faces the same way, wipe excess glue away, and let stand for two hours or overnight.

STEP 12
TRIMMING, PLUGGING, DRILLING, AND SANDING DRAWER FACES

Use a table saw to trim a half-inch from each end of each drawer face. Then tap glued plugs into the holes in the edges and let stand a half-hour.

Scribe a line 4⅛ inches from the top of each small drawer face and one 5¼ inches from the top of each large face. Make a small perpendicular mark at the center of each line, and mark the line for pull holes. If you're using Belwith P676-UW pulls, make marks 1⅞ inches left and right of center. Then center-punch and drill pull holes.

Sand the broad surfaces with a belt

SORTING DRAWER-FACE STRIPS

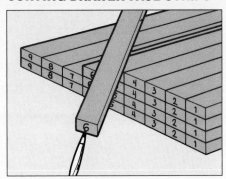

Sort 17-inch 1 × 2s into two sets of nine and two sets of six, and number one end of each set with a felt-tipped pen.

LAMINATING DRAWER FACES

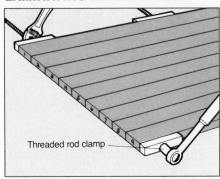

Laminate each set of strips into a drawer face with glue and three threaded-rod clamps.

MARKING AND DRILLING DRAWER FACES

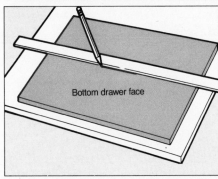

1. Scribe a line 4⅛ inches from top edge of each top-drawer face and 5¼ inches from top of each bottom-drawer face.

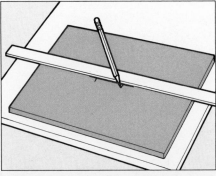

3. Mark for pull-screw holes 1⅞ inches left and right of the center mark.

MARKING FOR CLAMP HOLES

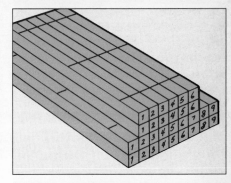

Scribe lines across the narrow edges of each set at 1½ and 8½ inches from each end.

TRIMMING DRAWER FACES

Use a table saw to trim a half-inch from each end of each drawer face.

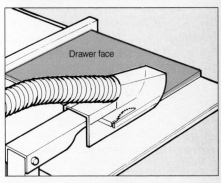

2. Mark the center of each line on each drawer face.

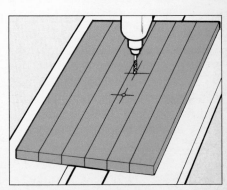

4. Drill two ¹³⁄₆₄-inch-diameter pull-screw holes in each drawer face.

sander and medium belt. Round over the ends of the face surface.

Use a pad sander and 120-grit sandpaper to sand all surfaces, and sand all but the rear surfaces with 220-grit paper, rounding over the ends and slightly rounding over edges and corners.

STEP 13
MARKING AND DRILLING DRAWER-FRONT STRIPS

Scribe lines two inches from each end across the broad surfaces of eight 13-inch parting-bead strips. Mark the center of each line, and drill an 11/64-inch-diameter hole at each spot. Then countersink with a #8 countersink bit.

STEP 14
ATTACHING CLEATS TO DRAWER PANELS

Prenail the remaining four 13-inch strips with three ¾-inch brads each. Run a thin bead of glue down the unnailed side; position each along the inside of a drawer rear panel, flush with the bottom; and drive and countersink the brads.

Mark the drawer side panels L and R. Then scribe a short line on the inside of each panel, at the bottom rear corner, one inch from and parallel to the rear.

Prenail the eight 18½-inch parting-bead cleats with four ¾-inch brads each. Then glue and nail along the bottom inside of each side panel, one inch from the rear edge.

STEP 15
ASSEMBLING DRAWERS

Run a bead of glue down one side of a rear panel, butt it to a side panel, and clamp with a corner clamp. Drive and countersink three one-inch brads through the side panel into the rear panel. Then attach the other side panel the same way.

Stand the assembly on its back, and apply glue to the front ends of the cleats. Attach a drilled parting-bead strip between the bottom front corners with countersunk holes inside, and drive a one-inch brad through each end into the cleats.

Apply glue to the ends of another drilled piece, and attach it between the top corners with brads.

Assemble the other drawers the

MARKING DRAWER STRIPS

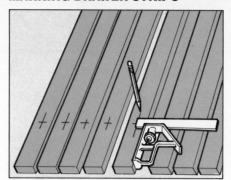

Mark eight 13-inch pieces of parting bead for centered holes two inches from each end.

DRILL-STARTER HOLES

Center-punch a drill-starter hole at each spot marked on each strip.

ATTACHING CLEATS TO DRAWER PANELS

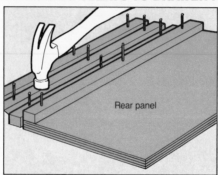

1. Attach a 13-inch parting-bead strip to the bottom inside of each rear panel with glue and three ¾-inch brads.

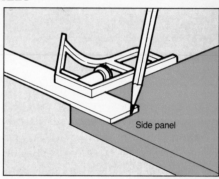

2. Scribe a short line on the inside of each side panel, at the bottom corner, one inch from the rear edge.

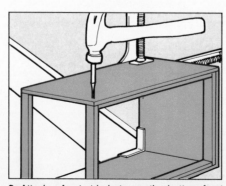

3. Attach an 18½-inch parting-bead strip along the bottom inside edge of each side panel, with glue and four ¾-inch brads.

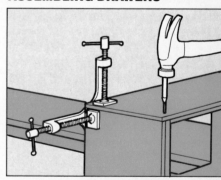

1. Apply glue to each side edge of rear panel; clamp side panels to it and then drive brads through side panel.

ASSEMBLING DRAWERS

MARKING DRAWER FACES

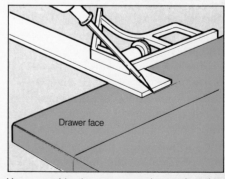

2. Attach a front strip between the bottom front corners and another between the top corners with glue and brads.

Use a combination square and scratch awl to etch guide lines on drawer faces as described in text.

same way, and let stand, with clamps in place, for an hour.

STEP 16
FINISHING DESK COMPONENTS

Apply a coat of Watco Medium Walnut Danish Oil Finish to all surfaces of the pedestals, top, drawer faces, and pulls. Let penetrate 30 minutes; wipe dry.

STEP 17
ATTACHING DRAWER FACES AND PULLS

Lay drawer faces face down, and make several marks one inch inside the side edges. Make several marks one inch from the bottom edge of the *top faces*. Then make marks a half-inch from the bottom edge of the *bottom faces*.

Stand a top drawer on a top-drawer face, and position it inside the marks, and clamp the bottom front strip to it with two spring clamps. Then attach with four 1 × 8 flathead screws.

Attach the other assemblies to the faces, then attach pulls with screws.

STEP 18
ATTACHING DRAWER SLIDES AND TOP

Attach drawer channels CR and CL to the channel strips and channels DR and DL to the drawers, according to the manufacturer's directions.

Measure four inches from the face frame, and mark the top of each pedestal side panel. Measure four inches from the inside of each side panel, and mark the top of the rear panel. Then mount a corner brace at each spot, flush with the top edge, using two ¾ × 8 flathead Phillips screws at each brace.

Lay the top upside down in the room where the desk will stand. Place a pedestal upside down at each end, aligned just inside the edge trim at the front of the top and two inches from the end. Then attach each pedestal to the top with eight 1¼ × 8 flathead Phillips screws.

Stand the desk upright, and slide the drawers in place. Lay drawer bottoms atop the cleats. Press a self-adhesive felt cushion in place near each corner of each drawer opening.

DRAWERS TO FACES

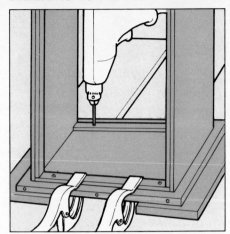

Align each drawer with the guide lines on a drawer face, clamp with two spring clamps, and attach with four 1 × 8 screws.

ATTACHING DRAWER PULLS

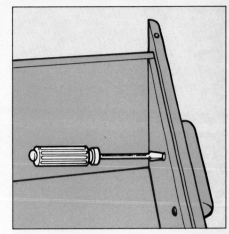

Attach a pull to each drawer with screws provided.

INSTALLING DRAWER SLIDES

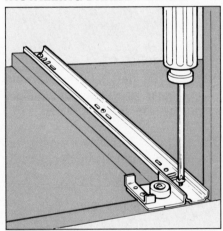

1. Attach a channel CR to each right channel strip in each pedestal and a channel CL to each left channel strip.

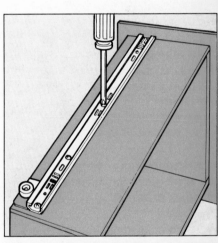

2. Attach a channel DR to each right drawer side panel and a channel DL to each left drawer side panel.

INSTALLING CORNER BRACES

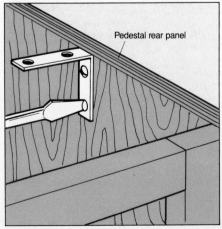

Pedestal rear panel

Attach corner braces to the top inside of each pedestal rear panel and side panel as described in the text.

ATTACHING PEDESTALS TO TOP

Align pedestal corner molding inside the front edge trim and pedestal side panel two inches from the end of the top.

Glossary

Abrasive Material used for smoothing, polishing, and lapping, such as sandpaper.

Air-dried Lumber that has been dried by exposure to air, usually in the open, without artificial heat.

Along-the-grain In the same direction as the grain; in plywood, the same direction as the grain of the face ply, usually the long dimension. Also referred to as *with-the-grain* and *cross-grain*.

Across-the-grain Perpendicular to the wood grain. Sometimes referred to as *cross-grain*.

Awl A pointed instrument used to pierce small holes in wood.

Back The side of a plywood panel having the lower-grade veneer.

Backsaw A short saw with a reinforced back.

Bandsaw Saw consisting of an endless toothed steel band passing over two wheels.

Bevel To cut edges or ends at an angle to make smooth mating joints between pieces.

Bit Removable drill or boring tool for use in a brace or drill press.

Bleeding The seeping of resin or gum from lumber.

Board A term generally applied to lumber 1 inch thick and 2 or more inches wide.

Bond To glue together, as veneers are "bonded" to form plywood. Pressure can be applied during the process to keep mating parts in proper alignment.

Brad A slender wire nail having either a small, deep head or a projection to one side of the head end.

Brace Piece of lumber or metal used to support or position another piece or portion of a framework.

Butt joint A joint formed by abutting the squared ends, or ends and faces, of two pieces. Because of the inadequacy and variability in strength of butt joints when glued, they are not generally glued.

Chalk line Also called *snap line*. A chalked string used to make a straight line on a surface by holding the string taut against the surface and snapping it to transfer the chalk.

Chamfer The flat surface created by slicing off the square edge or corner of a piece of wood or plywood, usually at a 45-degree angle to the adjacent faces.

Circular saw A power saw with a circular disk.

Clear lumber A term including the higher grades of lumber. It is sound and relatively free of blemishes.

Clamps Any of several types of devices used to hold a joint secure and as desired until glue has dried and/or while nails or screws are driven into place.

Cleat Wedge-shaped block fastened to a surface to serve as a check or support.

Combination square Adjustable device for testing squareness of carpentry work, consisting of a pair of straightedges fixed at right angles to one another.

Countersinking To position the head of a screw or bolt so as to be flush with or below the surface.

Cove Concave surface or molding.

Crook A distortion of a board in which there is a deviation edgewise from a straight line from end to end of the board.

Cross lamination In plywood manufacture, the placing of consecutive layers at right angles to one another to minimize shrinkage and increase strength.

Cross member A structural part of cabinetry, either horizontal or vertical, which adds stability.

Cross nail At a miter joint, nailing from each side through the joint for stability.

Cup A curve in a board across the grain or width of a piece.

Dado A joint formed by the intersection of two boards; one is notched with a rectangular groove to receive the other.

Dimension lumber A term generally applied to lumber 2 to 4 inches thick and 2 or more inches wide.

Dovetail Tenon broader at its end than at its base; a joint formed of one or more such tenons, fitting tightly within corresponding mortises.

Dowel Also *dowel pin*. A pin, usually round, fitted into holes in adjacent pieces of wood to align them or prevent slippage.

Dressed lumber Lumber after shrinking from the green dimension and being surfaced with a planing machine, usually 3/8 or 1/2 inch smaller than the nominal (rough) size; for example, a 2 × 4 stud actually measures 1½ × 3½ inches.

Drill press Drilling machine having a single vertical spindle.

Eased edges A term used to describe slight rounding of edge surfaces of a piece of lumber or plywood to remove sharp corners.

Emery board A small, stiff strip of paper or cardboard coated with powdered emery, used for grinding and polishing.

End grain The grain at the end of a board, in which the fibers have been cut perpendicular to their length.

Epoxy A synthetic resin used in some paints and adhesives because of its toughness, adhesion, and resistance to solvents.

Face The wide surface of a piece of lumber; the side showing the better quality or appearance on which a piece is graded.

Finished size The net dimensions after surfacing.

Good-one-side Plywood that has a higher-grade veneer on the face than on the back; used where only one side will be visible. In identifying these panels, the face grade is given first.

Grain The direction, size, arrangement, appearance, or quality of the fibers in wood.

Gusset Plate or wedge used to join structural members.

Hacksaw Saw for cutting metal, consisting of a narrow, fine-toothed blade fixed in a frame.

Hardwoods The botanical group of broad-leaved trees, such as oak or maple. The term has no reference to the actual hardness of the wood.

Heartwood The nonactive core of a tree, usually darker and more decay-resistant than sapwood because gums and resins have seeped into it.

Jig saw Narrow saw, mounted vertically in a frame, for cutting curves and other complicated lines.

Jointer A power tool used to finish an edge or face of a board.

Kerf A slot made by a saw; the width of the saw cut.

Kiln-dried wood Wood that has been dried in ovens by controlled heat and humidity to specified limits of moisture content.

Knot The portion of a branch or limb that has been surrounded by subsequent growth of the wood of the tree trunk.

Lag bolt A heavy wood screw having a square or hexagonal head.

Laminate To unite layers of a material, usually wood, by binding with adhesive and compressing.

Lap To position two pieces so that the surface of one extends over that of the other.

Loosened or raised grain A small section of the wood that has been loosened or raised, but not displaced.

Long grain The grain in the edge or face of a board, in which the fibers have been cut parallel to their length. Sometimes referred to as *surface grain*.

Lumber The product of the saw and planing mill manufactured by sawing, resawing, passing lengthwise through a standard planing machine, crosscutting to length, and matching.

Lumber-core Plywood construction in which the core is composed of lumber strips and outer piles are veneer.

Miter joint A joint formed by fitting together two pieces of lumber or plywood that have been cut off on an angle.

Miter box A fixed or adjustable guide for a saw used in making miters or cross cuts; usually a troughlike box open at the ends which guides the saw by slots on the opposite side.

Mortise Notch, groove, or slot made in a piece of wood to receive a tenon of the same dimensions.

Nail set A short rod of steel used to drive a nail below or flush with the surface.

Oven-dried wood Wood that has been dried so completely that it is without any moisture content.

Parting bead A strip of wood used to keep two parts separated.

Ply A single veneer in a glued plywood panel.

Plywood A panel made of three or more layers of veneer joined with glue and usually laid with the grain of adjoining plies at right angles. To secure balanced construction, an odd number of plies is almost always used.

Rabbet   A joint formed by cutting a groove in the surface along the edge of a board, plank, or panel to receive another piece.

Radial saw   Cantilevered circular saw adjustable at various angles to the length of the work and to the perpendicular.

Rail   The horizontal member of a frame.

Ripping   Cutting a board along the grain from end to end.

Scarf joint   An end joint or splice formed by gluing together the ends of two pieces that have been tapered or beveled to form sloping plane surfaces, usually to a feather edge.

Seasoning   Removing the moisture from green wood in order to improve its serviceability.

Select lumber   The higher grades of sound, relatively unblemished lumber.

Softwoods   The botanical group of trees that have needle or scalelike leaves. Except for cypress, larch and tamarack, softwoods are evergreen. The term has no reference to the actual hardness of the wood.

Solid-core   Plywood composed of veneers over a lumber core.

Split   A lengthwise separation of the wood, due to the tearing apart of the wood cells.

Surfaced lumber   Lumber that has been planed or sanded on one or more surfaces.

Table saw   A stationary power saw with an adjustable guide or fence that can be used for crosscutting, ripping, or grooving.

Tenon   Projection formed at the end of a piece of wood for insertion into a mortise of the same dimensions.

Toenail   Driving nails into corners or other joints at an angle.

Tongue-and-groove   A carpentry joint in which the jutting edge of one board fits into the grooved edge of a mating board.

Twist   A distortion caused by the turning or winding of the edges of a board so that the four corners of any face are no longer on the same plane.

Veneer   A thin layer or sheet of wood.

Warp   Any variation from a true or plane surface. The term covers *crook*, *bow*, *cup*, *twist*, and any combination of these.

Index

Metric Charts

LUMBER

Sizes: Metric cross-sections are so close to their nearest Imperial sizes, as noted below, that for most purposes they may be considered equivalents.

Lengths: Metric lengths are based on a 300mm module which is slightly shorter in length than an Imperial foot. It will therefore be important to check your requirements accurately to the nearest inch and consult the table below to find the metric length required.

Areas: The metric area is a square metre. Use the following conversion factors when converting from Imperial data: 100 sq. feet = 9.290 sq. metres.

METRIC SIZES SHOWN BESIDE NEAREST IMPERIAL EQUIVALENT

mm	Inches	mm	Inches
16 × 75	$5/8$ × 3	44 × 150	$1\frac{3}{4}$ × 6
16 × 100	$5/8$ × 4	44 × 175	$1\frac{3}{4}$ × 7
16 × 125	$5/8$ × 5	44 × 200	$1\frac{3}{4}$ × 8
16 × 150	$5/8$ × 6	44 × 225	$1\frac{3}{4}$ × 9
19 × 75	$3/4$ × 3	44 × 250	$1\frac{3}{4}$ × 10
19 × 100	$3/4$ × 4	44 × 300	$1\frac{3}{4}$ × 12
19 × 125	$3/4$ × 5	50 × 75	2 × 3
19 × 150	$3/4$ × 6	50 × 100	2 × 4
22 × 75	$7/8$ × 3	50 × 125	2 × 5
22 × 100	$7/8$ × 4	50 × 150	2 × 6
22 × 125	$7/8$ × 5	50 × 175	2 × 7
22 × 150	$7/8$ × 6	50 × 200	2 × 8
25 × 75	1 × 3	50 × 225	2 × 9
25 × 100	1 × 4	50 × 250	2 × 10
25 × 125	1 × 5	50 × 300	2 × 12
25 × 150	1 × 6	63 × 100	$2\frac{1}{2}$ × 4
25 × 175	1 × 7	63 × 125	$2\frac{1}{2}$ × 5
25 × 200	1 × 8	63 × 150	$2\frac{1}{2}$ × 6
25 × 225	1 × 9	63 × 175	$2\frac{1}{2}$ × 7
25 × 250	1 × 10	63 × 200	$2\frac{1}{2}$ × 8
25 × 300	1 × 12	63 × 225	$2\frac{1}{2}$ × 9
32 × 75	$1\frac{1}{4}$ × 3	75 × 100	3 × 4
32 × 100	$1\frac{1}{4}$ × 4	75 × 125	3 × 5
32 × 125	$1\frac{1}{4}$ × 5	75 × 150	3 × 6
32 × 150	$1\frac{1}{4}$ × 6	75 × 175	3 × 7
32 × 175	$1\frac{1}{4}$ × 7	75 × 200	3 × 8
32 × 200	$1\frac{1}{4}$ × 8	75 × 225	3 × 9
32 × 225	$1\frac{1}{4}$ × 9	75 × 250	3 × 10
32 × 250	$1\frac{1}{4}$ × 10	75 × 300	3 × 12
32 × 300	$1\frac{1}{4}$ × 12	100 × 100	4 × 4
38 × 75	$1\frac{1}{2}$ × 3	100 × 150	4 × 6
38 × 100	$1\frac{1}{2}$ × 4	100 × 200	4 × 8
38 × 125	$1\frac{1}{2}$ × 5	100 × 250	4 × 10
38 × 150	$1\frac{1}{2}$ × 6	100 × 300	4 × 12
38 × 175	$1\frac{1}{2}$ × 7	150 × 150	6 × 6
38 × 200	$1\frac{1}{2}$ × 8	150 × 200	6 × 8
38 × 225	$1\frac{1}{2}$ × 9	150 × 300	6 × 12
44 × 75	$1\frac{3}{4}$ × 3	200 × 200	8 × 8
44 × 100	$1\frac{3}{4}$ × 4	250 × 250	10 × 10
44 × 125	$1\frac{3}{4}$ × 5	300 × 300	12 × 12

NOMINAL SIZE	ACTUAL SIZE
(This is what you order)	(This is what you get)
Inches	Inches
1 × 1	$3/4$ × $3/4$
1 × 2	$3/4$ × $1\frac{1}{2}$
1 × 3	$3/4$ × $2\frac{1}{2}$
1 × 4	$3/4$ × $3\frac{1}{2}$
1 × 6	$3/4$ × $5\frac{1}{2}$
1 × 8	$3/4$ × $7\frac{1}{4}$
1 × 10	$3/4$ × $9\frac{1}{4}$
1 × 12	$3/4$ × $11\frac{1}{4}$
2 × 2	$1\frac{3}{4}$ × $1\frac{3}{4}$
2 × 3	$1\frac{1}{2}$ × $2\frac{1}{2}$
2 × 4	$1\frac{1}{2}$ × $3\frac{1}{2}$
2 × 6	$1\frac{1}{2}$ × $5\frac{1}{2}$
2 × 8	$1\frac{1}{2}$ × $7\frac{1}{4}$
2 × 10	$1\frac{1}{2}$ × $9\frac{1}{4}$
2 × 12	$1\frac{1}{2}$ × $11\frac{1}{4}$

METRIC LENGTHS

Lengths Metres	Equiv. Ft. & Inches
1.8m	5′ 10$7/8$″
2.1m	6′ 10$5/8$″
2.4m	7′ 10$1/2$″
2.7m	8′ 10$1/4$″
3.0m	9′ 10$1/8$″
3.3m	10′ 9$7/8$″
3.6m	11′ 9$3/4$″
3.9m	12′ 9$1/2$″
4.2m	13′ 9$3/8$″
4.5m	14′ 9$1/3$″
4.8m	15′ 9″
5.1m	16′ 8$3/4$″
5.4m	17′ 8$5/8$″
5.7m	18′ 8$3/8$″
6.0m	19′ 8$1/4$″
6.3m	20′ 8″
6.6m	21′ 7$7/8$″
6.9m	22′ 7$5/8$″
7.2m	23′ 7$1/2$″
7.5m	24′ 7$1/4$″
7.8m	25′ 7$1/8$″

All the dimensions are based on 1 inch = 25 mm.